DEVELOPING PUBLIC POLICY

DEVELOPING PUBLIC POLICY

A PRACTICAL GUIDE

Bobby Siu

Canadian Scholars' Press
Toronto, Ontario

Developing Public Policy: A Practical Guide
Bobby Siu

First published in 2014 by
Canadian Scholars' Press Inc.
425 Adelaide Street West, Suite 200
Toronto, Ontario
M5V 3C1
www.cspi.org

Canadian Scholars' Press Inc. gratefully acknowledges financial support for our publishing activities from the Government of Canada through the Canada Book Fund (CBF).

Library and Archives Canada Cataloguing in Publication
Siu, Bobby C. Y., author
    Developing public policy : a practical guide / Bobby Siu.

Includes bibliographical references and index.
Issued in print and electronic formats.
ISBN 978-1-55130-549-3 (pbk.).--ISBN 978-1-55130-550-9 (pdf).--
ISBN 978-1-55130-551-6 (epub)

    1. Political planning. 2. Political planning--Problems, exercises, etc. I. Title.

JF1525.P6S58 2013   320.6   C2013-905143-0

Text design by Aldo Fierro
Cover design by Em Dash Design

Printed and bound in Canada by Webcom.

Canadä

MIX
Paper from
responsible sources
FSC
www.fsc.org   **FSC® C004071**

*This book is dedicated to those public policy developers who work
hard to make the world a better place.*

CONTENTS

LIST OF FIGURES AND TABLES

Figures

Tables

PREFACE

Developing public policy is both a science and an art.

A public policy developer must have an academic mind and be capable of thinking as meticulously as a scientist. Public policy developers must ask the right questions, develop sound methodologies, and interpret findings in a proper context. A perceptive mind is needed to decipher the implicit interests of stakeholder groups and to understand the political context in which policy topics are being raised; such perceptiveness also allows public policy developers to empathize with politicians and recognize the immense pressure under which they work. Public policy developers must have the knowledge, skills, and patience to guide policy matters through the maze of internal scrutiny. Without these attributes, they may not be able to withstand the unexpected changes inherent to this process, and the criticism routinely directed towards policy matters by various external stakeholder groups, including the mass media and politicians from opposition parties. Responding to such changes and enduring this type of criticism not only requires a keen mind and a steady hand, but also perseverance.

When an idea goes through the process of development, academic robustness, professional expertise, and scientific evidence are not the only facilitators of this movement. Public policies emerge from a democratic tradition; they are the embodiment of political agendas, ideologies, stakeholder interests, public opinion, personal determination, and structural and financial constraints. Awareness of these factors and the ability to incorporate them in a balanced manner are the artistic components of public policy development.

Having worked in both the public sector (in the domains of public policy development, program implementation, and public administration) and academia, I have a solid understanding of what is expected in a government context, as well as insight into the current status of the post-secondary education programs that are preparing the next generation of public policy developers.

The prevailing method of equipping students with a macroscopic knowledge of policy patterns and trends, historical context, government structures, and policy ramifications is certainly beneficial, as it provides the big picture of how government processes work. Unfortunately, by heavily emphasizing an academic knowledge of public policy development, the other professional attributes required to be an effective public policy developer become obscured. While excelling in theoretical and historical understanding may earn a student high grades, it may not yield the professional skills required for public policy development.

A balance of academic robustness and professional development is not yet in place in public policy and management programs, and needs to be promoted and established at the college and university levels. Treating public policy development and management as both an academic and professional discipline would bring many advantages—the professional mindset and skills needed to enter the cadre of public servants can only complement a foundational knowledge of our government's structure and history.

The purpose of this book is to enrich the existing material on public policy development by providing practical ideas for readers on how best to prepare for a career in public policy. Current literature on public policy development has a tendency to focus on macroscopic aspects (changing global contexts and community dynamics) and organizational issues (management structures, government constraints, and emerging public sector issues). This book is intended to build on this large reservoir of scholarly knowledge by moving public policy development from the macroscopic to the microscopic, from the academic to the practical, and from the outside looking in to the inside looking out.

This book adopts a practical approach to public policy development. An intimate knowledge of the public sector and the dynamics of government activities is definitely an asset when developing public policies; however, this book does not assume that every reader has this level of knowledge. It does assume a cursory understanding of the government and how public policy development generally works. After laying the primary components of public policy development as groundwork, this book provides a compass and road map to navigate the public policy development process—from idea to policy—making it an essential pocket guide. Given the fluid and complex nature of public policy development, this book does not provide a step-by-step guide; as the public policy development process is in a constant state of evolution, such a manual would be both useless and misleading. Instead, I hope to impart a clear picture of how public policies are developed, and provide an array of guiding principles to help readers tackle the many grey areas of policy development and strategies to meet the daily challenges of a fast-paced work environment.

The best way to learn how to develop public policy is to do so; through this experience, in concert with the shared knowledge and observations of more experienced professionals, you will gradually acquire the knowledge and skills necessary to succeed. Due to the book's emphasis on the practical side of public policy development, you will find that it focuses on both the requisite soft skills (political astuteness and communication) and hard skills (research methodology and writing techniques). This combination of knowledge and skills will make the public policy development process methodologically robust and personally rewarding, and the policies developed likely to be accepted by cabinet.

STRUCTURE OF THE BOOK

Developing Public Policy is divided into two parts. Part I presents a generic framework of the structural components and processes of public policy development, and is meant to outfit readers with the knowledge, principles, strategies, and tactics required to develop public policies. This book focuses exclusively on the federal and provincial governments of Canada, and does not discuss the public policy development process in territorial and municipal governments. Because the structures and processes of the federal and provincial governments (which are based on the British parliamentary system) are quite different from those of the territorial governments (which are intertwined with Aboriginal traditions) and those of municipal governments (which do not have a cabinet system), it would be too cumbersome to attempt to describe here how to develop public policies in each of these very different systems.

An overview of government structures, required attributes, and the elements of good public policy are discussed in the first part. In addition, it addresses the four major components of public policy development: identifying public policy issues (chapter 6), conducting research and analyzing information (chapter 7), formulating policy options and recommendations (chapter 8), and determining public policies for implementation (chapter 9).

For our purposes, the term *public policy development* is defined as the process of creating a public policy from an idea into a full-blown piece of legislation, an amendment to an existing law, or a budgetary item officially passed in the legislature. The term does not cover the activities that take place after cabinet approves the public policy and the bill or estimate has passed in the legislature. It does not cover activities related to the translation of public policies into programs, or the implementation and evaluation of these programs. Both implementation and evaluation of programs and services require particular sets of knowledge and skills that are distinctly different from those required for public policy development. Furthermore, in practical terms, program administrators often carry out program activities in a government department that is separate and different from the policy development department. This book does not include the public policy development processes in non-governmental sectors (such as think tanks, industrial or business associations, labour unions, and special interest groups) because they have different public policy development structures and processes. This does not mean that the practical ideas in the book could not be applied to public policy development in other types of organizations; in fact, public policy developers working in non-governmental sectors may find this text insightful and relevant when developing recommendations, advocating, and lobbying for or consulting on public policies in their sector.

As there are many similarities between the public policy development processes of the federal and provincial governments, the book uses generic terms to denote government organizations, in spite of the variation in their names in common usage. There are three areas in which generic terms are used to avoid repetition and redundancy. Firstly, the term *legislature* is used in the academic sense to denote a place where laws are made, amended, or repealed by elected politicians (known as members of parliament or members of provincial parliament) at both the federal and provincial levels. There are occasions in this book when the term *parliament* or *House of Commons* follows *legislature* in brackets to emphasize that the content is applicable to both levels of the government. Secondly, as each provincial government and the federal government have different names for departments that perform similar functions, generic names (such as *management board* or *department of finance*) are used. Thirdly, the terms *ministries, line ministries, departments,* and *line departments* are used interchangeably throughout the book to denote the generic names of different government bodies.

The chapters in part I are enhanced with figures that illustrate how public policy components move within a government structure and flow from one stage to another; they also depict the relationships between these components. These figures employ three kinds of text boxes: some outlined with solid thick borders, others with solid thin borders, and others with dotted borders. The text boxes with solid thick borders represent the key topical component(s) of the section in which the figure is located; those with solid thin borders are activities or structural parts that are related to the material in boxes with solid thick borders; and those with dotted borders represent activities that take place in the background to move the process forward. Questions for critical thinking that can be used for group discussion or individual reflection are provided at the end of each chapter.

This book takes a learning-by-doing approach. To help readers acquire and apply the soft and hard skills described throughout the first part of the book, part II offers 14 practical exercises. These exercises are based on real issues (with some modifications) that exist within the federal and provincial governments, specifically in the fields of energy, employment, the environment, education, training, tourism, health care, gaming, immigration, international trade, equity, telecommunication, and public housing. Readers are invited to imagine themselves as public policy developers who have been asked to develop public policy products on a broad range of policy matters based on the provided information. While these scenarios provide basic information, readers may be required to do additional research or make educated assumptions; it is critical that these assumptions be described and documented, as different information may result in different policy directions. There is no single correct answer to any of these exercises; however, as the exercises progress, readers will get a better sense of what policy issues are priorities and how best to write about or present them. Following part II is glossary of key terms and their working definitions in the context of this book.

A FRAMEWORK FOR PUBLIC POLICY DEVELOPMENT

INTRODUCTION

DEFINING PUBLIC POLICY

In this chapter, we will begin by establishing a working definition of the term *public policy* that brings together several key components put forward by social scientists. Developing a definition that is acceptable to everyone is difficult because different people have varying conceptions of what constitutes a public policy. This term has been appropriated as a generic concept that covers many activities performed by politicians, bureaucrats, and government agencies vaguely related to policy matters. People are sometimes surprised to learn that not all government programs are public policies of the government in power, and that public policies are not always formal pieces of law created by government. It is a commonly held notion that public policies must be consciously made, but sometimes a government's silence or inaction is de facto public policy. There are a number of reasons why this may occur; a lack of time, effort, or priority can result in an issue falling through the cracks as the government tries to meet the many challenges and demands made by the public.

This book adopts the following working definition of *public policy* to anchor our discussion on the topic: a public policy is an embodiment of both formal and informal actions (or inactions) carried out by the government on specific issues that have significant social, economic, political, and/or environmental impact on specific population groups or the public at large. It is usually carried out in the name of the public good and represents the government's position. This position is often, but not necessarily, supported by human and financial resources, organizational structures and processes, ideological justifications, or legal, financial, and/or military sanctions.

While it may not be perfect, this definition incorporates several key components of what constitutes a public policy as proposed by a number of social scientists. This definition aligns with, but does not duplicate, Jackson and Jackson's (2001, p. 499) definition, which is characterized by its public sector origin and enforcement through legal or other coercive sanctions; Dye's (1978, p. 3) definition of public policy as "whatever governments choose to do or not to do"; and Pal's (1992, p. 2) definition as "a course of action or inaction chosen by public authorities to address a given problem or interrelated set of problems."

THE VALUE OF PUBLIC POLICY DEVELOPMENT

Public policy development provides opportunities for the government to consult the public and stakeholder groups

Part of the public policy development process is to identify public issues and analyze relevant information through consultation with the public and stakeholder groups. This process facilitates a deep understanding of the segments of the population that may be affected by a change to the status quo. The perspectives that emerge from this dialogue can unfold as integral parts of a public policy.

Public policy development enables the government to translate its vision in a systematic manner

A political party usually has a vision, which may be articulated in a written political platform and publicized during the election process, or may simply exist as a set of vague ideas about issues that remain abstract. To translate this vision into action, it is critical to undergo a comprehensive public policy development process in which the following occurs:

- core issues are identified
- research is conducted
- relevant information and data are analyzed
- stakeholder groups are consulted or collaborated with
- legal opinions and implications are sought
- financial costs and risk factors are considered
- organizational, political, and administrative implications are examined
- policy options are formulated and debated by politicians

Going through this rigorous procedure enables the government to have full knowledge of the benefits and risks of a particular public policy prior to its implementation. Realistically, the process cannot anticipate all of the scenarios that may arise when a vision is put into operation, but at the very least, inconsistencies will be minimized.

Public policy development provides a framework for developing legislation and regulations

A piece of legislation and its regulations may not consist of all the policy details; however, thinking through as many aspects as possible during the development process certainly assists in the drafting of legislation that is consistent with the original policy intentions. Public policy development, at its most comprehensive, should accomplish the following:

- establish the policy principles, objectives, and scope of impact
- identify target groups and institutions, and formulate their duties and obligations
- strengthen accountability
- define the roles of the government and related agencies
- decide on mechanisms of monitoring and enforcement
- organize the structure and processes required for implementation
- estimate the financial requirements, derive the human resources implications, and calculate a time frame for implementation

If the government chooses to go the legislative route, this articulation of details at the public policy development stage lays the groundwork for future legislative and regulation development.

Public policy development provides the government with a framework for action

When a public policy is created through this process, it is an embodiment of public consultation, documentary research, external interviews and focus groups, and internal discussions among politicians and public servants. When the policy is officially adopted by the cabinet—and potentially followed by a piece of legislation—it provides a framework within which programs or services can be designed and implemented. Although the policy framework is merely one of many factors (including, but not limited to, finance, resources, regional differences, culture, and time) considered in the design of programs and services, it is of the utmost importance as its principles and objectives are the reference points against which program and service details are measured.

Public policy development enables the government to clearly communicate its rationale and supporting evidence to the public

An understanding of stakeholder interest and public opinion, obtained through consultation, provides politicians and public servants with the opportunity to customize their communication messages. Since communication and public policy development occupy different spheres in separate departments of the government, public policy documents (such as briefing notes) assist public servants in charge of communication to write public messages that align with the public policy.

While these five benefits may not be immediately obvious to politicians and public servants, they are usually grateful that a comprehensive and rigorous policy development process has taken place, as this increased level of detail makes their interactions with ministers, legal counsel, program designers, internal and external stakeholder groups, and the public much easier.

THE BENEFITS OF A COMPREHENSIVE PUBLIC POLICY DEVELOPMENT PROCESS

A comprehensive public policy development process

- ensures that the government is made aware of the interests and opinions of stakeholder groups and the public though consultation;
- enables the government to translate its vision into policy in a systematic and transparent manner;
- provides a framework for developing legislation and regulations;
- provides a framework for the government when considering and executing its actions; and
- equips the government with rationales and supportive evidence to communicate to the public.

SCOPE AND IMPACTS OF PUBLIC POLICIES IN CANADA

Although public policies are abstract notions, their existence affects our behaviour on a daily basis. They have great bearing on our society's structure and future. Public policies inform the way people make decisions—how to save for retirement, educate and arrange care for children, utilize health care facilities, access housing, and so on. Governments are widening the breadth of their involvement in the everyday lives of citizens. The vast number of bills with personal and institutional implications that are passed in parliament every year attests to the importance of public policies (Inwood, 2009, p. 134).

An example of the broad scope and impact of public policy is the federal government's adoption of a Keynesian economic approach in the early 1940s. The theory maintains that the best way to fight a recession is to increase government spending; accordingly, the military expenses during the Second World War may be seen as having ended the Great Depression of the 1930s. After the Second World War, the federal government continued to endorse a Keynesian policy to stimulate economic growth and employment, in spite of mounting debts and deficits (Miljin, 2008, p. 134). The momentum of this policy continued unabated until the Liberal Party acknowledged in 1994 that debt was the root cause of Canada's economic decline and high unemployment. At that time, the government decided to abandon the policy, and this helped to arrest the pace of the accumulation of debt in the late 1990s (Miljin, 2008, pp. 123–124). Scholars who believed that globalization was the actual source of high unemployment did not support such an abrupt change in policy direction (Capeheart and Milovanovic, 2007, pp. 81–87; Cramme and Diamond, 2009, pp. 9–12).

Although the federal government had largely abandoned the Keynesian method in the 1990s, it once again adopted this type of policy in response to the near collapse of the financial sector in the United States in 2008, creating a stimulus plan to spend $47 billion on the Canadian economy. The thinking behind this implementation was to allow an easier flow of capital, create jobs, stabilize the economy, and restore public confidence. The impact of this policy remains unmeasured; there are indicators that suggest that the economy may have stabilized, but the unemployment rate is still high and the federal government has resumed its pattern of an annual deficit and high national debt (Palmer and Egan, 2011, p. B8).

Another example of the broad scope and impact of public policy is Canada's official bilingualism policy, which has had a profound effect on Canadians. The *Official Languages Act* of 1969 guaranteed language rights to individuals, equitable representation of the two official linguistic groups—English and French—in the federal public service, and the right to work in the language of one's choice. As a result of this policy, there are more bilingual public services, official bilingual communications, and French-language schools and programs throughout Canada, and there is more francophone work in the federal government and financial assistance for extending the rights of official-language minorities and francophone culture.

The federal and provincial financial support policies for the elderly or disadvantaged provide another example of public policies with a broad scope and impact. Those eligible may receive income support in the form of social assistance, Old Age Security, Guaranteed Income Supplement, or Employment Insurance. There are additional income support programs at both federal and provincial levels, such as the Canadian Pension Plan, Spousal Allowance, Disability Allowance, drug subsidies, and social housing options. The federal income support policy consumes a sizable sum of money and has a broad effect on many Canadians. In 2004–2005, the federal government spent $23.6 billion on the Canada Pension Plan, $22.2 billion on Old Age Security, and $23 billion on Employment Insurance and social assistance. One-quarter of Canadians in the labour force collected Employment Insurance payments at some point in recent years, and approximately three million Canadians receive welfare support annually (Miljin, 2008, pp. 161–162). This public policy meets the financial needs of Canadians at various stages of their lives and has a redistributive effect on income.

SUMMARY

Although there is a lack of consensus on the concept of public policy, the working definition put forward here captures the key components that different social scientists consider integral to the concept. Public policy development is beneficial to the government because it puts forward a systematic approach, solicits public and stakeholder input, lays the policy foundation for legislative change, aligns policy and programs properly, and promotes clarity in public communication.

QUESTIONS FOR CRITICAL THINKING

1. List 10 things in your environment, or activities that you have carried out recently, that are the result of government regulations.
2. This chapter provides a working definition of public policy. What are the limitations of this definition? How would you address these limitations in your own definition?
3. If public policies affect Canadians, and the developmental process they undergo is beneficial to the government, what reasons would the government have for not undertaking a comprehensive development process for every public policy on its agenda?

PUBLIC POLICY DEVELOPERS

INTRODUCTION

Formulating social, economic, cultural, and environmental policies in the public sector is one way to instigate change in the private and public spheres of everyday life. An interest in producing a lasting and positive impact on people and society is what usually leads a person to pursue a career in public policy development.

This chapter focuses on the people who develop public policies, the kind of work they do in the public sector, and the basic ingredients needed for their work to be effective. These ingredients include general and specialized knowledge, as well as a specific skill set. To perform well, public policy developers must also be cognizant of their work environment, develop survival strategies, and utilize their knowledge and skills in an adaptive manner. To guide and assist developers in their work, a generic framework of public policy development will also be outlined in this chapter.

WHO DEVELOPS PUBLIC POLICY?

Public policy developers are usually public servants working in the government. While there are no formal studies on the backgrounds or attributes of these public servants, general observation suggests that this work attracts young, university-educated men and women. Some are fresh out of university, others have transferred or been promoted from the program side of other departments, and a few come from the community or non-profit sector. Many of them occupy positions at a more junior level, working as research assistants, researchers, junior policy analysts, and policy analysts. Those who are promoted from within the government and have a background in policy usually occupy more advanced positions, such as policy or senior advisor, as they already have several years of policy or planning experience. A few may be political aides who come from the offices of ministers. A limited group is from the private sector, and they usually join government departments that deal with the economic, commercial, financial, or industrial sectors. As public policies increasingly expand into new domains, there are indications that people with private sector experience are apt candidates for senior policy positions. All of the public servants who occupy the junior and senior positions discussed above are, loosely termed, public policy developers.

The educational qualifications for public policy developers have increased over the last decade. From 1960s to the 1990s, a general undergraduate degree was a sufficient qualification for a public policy developer. Due largely to the high supply of undergraduate applicants in the public sector, graduate degrees are now generally required. To work at a senior level in this field, a postgraduate degree along with several years of policy work is desirable. This tends to give an edge to academics who have university research experience. Before the turn of this century, it was uncommon to find PhDs working in government—this is no longer the case.

FUNCTIONS OF THE PUBLIC POLICY DEVELOPER

Public policy developers are employed in almost every line department and central agency in the government. Line departments or ministries are headed by ministers (or line ministers) and are responsible for specific portfolios, such as education, employment, and economic development. Central agencies are government bodies that review and approve public policies, and legal, management, and funding issues. Public policy developers in line departments focus on developing public policies related to the mandates of their departments, whereas those in central agencies focus on analyzing and coordinating policy documents from line departments, and developing policies related to the mandates of their agencies.

In terms of reporting arrangements, public policy developers report directly to either their manager or director of public policy development. These managers and directors report to assistant deputy ministers, who have public policy development in their portfolios, among other responsibilities. An assistant deputy minister reports to the deputy minister. Deputy ministers report to the ministers of their line departments. Although public policy developers report to a manager or director, policy products are typically customized to the minister of their department or central agency.

Public policy development work covers a broad range of policy-related activities. For people who do not work in government, the most obvious question is: What does a public policy developer in the government do on a daily basis? This question sounds simple, but the answer varies depending on the resources and structures of the organization in which the public policy developer works. A department with a large budget and an important portfolio (such as health or community services) usually has a greater division of labour based on functions—policies, programs, financial administration, communication, and external liaising—that are demarcated in different branches. For example, a large department may have a policy branch, a planning branch, a communication branch, a legal branch, and numerous program or service branches. Alternatively, a minister of a smaller department may have fewer resources, and therefore the structure of his or her department is more compact; for example, the public policy development and analysis function, planning function, and a program evaluation function may all be under the umbrella of a single branch manager.

FIGURE 2.1: ORGANIZATIONAL STRUCTURE OF A LARGE GOVERNMENT DEPARTMENT

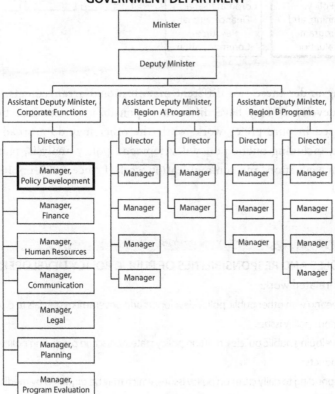

FIGURE 2.2: ORGANIZATIONAL STRUCTURE OF A SMALL GOVERNMENT DEPARTMENT

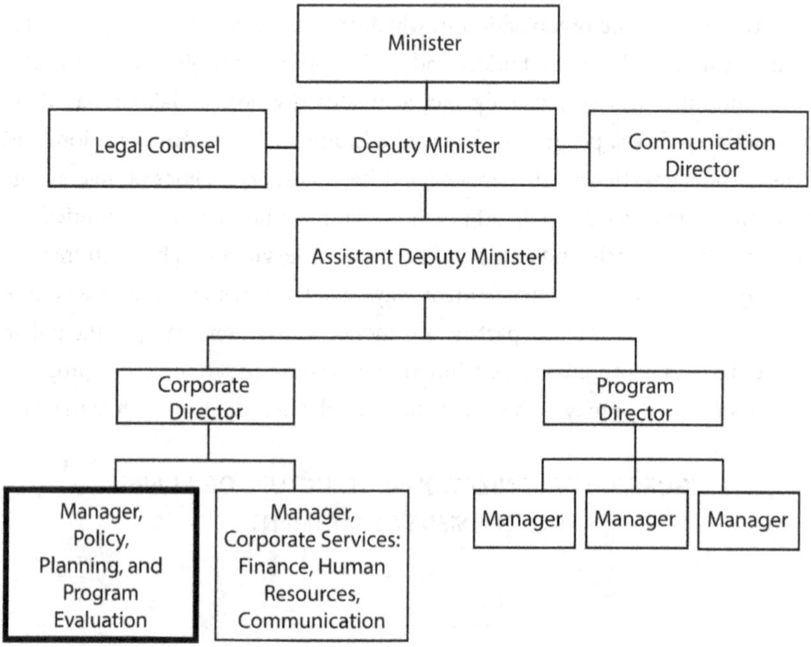

Working under these two different organizational arrangements, public policy developers may have different responsibilities: one may be very specialized in pure policy work, while the other may do a broad range of work, including public policy development, policy analysis, planning, program evaluation, and communication work (Prince, 2007, pp. 166–167, 178–180).

ROLES AND RESPONSIBILITIES OF PUBLIC POLICY DEVELOPERS

Policy-related work:

- meeting with other public policy developers and government officials to discuss various policy issues
- developing public policies, drafting policy statements, and producing policy products
- responding to daily crises on policy issues, which may be triggered by media coverage, stakeholder statements or announcements, and public opinion

- briefing and advising politicians (and their aides), ministers, and senior bureaucrats
- developing policy guidelines and public education materials
- making presentations to cabinet committees and other central agencies
- preparing briefing notes, briefing binders, presentation notes or slides, policy papers, consultation papers, cabinet submissions, management board submissions, and other policy products
- providing legislative supports and ensuring policy consistency in new legislation and regulations, or amendments to existing legislation and regulations
- liaising and collaborating with stakeholder groups and organizations
- arranging and conducting consultations, interviews, and focus groups with stakeholders and segments of the public, as well as creating partnerships and collaborative relations with these groups

Program-related work:
- identifying and reviewing programs with similar objectives in other jurisdictions
- designing new programs derived from public policies
- reviewing program data and reports to identify policy issues
- assisting the development of program administration policies or guidelines
- assisting program staff to establish monitoring and enforcement mechanisms to ensure compliance with public policies
- evaluating programs and assessing their effectiveness and efficiency

Planning-related work:
- developing strategic plans for the ministry
- liaising with external agencies and stakeholder organizations, and managing interdepartmental and cross-jurisdictional relations
- collaborating with the communications department and developing public communication plans
- preparing and analyzing budgets, and determining the allocation of future program funding
- collaborating with other jurisdictions to jointly plan future policies and programs

Communication-related work:
- drafting correspondence in response to public inquiries or complaints
- providing guidance on public education and training (such as e-learning modules or web pages) related to new public policies and programs
- implementing public communication activities (such as hotlines, seminars, webinars, and speaking tours) related to new public policies and programs
- assisting with writing press releases
- drafting speeches for senior bureaucrats
- arranging training workshops and conferences
- managing internal and external stakeholder groups' requests
- briefing international delegates on policy issues and program activities

SCOPE OF KNOWLEDGE

Public policy developers require a combination of knowledge and skills to fulfill this broad range of responsibilities. The traditional public policy developer, who has a narrow specialization of knowledge, is being replaced by professionals who have a broad spectrum of knowledge as the result of post-secondary education and years of work experience.

Thirty years ago, a background in economics was common among public policy developers. Knowledge of macro- or microeconomics often placed public policy developers in a good position to make a diagnosis or forecast of the economy, or to conduct a cost-benefit or market analysis. A specialized economic knowledge base limited public policy development to a technical analysis mode, and restricted full comprehension of the complete public policy development process, including political agenda setting (Mintrom, 2007, pp. 152–154).

Today, while economic knowledge is still needed for policy development, an interdisciplinary knowledge base is provided by public policy developers who have been educated in various social sciences and humanities disciplines, such as literature, fine art, anthropology, psychology, sociology, law, political science, business administration, urban planning, and social work, as well as the natural and physical sciences, including agriculture, climatology, engineering, marine sciences, and geography. There is value in bringing the diverse and sophisticated perspectives of generalists, specialists, and interdisciplinary experts together to formulate public policies. Mintrom (2007, pp. 155–157) argues that public policy development may be experiencing a paradigm shift, as the mainstream policy perspective must now be augmented by an alternative policy perspective to meet the demands created by expanding policy domains. Meanwhile, Prince believes that with the introduction of the relatively new role of public policy developers as advisors, public policy development has become a "soft craft" that requires "enthusiasm, conviction, and instincts for survival" (2007, pp. 164–165). Public policy developers must use scientific knowledge, statistical data, social psychology, and human relations to adapt to constantly changing political environments and organizational contexts.

A background in these disciplines is an asset, but is not adequate on its own. It establishes a foundation upon which specialized policy-related knowledge can be acquired. Public policy developers must be well read in research reports, conference proceedings, academic studies, current media reports, and government documents. Furthermore, on a regular basis, they need to tap into the professional, technical, and business knowledge of those working in specialized policy fields. They also have to be well informed of the opinions and positions of stakeholder groups and those with direct field experience.

SCOPE OF SKILLS

Along with a broad knowledge base, it is equally important that public policy developers possess a wide range of skills. This raises the question of how many generalist and specialist employees one policy department needs. In addition, it raises the issue of outsourcing public policy development projects to private consulting firms, the academic sector, or think tanks (Howlett and Lindquist, 2007, pp. 91–92). The availability of financial resources and government priorities largely determines the answers to these issues.

Since the 1960s, a centralized parliamentary federalism has gradually changed to become a decentralized system focused on fiscal restraints. These changes have necessitated a shift in public policy development from a rationalistic, client-based, argumentative style to a focus on process, interaction, and participation. With these changes, the skill set required of a team of competent public policy developers has also changed (Howlett and Lindquist, 2007, pp. 104–105). It is essential that current and future generations of public policy developers be well trained in conducting research and have good communication skills and consultation, facilitation, and negotiation abilities, as well as excellent time management, interpersonal, networking, team-building, and advising skills.

These skills can be learned and acquired through professional development courses offered by colleges, universities, consulting firms, and internal government training centres. Better still, potential public policy developers may gain these abilities in an incremental manner through hands-on experience in the workplace, and during mentorships, internships, job shadowing, secondments, acting positions, committee activities, and volunteer positions.

Research Skills

Public policy developers need to be able to develop appropriate research methodology. The term *methodology* encompasses many activities, including how to pose research questions, apply measurement indicators and tools, and collect, compile, and tabulate data. Developing a methodology with pertinent research questions is key to resolving policy issues.

Citing several studies of public administration doctoral programs in the United States, Waugh, Hy, and Brudney (1991, pp. 49–56) noted that the traditional academic research methods taught in these programs have a limited impact on the outcome of government decisions when used in the public sector. While these are American findings, observation of the contemporary Canadian public sector suggests they may also be applicable to Canada. Traditional academic research methods (such as field surveys and experimental assessments) are time-consuming in practice, and cabinet ministers see their findings as largely irrelevant and inapplicable (LaPlante, 1991, pp. 57–65). Today, public policy developers in Canada seldom utilize the sophisticated research methods taught by university professors, and their research findings are rarely presented in an academic manner. Recent graduates may need to adjust their research methods and move away from an academic style of presentation, taking into consideration cabinet ministers' needs, priorities, and political interests. Contemporary public policy developers must employ simplified research methods (which may yield rudimentary, but still useful, findings) and present their findings in a user-friendly manner.

In addition, public policy developers must analyze information accurately. There are challenges associated with drawing exclusively on secondary sources such as academic studies and research reports. While the information and data derived from secondary sources may appear to be relevant to a particular policy issue, it is important to keep in mind that the researchers who collected this information may have done so with different objectives in mind. As a result, the studies may measure different aspects of the same subject; therefore, the research findings may not necessarily be applied to the present policy issues.

Public policy developers need to have the analytical skills to determine the applicability of data to the policy issues that they are working on.

The research skills public policy developers employ are essentially the same as those used for academic research; the difference, in many cases, is that the methodology is simplified, more secondary sources are utilized, and only data relevant to policy issues is scrutinized. While academic research studies are geared towards theoretical insight, critique of existing studies, and discovering new empirical findings, policy research studies are geared toward the pragmatic end of the formulation of a public policy. Further discussion of research is included in chapter 7.

Communication Skills
Effective public policy communication is brief, clear, jargon-free, simplified, and easy to understand. Public policy developers must communicate in a manner that is sensitive to the political context and the people involved. As they are often asked to make verbal presentations to senior managers, ministers, and internal and external stakeholder groups; write papers to express their ideas, highlight consultation results, and brief senior bureaucrats on policy issues; and dispatch correspondence, the ability to write and speak effectively is essential for public policy developers to perform well in a government environment. On many occasions, public policy developers have to present technical information and write briefing notes, memoranda, letters, discussion papers, options papers, consultation papers, proposals, orientation or training materials, progress and research reports, summary notes, and cabinet submissions. They are required to facilitate meetings, conduct focus group discussions, negotiations, and interviews, and lead public or stakeholder consultations.

On rare occasions, public policy developers are asked to speak to the public to clarify policy or program issues. Not only are they required to know how to speak and write articulately, they are sometimes asked to explore the use of media technology (such as Twitter) to discuss ideas and positions. Despite the increasing importance of and reliance on social media as a means of broadcasting information, governments are slow to inform and communicate with the public using these channels. The organizational culture of the public sector, which embraces less-than-transparent public policy development and the hierarchical management of information, constitutes a major barrier for making public policy development a completely open and trusting process (Fyfe and Crookall, 2010). The government is still very risk-averse in its democratization of the public policy development process, and there is a long way to go for the public sector to utilize social media to its optimal capacity. For these reasons, the communication skills that public policy developers must possess are largely limited to those needed to understand and use traditional methods and media.

Consultation Skills

A consultation is a conversation between two or more parties in which the objective is to exchange ideas and find solutions to perceived problems. These problems may not affect all parties equally, but each will have a vested interest in finding a resolution. From the government's perspective, consultations with external and internal stakeholder groups enable public policy developers to discover concerns and proposed solutions. External stakeholder groups may include community organizations, associations, unions, or institutions. Internal stakeholder groups include only internal government departments. To conduct a consultation, a researcher, acting as a representative of the government, must focus on issues that the government wishes to tackle. The primary objective of a consultation is to elicit and probe issues beyond a superficial level of understanding; this is only possible if the researcher can make people feel comfortable enough to share information, and if he or she listens carefully to what they have to say without prejudice and without losing sight of the key issues. During a consultation, there is always the possibility that the researcher will have to defuse inter-group tensions that may arise as a result of competing or conflicting interests. He or she may also have to identify and highlight recurring themes and issues, and find common ground among stakeholder groups. The following section describes two types of consultation skills that are seldom discussed in relation to public policy development.

Research and Communication in Consultation

Consultation skills are connected to research and communication skills. Sometimes, cabinet ministers (policy decision-makers) do not see the value of the research techniques used or findings produced by public policy developers. This may be because the public policy developer has not properly consulted with the minister, or listened carefully to his or her concerns. Perhaps as a consequence of their post-secondary education, some public policy developers have a tendency to fixate on learned research methodologies without taking their environment into consideration or adapting their methodologies to the policy issues under examination. Their hesitance to customize their methodology in turn affects their ability to determine proper indicators to measure the policy variables at stake, and may therefore yield results that cabinet ministers do not consider pertinent or actionable (LaPlante, 1991, pp. 57–65).

Listening well to the minister's concerns is an important part of the consultative skill set. Research findings can be difficult for the layperson to understand; therefore, connecting these findings to political issues that are relevant to the minister and presenting this information in a user-friendly manner in plain language is imperative. It is also beneficial for public policy developers to confer with cabinet ministers to find out what they are looking for in research briefings, so that the policy developers can frame their findings in ways that are intelligible and pragmatic. One of the aims of consultation is to find the best way to present research methods and findings to an audience—which, it can be safely assumed, is not intrigued by academic jargon or sophistication, but is interested in knowing only the relevant facts on which to base decisions.

Non-Verbal Language in Consultation

In addition to verbal and written skills, public policy developers should also be capable of communicating non-verbally by interpreting facial expressions, hand gestures, and body posturing (Waugh and Manns, 1991, p. 139). These visual cues convey specific messages, and should be observed to detect indications of discomfort, annoyance, or acceptance among members of stakeholder groups. While there might be different styles of consultations, a public policy developer's ability to decipher both explicit and subtle messages from stakeholders and members of the public at any session is invaluable. Mintrom (2007, p. 154), who maintains that the narrow technical training of public policy developers in university may not include teaching the variety of soft skills that contemporary public policy development demands, includes interpreting non-verbal language as one of these skills.

Beyond interpreting other people's gestures, it is also important for public policy developers to remember that their own non-verbal cues, whether conscious or unconscious, are being observed by the public. Audience members may interpret dismissive gestures, such as frowning, eye rolling, lip twisting, and eyebrow raising, as a signal that the government (as represented by public policy developers) has already made up its mind on certain issues and may not be interested in exploring other options. Consequently, this non-verbal language is part of the consultation skills that public policy developers must hone to do their work in a politically sensitive environment.

Facilitation Skills

Stakeholder consultations may be conducted on an individual or public level. In either type of meeting, the ability of a public policy developer to facilitate is crucial. Prior to a session, public policy developers need to determine what they wish to accomplish during the consultation and clearly communicate their goals to the audience. This information should be shared up front with participants, so that they can align their expectations with the intentions of the consultation. Establishing transparency, as well as setting up a structured environment by outlining the rules, process, scope, topics, time frame, and agenda, may also contribute to the success of a consultation. This kind of facilitation was not part of traditional public policy development work. In the past, public policy developers needed only to research, analyze, and formulate reports. In contrast, consultation is now a fixture in public policy development and, as a result, public policy developers must have strong facilitation skills. This is especially important when consultation sessions are conducted with rival and competing stakeholder groups or between multiple parties—it is not uncommon for these meetings to deteriorate into shouting matches. Public policy developers need to manage participants' expectations, as well as the pace and intensity of the consultation.

Negotiation Skills

When developing a public policy, there are occasions on which public policy developers have to organize negotiation sessions between multiple stakeholder groups. To strike a balance among the opinions of various groups, public policy developers may need to play the role of mediator while negotiating specific policy issues. It is important to recognize that the government is not neutral during mediation—just like the stakeholder groups, it has interests, too. When acting as mediator, the public policy developer's objective is to find a compromise that each party (including the government) can accept. During negotiations, trade-offs are expected; a series of policy issues can be packaged together in such a way that one stakeholder group is satisfied by some proposed solutions, while another is pleased with the others.

Empathy, critical analysis, and sensitivity help public policy developers determine the priorities and inclinations of an individual or group. By utilizing both instinct and awareness, public policy developers can gauge an audience's disposition and anticipate its potential acceptance or rejection of particular solutions. This perceptiveness optimizes their ability to respond, and allows them to think quickly to figure out how to dissect an issue and repackage it to reach a compromise that is well received. It is not uncommon to surreptitiously conduct research to assess a stakeholder group's willingness to accept proposed policy packages, or to launch trial balloons to discover the limitations and expectations of a particular stakeholder. It may be argued, according to Geva-May and Maslove (2007, pp. 186–187), that this tactical manoeuvring requires more than a textbook education. These covert processes are most effective when one is attempting to find a policy solution that involves stakeholder groups with diametrically opposed interests. Because going through the negotiation process enables stakeholders to be cognizant of the constraints and compromises that need to be made to reach a satisfactory conclusion, those that do tend to accept negotiated policy packages in spite of their less-than-ideal contents. McArthur (2007, pp. 257–258) claims these "truly integrative" packages generally work well and are the key to successful public policy development.

Time-Management Skills

Good time management is often based on a comprehensive understanding of the political environment within and procedures under which public policy developers work. The time frame in which public policy developers must do their research, collect data, and analyze information is usually very short because of the high volume of inquiries that ministers receive on a daily basis. On top of practical development-related duties, public policy developers also monitor media coverage of events and attend meetings, conferences, and daily question periods in the legislature. During these activities, ministers need to have information and answers as quickly as possible, which reduces the turnaround time for briefing notes, speeches, documents, letters, and background information. As a result, public policy developers often do not have enough time to do extensive research or analysis. Strategies on how to deal with short turnaround time for policy products will be dealt with later in this chapter.

Academics commonly view research as a process that includes the following: posing the research hypotheses, designating a research methodology (which includes identifying research techniques, indicators, measurement, and coding), implementing the research, compiling, tabulating, reviewing, and analyzing data, and writing a research paper. This is not enormously different from the method ordinarily employed by public policy developers—except that the time typically allocated in the public sector for research and results is much briefer. Depending on the policy requests from the minister's office, the entire research process is often compressed to weeks, days, or even hours. There are exceptions, such as those requiring a new piece of legislation or amendments to existing legislation, which may take place over a period of a year or more. The legislative route requires additional research and negotiation on the part of lawyers to ensure legislative consistency across different pieces of law, and a certain degree of consensus among the ministers responsible for implementing the proposed amendments to the existing legislation. Additional time is also needed for negotiation among ministers regarding the organizational and resource implications for their ministries under the proposed legislation or amendments. In some cases, federal and provincial governments may need to come to an agreement on the proposed legislative changes. However, even within these exceptions the research process is often quite compressed, unless the public consultation process is built in or the cabinet has changed its policy priority.

In a fast-paced policy environment, a lot of groundwork must be completed prior to taking on new policy work—false starts in research should be avoided. This groundwork (which is discussed in detail in chapters 6 and 7) includes posing proper policy questions and developing a research plan to address these questions. It is critical to set priorities for different types of public policy development activities, such as documentary review, stakeholder consultations, and focus groups. If it is suspected that a new public policy may have major implications—and it is expected that a piece of new law or legislative amendment may be an end product—policy work is often done as a team (often made up of those seconded from other departments) or outsourced to external consultants when financial resources are available. Teamwork is required to set in motion numerous public policy development tasks, such as research and consultation. These activities tend to produce more documents and issues that need to be resolved, including issue integration, policy quality control, and synchronization of activities. Ultimately, on an individual level, the time saved by working as a team is often consumed by the new duties it produces.

Team-Building Skills

Major public policy development undertakings sometimes require a team of public servants to work together. The team may be small or moderate in size, and the members may be colleagues within the same policy department or from different departments. The composition of the team is largely a function of the complexity of the policy matter, expertise required, availability of financial resources, and time allocated for the work.

The core objective of team building is usually to maximize performance levels and work quality. Whether steered by a leader or not, all activities performed by the team members should be coordinated and synchronized. Policy issues must be integrated to ensure consistency and coherence. For collaborative purposes, public policy developers need team-building skills. These skills consist of the ability to communicate honestly and clearly, understand group dynamics, compromise on common terms of reference and definitions, plan protocols and procedures collectively, provide input and receive feedback from others, solve problems collaboratively, adhere to timetables, focus on getting results, and interact socially with other team members. This is not an exhaustive list of skills, but it provides a broad idea of what team members must bring to the table when working in a group.

Interpersonal Skills

In the past, when most public policy development work depended on technical research and analytical skills, working in isolation was sufficient. However, contemporary public policy development requires an ability to work with other people, including those employed in similar and other policy areas, as well as members of internal and external stakeholder groups (Mintrom, 2007, p. 146). Interpersonal skills include the ability to communicate, listen, empathize, relate, connect, and collaborate with people regardless of their diverse statuses, backgrounds, or working styles.

In order to formulate policy issues, public policy developers are usually required to interview and consult with members of different segments of the population with diverse cultures, worldviews, values, attitudes, and behavioural norms that may differ from their own. To be able to mingle with and relate to a broad range of people on a daily basis requires a clear and respectful demeanour, and the ability to listen attentively and watch for non-verbal communication to reduce potential misunderstandings. It is also important to be able to explain and clarify, show a genuine interest and demonstrate empathy, smile and make eye contact, be positive and confident, and inspire trust.

Networking Skills

Networking skills are necessary to broaden a public policy developer's circle of reference. Like interpersonal skills, networking skills are not always innate, but they can be acquired. The ability to branch out and build relationships with members of other segments of the community is useful when public policy developers require referrals or esoteric information. Usually, these skills are enhanced when a networking strategy, which articulates clear goals and timetables, a list of people to be met, a database of contacts, and networking methods, is in place. They are also complemented by an inclination for team-work and helping others, and a large reservoir of sustained motivation and enthusiasm. A public policy developer may draw upon his or her network to resolve some policy issues; a network of reliable contacts can be counted on to provide connections to additional contacts or to keep a vigilant eye on activi-ties within communities. This is especially important when time constraints are demanding.

Networking skills allow public policy developers to remain up-to-date on the current situations of both external and internal stakeholder groups. Through their contacts, public policy developers are able to discover what involved parties are doing or planning, and the rationale behind their activities. This information is helpful when developing public policies because it creates a lens through which different stakeholder groups can be understood, and ultimately helps public policy developers determine what these groups may perceive as acceptable or unacceptable.

Advising Skills

Mintrom (2007, p. 146) maintains that the role of public policy developer has shifted from analyst to advisor. This means public policy developers are expected to provide timely, educated advice, rather than just reporting on re-search findings to politicians. Policy analysts currently provide policy advisors with the research material they need to analyze the most up-to-date informa-tion, create political arguments, provide ideas on resolutions, and make rec-ommendations. Unlike an oral defence of a doctoral dissertation, public policy developers are not present to defend their policy positions in person. In order to advise politicians, public policy developers have to know their audience, the political context, the history of the issues at stake, the availability of feasible options, and the potential effects on the jurisdiction. Advice must be presented in a tactful, succinct, and clear manner; according to Prince (2007, p. 165), "effective policy advising is astute, shrewd, and subtle." In reality, public policy developers must customize their approach to giving advice to the minister's temperament. Some advice is easily adopted when it is presented flexibly and supported by sound evidence; other advice is taken only when the political and fiscal contexts are taken into consideration.

Advising requires astute perception and the ability to develop trusting relationships with senior management and politicians. Some public policy developers have identified gaining the confidence of a minister's executive assistant as a critical step to securing the minister's trust.

CHARACTERISTICS OF THE PUBLIC POLICY WORK ENVIRONMENT

When public policy developers are equipped with the knowledge and skills discussed above, they may be in a position to perform well in the public sector; however, they must also be cognizant of the features of their work environment and how to use their knowledge and skills within this sphere. The following section will help prepare the prospective public policy developer deal with quick turnaround times, the requirement of up-to-date and accurate information, stakeholder groups with competing or conflicting interests, recurring issues, the benefits of institutional memory, and the necessary communication between line departments and central agencies.

Short Turnaround Time

The concrete deliverables for public policy developers are policy products. These are mainly internal documents (e.g., briefing notes, cabinet submissions), although some are for external use (e.g., public consultation papers, policy statements). Policy products will be further discussed in chapter 4.

As previously mentioned, time for carrying out policy activities and delivering policy products is often extremely limited. This time crunch may be due to any number of reasons, ranging from breaking news to editorial comments. When issues become urgent unexpectedly, public policy developers must quickly provide specific policy products (e.g., briefing notes) to ministers based on their requests for up-to-date information. Sometimes this involves working with people at different levels or within various departments of the government bureaucracy. Draft papers are vetted by various colleagues in other departments and, by the time their comments and input are circulated back into the hands of public policy developers, the time left for revision and completion is rather limited. Public policy developers then have to review the suggestions, integrate the revisions, and finalize the documents to meet the deadline.

At times the decision-making process moves slowly because many urgent items are already lined up on the minister's desk for his or her review or approval—this bottleneck tends to increase at the top level of the government. There are also situations in which ministers cannot make decisions on policy work because other issues (such as complaints from constituents or recent court decisions) have arisen and assumed a higher priority, or new information has emerged that affects the policy direction and the minister needs more time to consult his or her colleagues. After a minister has consulted with his or her colleagues, and reviewed and commented on policy products, they are usually sent back to public policy developers for revision or additional research without changing the original due date.

The Need for Up-to-Date, Accurate Information

Ministers and senior bureaucrats depend on public policy developers to have the most up-to-date information, obtained through research and consultations with stakeholder groups, on policy matters. To enhance the quality of their policy work, it is also important for public policy developers to be familiar with the latest Statistics Canada data, relevant developments in other jurisdictions and countries, new publications on academic research, news related to community or institutional development, and recent public opinion polls.

A public policy developer's ongoing task is to collect information and update senior officials on the latest development of a policy matter. As such, public policy developers are expected to read diligently, liaise frequently with stakeholder groups, attend relevant functions, network widely, and manage their time well. In other words, public policy developers must always be in a state of preparedness. Out-of-date and inaccurate information reflects poorly on a public policy developer's performance and the quality of his or her work. Furthermore, if a public policy developer provides incorrect information that is then quoted by a minister, the minister may suffer public embarrassment.

The Presence of Stakeholder Groups with Competing or Conflicting Interests

A public policy seldom affects only one stakeholder group. It usually impinges on several groups with competing interests and different power bases or resources. Some stakeholder groups may have conflicting values and interests, as well as a long history of tension between them. Policy matters are commonly accompanied by the historical baggage of polarized opinions; examples of such issues include Aboriginal land claim violations, pollution sources, end-of-life support, and foreign ownership of Canadian resources.

When developing a public policy, the position of stakeholder groups, the government, and what we may call the public good must all be taken into consideration. The current emphasis on consultation and negotiation in public policy development implies that policies should be developed face-to-face with stakeholder groups, which may be uncomfortable and burden the public policy developer with defusing tensions and finding common ground.

Recurring Issues and Institutional Memory

Research publications, documents related to policy issues, and internal policy documents may be used more than once during a public policy developer's tenure. Because different stakeholder groups may not be satisfied with the resolution of a particular policy issue, these issues can surface and resurface, each time in a different configuration of contentious issues or with a shift in foci and priorities. Due to changed circumstances or the emergence of new stakeholder groups and alliances, each time these policy issues resurface, there tend to be different preferences expressed with varying degrees of intensity. As a result, they warrant new approaches and options. In spite of this, having institutional memory on these policy items can go a long way toward understanding their dynamics.

The Importance of Communication between Line Departments and Central Agencies

Public policy development is not an isolated act and public policy developers do not work in a vacuum; therefore, development is the joint effort of many players inside the government. It is usually carried out by those in line departments (e.g., the ministry of education) and central agencies (e.g., the treasury board secretariat or the cabinet office). As central agencies are in close contact with each other and the political and bureaucratic sides of the government, those working within them are in an advantageous position to know the political agenda and mindset of ministers. This helps them to determine how and what will work. As line departments often work through ministers and deputy ministers, they receive news on the development of policy issues through their interactions with the central agencies. Public policy developers usually work at the mid-level of government bureaucracy and follow the directions of their ministers and deputy ministers to refine policy issues.

Public policy developers not only revise policy products as part of their daily duties, but they must also engage in ongoing negotiations and find compromises to deal with the conflicting demands of different players in the government. Every time a request for a major revision of a policy direction is received, public policy developers have an obligation to identify the implications and effects of such a change on the overall policy framework. In addition, they have a responsibility to assess whether these requests dilute or undermine the principles of good public policy, and the extent to which each revision would upset the delicate balance of these principles.

PROACTIVE STRATEGIES FOR PUBLIC POLICY DEVELOPERS

When public policy developers are faced with competing or conflicting interests, a proactive strategy that will allow them to perform their duties quickly and effectively is imperative. Below are a few suggestions that have worked successfully in the past.

Establish a Broad Network

An extensive network of knowledgeable and well-connected people enables public policy developers to get background information from individuals with long institutional memories and to obtain up-to-date and accurate information, both of which help them produce policy products within tight time frames.

Networking enables public policy developers to liaise with stakeholder groups and gather intelligence about their communities or members. This may include the moods, mindsets, orientations, beliefs, preferences, and commitments among stakeholder groups, which helps public policy developers to be sensitive to the subtle inner workings of policy issues.

Access and Maintain Extensive and Up-to-Date Knowledge

Public policy developers need a broad knowledge base of the policy issues for which they are responsible. This can be acquired by reading the latest developments in their policy field in print or electronic media; subscribing to the electronic newsletters of relevant associations, organizations, or institutions; and maintaining relationships with community agencies. Statistics Canada's updates on the latest data and survey findings are also essential to keeping abreast of new developments. Social media utilized by professional or business associations, trades councils, and consulting firms are also good sources of information.

Through networking, public policy developers can make connections with scholars, experts, and colleagues who work in similar policy fields or the government; such contacts are great sources of information about what different jurisdictions are doing. Because turnaround time for policy products is usually short, having both a deep understanding of policy issues (including past developments) and a reservoir of the latest information enables effective and informed communication with central agencies, helps to avoid false starts (such as identifying the wrong policy questions for research or trying to obtain information from incorrect sources), and cuts down on developmental lead time.

Build an Effective Filing System

Cultivating a good electronic or manual filing system for documents related to relevant policy fields is a wise investment of a public policy developer's time. Because issues surface and resurface, public policy developers who are able to quickly access historic documents, research notes or briefing books prepared for previous projects, and archived publications (including political party platforms, reports of previous governments, estimates, and speeches) are in a much better position to brief their ministers and senior bureaucrats.

It is a good habit to continually collect relevant information on policy issues and sources. In addition, public policy developers should develop an inventory of web addresses for sites that provide reliable information on various policy matters on which they are working. Websites of different governments, professional associations, global consulting firms, colleges and universities, and international government bodies (such as the World Health Organization) are useful sources of recent publications and policies.

GENERIC FRAMEWORK OF PUBLIC POLICY DEVELOPMENT

Equipped with the appropriate policy knowledge and skill set, public policy developers are in a position to meet the challenges posed by the workplace and to complete the essential components of policy work, outlined below:

> *Identifying the issues:* Public policy developers must determine and identify which of the problems defined by stakeholder groups or individuals are public policy issues that will be placed on the government agenda and which are not. This is discussed in greater depth in chapter 6.

> *Conducting research and analysis:* Once the policy issues have been identified, the public policy developer ascertains how he or she can collect and analyze information to understand the policy issues and to find solutions. This is discussed in further detail in chapter 7.

Presenting policy options and recommendations: After public policy developers have analyzed the research data, they determine the viable policy options for ministers to consider and formulate recommendations. This is discussed in further detail in chapter 8.

Making decisions: The cabinet-approved public policy is tabled and debated in the legislature. The decision-making process involves the interplay between government and opposition parties in a formalized structure. This is discussed in greater depth in chapter 9.

FIGURE 2.3: A FRAMEWORK FOR PUBLIC POLICY DEVELOPMENT

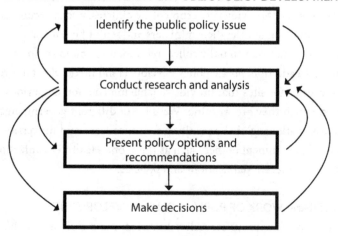

The components of public policy development illustrated in this framework are interconnected. They follow a more or less linear progression from identifying issues to conducting research to providing policy options and recommendations to cabinet ministers on which they will base their decisions. This linear progression is interrupted by research activities, which take place throughout the process; they play a key role in identifying the issue, formulating policy options and recommendations, and, occasionally, in making decisions. This framework of public policy development is consistent with other scholarly typologies in the public policy field. There is more or less a consensus among social scientists on the process of developing public policies in government, although different terms have been used to describe similar processes in the federal and provincial governments. Here are a few examples of frameworks expounded by social scientists specializing in the public policy field:

1. Chandler and Chandler (1979, pp. 121–123) categorized public policy processes into four stages: the identification of a problem, formulation of solutions to the problem, selection of particular solutions, and implementation of the selected solutions.

2. Doern and Phidd (1983, pp. 95–96) articulated a six-stage model of public policy: identification of the problem; definition of the nature of the problem, issues, and potential results; alternative search for various solutions to the problem; choices for making decisions on various options; implementation as the actual translation of the policy decision into a program; and evaluation of the outcomes and impacts of the program. This framework is often described as a policy cycle in which the feedback from the final stage—evaluation—provides information about the first stage—identification—that may lead to another round of public policy development.

3. Wu, Ramesh, Howlett, and Fritzen (2010, pp. 7–9) presented a framework, similar to Doern and Phidd's, which is made up of five components: agenda setting, policy formulation, decision-making, policy implementation, and policy evaluation. These five components cover the identification and selection of policy issues to be placed on the political agenda; development of various alternative means to address the policy issues selected by politicians; the decision by politicians to adopt a specific course of action for implementation; putting into action the policies approved by politicians (often in the form of legislation or programs and services); and evaluation of the public policy in terms of its objectives and impacts.

4. Bardach (2009, pp. xvi, 1–64) focuses on only the first four stages of Doern and Phidd's framework (or the first three components presented by Wu and colleagues) and breaks these down further into eight components: define the problem, assemble some evidence, construct the alternatives, select the criteria, project the outcomes, confront the trade-offs, decide, and tell your story. These components are sequential.

The framework used in this book is consistent with and derived from the components of the models described above; however, the framework used here does not deal with the components—implementation and evaluation—that take place late in the process, after the public policy has been passed in the legislature and received royal assent. The framework used here will be discussed in greater detail in chapters 6 to 9. A comparison of the frameworks described above is presented in table 2.1.

TABLE 2.1: A COMPARISON OF PUBLIC POLICY DEVELOPMENT MODELS

Chandler and Chandler's Public Policy Process	Doern and Phidd's Policy Cycle	Wu et al.'s Public Policy Model	Bardach's Policy Analysis Process	Siu's Public Policy Development Framework
Identification	Identification	Agenda setting	Define the problem	Identification of public policy issue
	Definition		Assemble some evidence	Research and analysis of information
Formulation			Construct the alternatives	
	Alternative search	Policy formulation	Select the criteria	Formulation of policy options and recommendations
			Project the outcomes	
			Confront the trade-offs	
Selection	Choice	Decision-making	Decide	Determination of public policies for implementation
			Tell the story	
Implementation	Implementation	Policy implementation		
	Evaluation	Policy evaluation		

SUMMARY

To be prepared for work in public policy development, public policy developers need a broad scope of knowledge and skill set, which includes research, communication, consultation, negotiation, time-management, team-building, interpersonal, networking, and advisory skills. The work environment in which public policy development is conducted is unique in that there is usually a tight time frame to produce policy products. The job of a public policy developer involves possessing up-to-date and accurate information, having access to an institutional memory, working with stakeholder groups with competing or conflicting interests, and communicating with line departments and central agencies.

These workplace characteristics and specializations necessitate the development of an effective strategy to manage the process of public policy development. This strategy usually involves assembling an extensive network, a broad and up-to-date knowledge base, and an effective filing system. The framework of four key components of public policy development outlined here can be used as a navigational guide to approaching and resolving policy issues.

QUESTIONS FOR CRITICAL THINKING

1. In what ways could college and university programs be modified to help students acquire the professional skills needed to successfully develop public policy?
2. Which three skills required by public policy developers described in this chapter are most important and why?
3. What are the implications of public policy development being increasingly dependent on consultation and negotiation rather than research?

PUBLIC POLICY AND THE GOVERNMENT

INTRODUCTION

There are multiple similarities between the structures of Canada's federal and provincial governments in terms of their public policy decision-making processes. At both the federal and provincial levels, the centralization of public policy development in the offices of the prime minister and the provincial premiers is growing increasingly obvious.

An understanding of how the federal and provincial government systems are structured is fundamental to a public policy developer's ability to utilize his or her knowledge and skills in a way that aligns with the expectations of the minister and the cabinet. This chapter illustrates that the responsibility for public policy development extends beyond public policy developers to many internal stakeholder groups within the government. It presents an overview of federal and provincial systems as they relate to public policy development. The terms used to describe their functions (such as *boards, councils, offices, committees,* and *departments*) are generic and may not correspond strictly to those used in a particular government.

FEDERAL GOVERNMENT STRUCTURE

McArthur (2007, p. 238) argues that most public policy development work is done at the provincial level because the provinces are responsible for two-thirds of government services provided to citizens. He suggests that the federal government's major activity is merely the passive transfer of funds based on federal-provincial negotiations, rather than actual policy work. McArthur's position on public policy development is flawed, as it is based on the incorrect assumption that public policy development takes place only when direct services are being provided. The federal government may not provide many direct services, but it does have a jurisdictional role to play; it must ensure that national standards are met and provide direction for its federal services, as well as those provided by provincial governments. As a result, public policy development must take place at the federal levels.

Cabinet System and Central Agencies

The structure of the federal government is based on a cabinet system with a mandate to develop public policy, central planning, and public management. Johnson (2004) argues that it was the Co-operative Commonwealth Federation (CCF) in Saskatchewan that pioneered this socialist model of central planning and public policy development. This model, which was thoroughly studied by Lipset (1959), includes a central cabinet office that oversees, coordinates, and assesses public policy development in line departments. The federal and some provincial governments have adopted such a model since it was first introduced by the CCF (Dunn, 1995, 1996b).

In the federal government, the prime minister appoints cabinet ministers and chairs the cabinet. Within the cabinet, committees are set up to deal with different policy issues. Acting as a central coordinating body, the Privy Council controls the flow of policy matters by distributing policy documents (which come from the line departments) to the appropriate cabinet members. The latter, in turn, discuss these policy matters in their own cabinet committees to determine and recommend policies for the cabinet to adopt. The cabinet is responsible for setting the overall government agenda and determining policy directions for the country. The Privy Council Office, which is staffed by public servants, briefs the prime minister as well as the chairs of the cabinet committees. This office plays a pivotal role in (a) supporting cabinet committees in various capacities, including communicating decisions and documents; (b) managing the cabinet business processes in accordance with the prime minister's instructions and standards; and (c) facilitating public policy development by collaborating with departments and agencies on proposals, as well as integrating new policy proposals with existing policies and the government's agenda. To execute these roles effectively, the Privy Council Office has established numerous internal secretariats, each of which specializes in a specific function, and all of which are coordinated by the Clerk of the Privy Council Office and the secretary to the cabinet. The Privy Council Office's internal secretariats include:

- cabinet documents
- communications
- economic development
- federal-provincial relations

- intergovernmental affairs
- international relations
- operations
- planning and priorities
- security
- social development

Although policy capabilities in the federal government are spread across line departments and coordinated through the Privy Council Office, in the past decade line departments have been perceived as weak in terms of producing any significant long-term policies from within their departments; this is due to a lack of resources. During this period, the Privy Council has not played a leadership role in developing public policies with long-range significance. Furthermore, policy research capacity is uneven among federal departments, as some have strong internal teams while others have had their policy capacities eroded by budget cuts (Voyer, 2007, pp. 227–232). Increasingly, the lead role for public policy development has been shifted to the Prime Minister's Office.

To mitigate the problems caused by short-term thinking and uncoordinated actions, the federal government has a strategic planning component in which cabinet members participate and make decisions. The planning component is coordinated by the central agencies, the most important of which are the Prime Minister's Office, the Privy Council Office, the Treasury Board, and the Department of Finance (Jackson and Jackson, 2001, p. 275). These agencies have centralized power to integrate, coordinate, monitor, and assess nationwide activities.

The Prime Minister's Office has an overarching role in shaping the policy direction of the country, usually in consultation with cabinet members. The office has a planning and priorities board (known as the Planning and Priorities Committee under the current Conservative government), which determines the direction and agenda of the government, and is the key leader of the cabinet. The office also has a policy bureau; its staff members actively monitor the pulse of the public and stakeholder groups by conducting research, including surveys and consultations, and participating in public events. These policy staff members also monitor all of the core policy issues discussed in cabinet committee and line department briefing notes. The Prime Minister's Office, in consultation with ministers and advisors, prepares the speech from the throne, which outlines the policy directions and key initiatives of the government. Public policies and programs are typically derived from the directions identified in this speech.

FIGURE 3.1: THE FEDERAL CABINET SYSTEM AND PUBLIC POLICIES

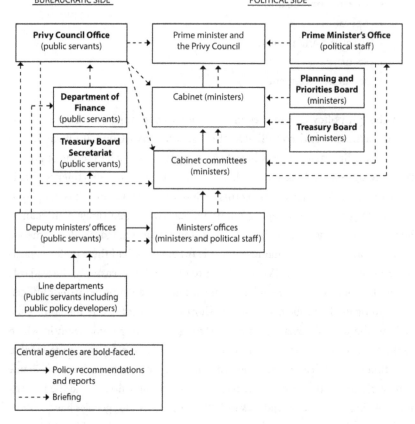

The Privy Council is made up of previous and current ministers of the Crown. The cabinet is a committee within the Privy Council. The Privy Council Office is the main body that provides support to the prime minister and the cabinet. Unlike the Prime Minister's Office, the Privy Council Office is staffed by public servants who develop and coordinate policy matters for the entire government. It briefs both the Prime Minister's Office and the cabinet committees. While the Privy Council Office is composed of many functional units (such as intergovernmental affairs, planning and priorities, and operations), it has a special policy function to coordinate all policy activities, both domestic and international, within the government. The Clerk of the Privy Council Office is the country's top public servant; he or she is the go-between for the Prime Minister's Office, the cabinet, and the federal bureaucracy. As the Privy Council Office is not an elected body, it can only provide information that is as objective and non-partisan as possible; it plays the role of advisor to the elected politicians who sit in the cabinet.

The Treasury Board is a committee of the Privy Council, and is composed of cabinet ministers. It has the mandate to oversee government spending and human resource management. The board brings a realistic perspective to the financial and human resource implications of the programs and services of recommended public policies. The Treasury Board is supported by the Treasury Board Secretariat (run by public servants), which has developed a management system to connect government agenda, policy directions, and finance.

In terms of public policy, the Department of Finance is interested in taxation and fiscal policies, as well as their implications for the Canadian economy and international business initiatives. Its economic and financial research work and forecasts help other government departments develop policies in their own domains. Due to its central role in planning and budgeting, it plays a dominant part in shaping the policies of all other departments.

These four central agencies—the Prime Minister's Office, the Privy Council Office, the Treasury Board, and the Department of Finance—collaborate with each other to ensure that, at least in theory, public policies represent the coordinated efforts of the key central agencies and line departments.

Patterns of Federal Public Policy Development

Although the structure and process of the federal system has been instituted to accommodate public policy development, government priority in pursuing particular issues and implementing corresponding policies waxes and wanes. In the 1960s, when the Canadian economy was doing relatively well, the federal government had built up a large internal capacity for public policy development, and this capacity helped the federal government to develop policies well into the 1970s (Pal, 2010, p. 27). But when the Canadian economy shrunk in the 1980s, cutbacks to policy capacities in the federal government were carried out, responsibility in public policy development diminished, and/or public policy positions or departments were made smaller or eliminated. At that time, building an internal policy capacity was no longer a priority and external think tanks began to fill the vacuum (Mintrom, 2007, p. 146). With the changing political landscape in the 1990s, which included the collapse of the Soviet Union and the rise of political polarization in Canada, there was a growing interest in and prioritization of a stronger government, economy, and public policy development procedure.

Since then, little progress has been made to strengthen the federal capacity for public policy development (Pal, 2010, pp. 27–28; Voyer, 2007, pp. 220–221). The destruction of the Twin Towers of the World Trade Center in New York City in 2001, the near collapse of the financial sector in the United States in 2008, and the present unstable global economic environment strengthen the government and its leadership in the market economy of the country, as the public looks to the government to take greater control over the direction of society. It is here that public policy development has an integral role to play.

The Conservative government, which won a majority in May 2011, has strengthened its lead on public policy development. It has shown signs of neutralizing the bureaucratic side of public policy development by creating a parallel pool of political aides to develop and manage public policies. Public and stakeholder consultations on policy issues have been minimized, policy positions emerge from ministers' offices without much research or analysis, and policies are often rushed through the ratification process in Parliament within omnibus bills (which cover a broad range of unrelated policy matters that have been packaged together). This is very similar to the speedy process used in Ralph Klein's government in Alberta (1992–2006) and Mike Harris' government in Ontario (1995–2002).

PROVINCIAL GOVERNMENTS

Canada is a federation of ten provinces and three territories, each of which has its own jurisdictional powers. Prior to World War II, the federal and provincial governments acted relatively independently; however, they are now more intertwined. A few social scientists, including Dyck (1996, p. 2), maintain that the provinces are growing in terms of power, revenues, and bureaucracies, but this does not mean the federal government is being displaced. Others, such as Inwood (2009, pp. 177–180), suggest that negotiations between the two levels of government have created an opportunity for a few, but not all, provinces (notably Alberta and Quebec) to wrest some power from the federal government.

In spite of the ascendency of the provinces, not much research has been done on the internal operation of their governments (McArthur, 2007, pp. 238–239). As a result, not much is known about the inner workings of their public policy development components. Dyck (1996, pp. 644–656) suggests that while provinces are distinct entities in terms of their political culture and leadership, they are increasingly similar to each other in terms of organizational structure, which includes cabinets, legislatures, and bureaucracies.

Towards the end of the twentieth century, structures created for public policy development were strikingly similar among the provinces, especially in the context of financial constraints.

Cabinet System and Central Agencies

As in the federal government, a formal structure consisting of the cabinet, its committees, and central agencies has been put in place in every provincial government in Canada (Dunn, 2002; Bernier, Brownsey, and Howlett, 2005). The cabinet system is the centre of the policy process, as it has responsibility for "the formulation, coordination, and implementation of policy" (Chandler and Chandler, 1979, p. 98). Provincial governments are headed by a premier, under whom is a cabinet of premier-appointed ministers. The provincial government is a decision-making body for all provincial matters, including public policies, central planning, and public management. A cabinet office (made up of public servants) supports the cabinet. Its policy roles are to guide ministries in their alignment to government priorities and fiscal direction, as well as to assist in their development of policy options and inter-ministerial initiatives. The cabinet office's responsibilities include briefing the premier, cabinet committee chairs, and cabinet members, and supporting the cabinet, planning and priorities board, and cabinet committees.

The planning and priorities board consists of ministers who chair the cabinet committees; their involvement ensures policy alignment. This board coordinates work related to the cabinet committees on policy and management issues. It also recommends public policies to the cabinet for final approval. Central agencies—such as the treasury board and the management board—are established to deal with, review, and recommend policy matters related to finance and management matters. Some provinces combine these two matters under one board for a certain period of time, usually to streamline processes or to reduce costs. For policies with legislative implications, some provinces create a statutory committee to deal with legislation and regulations. The ministry of finance is one of the central agencies, as it deals with financial planning and projections, and is in a strategic position to advise the cabinet of the province's current and anticipated financial situation. Its advice has major financial implications for the planning and priorities board (responsible for coordinating policies, departmental plans, and government initiatives), the treasury board (responsible for human resources), the management board (responsible for management issues), and the statutory committee (responsible for new legislation).

FIGURE 3.2: THE PROVINCIAL CABINET SYSTEM AND PUBLIC POLICIES

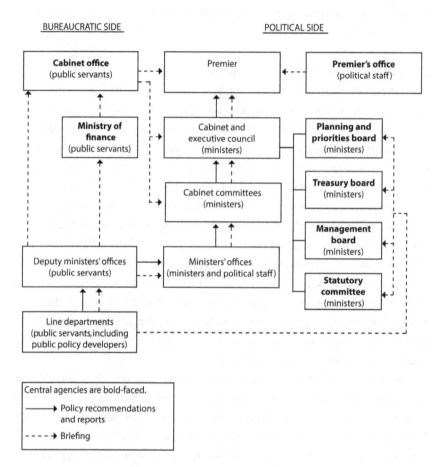

Central agencies review policy proposals and assess their financial and management implications. Due to their strategic position between the cabinet, line departments, and the premier's office, they play a key role in shaping public policies. The provincial finance ministries, due to their special role in research, and economic and financial forecasts, can readily influence public policies that have financial implications for the provinces (Dunn, 1996a, pp. 198–200).

The cabinet office, treasury board secretariat, and management board secretariat—all of which are staffed by public servants—work together to support elected politicians and ensure that public policies and programs are financially sustainable. Although government ministries may initiate particular policies, the provincial structure requires some checks and balances to assess the ramifications of policies for different ministries. Some differences are found in the policy capacities of line departments; some ministries have their own public policy development offices, while others do not. The ministries without a separate public policy development office often find themselves doing the policy work in their program offices.

The cabinet provides direction to the cabinet committees. Each provincial government has its own set of committees (such as the cabinet committee on environmental policy, the cabinet committee on economic policy, and the cabinet committee on social justice policy), which have different portfolios of high priority to the political party in power. The cabinet committees create forums for these ministries to discuss policy proposals and their implications collectively. They have regular meetings during which cabinet ministers, sometimes accompanied by deputy ministers, discuss relevant issues and the pros and cons of proposed policies. These cabinet committees receive direction and instruction from the planning and priorities board through the cabinet. Some of these committees have working groups that conduct research and information gathering; these staff working groups are made up of public servants (policy directors and managers) from different ministries who discuss policy issues from the perspectives of their own ministries.

In addition to public policy development, the cabinet office and cabinet committees have strategic planning functions. As the provincial government does not deal with one issue at a time, it has to juggle issues and balance the interests of various stakeholder groups. Negotiations regarding which issues to prioritize are played out at the planning and priorities board and cabinet meetings, and to a lesser extent, at the cabinet committee meetings. Knowledge of the strategic planning process is important to public policy developers, as it is often the key determinant of how policies are shaped, prioritized, and scheduled.

Patterns of Provincial Public Policy Development

General observation suggests that public policy development in provincial governments ebbs and flows; cycles of public policy development do not coincide with those found in the federal government. For example, when the federal government was pushing for stronger policy capacity in the mid-1990s, the Government of Ontario was restructuring and redefining the public service sector, as well as cutting costs and marginalizing public policy development. The Common Sense Revolution of the Progressive Conservative Party (PC) in Ontario in the 1990s had already outlined its policy framework, and there was no need to have much policy capacity in the government. During that pe-riod, policy decisions of immense social and economic significance were made swiftly, without consulting with public servants or the public, and without much research or evidence-based analysis.

The centralization of policy functions has a significant impact on public policy development at the provincial level (Howlett and Lindquist, 2007, pp. 95–96, 102–103). McArthur (2007, pp. 247–248) observed, and Bernier, Brownsey, and Howlett (2005) confirmed, that as public policy development has become increasingly centralized in the premier's office, the cabinet, and the cabinet committees, there has been a hollowing out of the public policy capacity in line departments. Instead of developing public policies, public servants coordinate or implement them. The 1980s and 1990s witnessed an increase in the policy capacity of political offices—the direct influence of the premier and the cabinet office weighed heavily on the development of public policies (Dunn, 1996a, p. 193). The influence of political aides in the premier's and other ministers' offices has been steadily increasing; these aides often act as gatekeepers and compete with public servants for policy control. Incidentally, during the last two decades expenditure of government departments has been reduced, which may have had a negative impact on the position of public policy developers.

The centralization of public policy development was an offspring of the tension between elected politicians and public servants. The policy exper-tise provided by public servants has been questioned by politicians who are of the opinion that the intuition and information sources of elected officials are more reliable than those of public servants. Some politicians perceive that public policy development is skewed to protect the interests of public servants rather than those of elected politicians, for example, when preserving existing programs or resources (McArthur, 2007, pp. 240–241). This perception has often resulted in politicians replacing existing deputy ministers with those of their own choice when they come to power. Meanwhile, a politician may strengthen the policy role of their own assistants (political aides) to compete with and ultimately replace public servants in public policy development. This shifting of policy influence from public servants to elected politicians' offices has occurred in several provincial governments, including Bob Rae's New Democratic Party government (1990–1995) and Mike Harris' Progressive Conservative government (1995–2002) in Ontario, Grant Devine's Conserva-tive government (1982–1991) in Saskatchewan, and Gordon Campbell's Liberal government (2001–2011) in British Columbia.

IMPLICATIONS OF GOVERNMENT STRUCTURES AND PROCESSES

There are many people involved in the federal and provincial government structures who have significant influence on public policy development and developers. Primarily due to the vast number of ministers and public servants in line departments and central agencies, a policy-in-the-making has to go through many levels of negotiation. Each internal stakeholder group (individual line department) is responsible for its own portfolios under legislation and is sensitive to the interests of its external stakeholders (outside of government). Each line department has a tendency to be protective of its services, programs, and resources. And each minister should listen to his or her constituents and adhere to cabinet priorities and decisions. Each central agency, due to its high level of knowledge of the government, is mandated to balance the interests of internal stakeholder groups and be cognizant of the consistency, resources, and public perception of government activities. In combination, these internal negotiations should result in balance and compromise.

Due to the back-and-forth nature of developing policy products—as they move between public policy developers, senior management bureaucrats, and ministers—the public policy development process is usually slow. Many new policy questions are posed sporadically throughout the process for public policy developers, and answers are expected in short duration. It is not uncommon for some policy matters to be shelved as ministers' priorities shift; however, this can quickly change if a particular policy matter is identified as urgent by cabinet members. This may occur for a number of reasons: a natural disaster, large-scale human tragedy, persistent negative media coverage, strong public opinion, scandal, or massive protests and violent action. Under urgent circumstances, policy matters may go through multiple layers of review and be approved by the cabinet very quickly.

The dichotomy between the political (elected politicians and political staff members) and the bureaucratic (non-elected public servants) sides of government often creates tension. While a public servant may work in a department for many years, it is not uncommon for a minister to be put in charge of a department with which they are unfamiliar. The knowledge of public servants is helpful when they brief their minister; however, when new policy matters arise, the institutional memory and knowledge of public servants may dampen the enthusiasm of ministers when they wish to pursue particular policy directions. This tension is usually resolved when public policy developers adopt the perspectives of their ministers because, after all, they are the servants, and the ministers are the masters.

Due to the fact that ministers and other senior bureaucrats have many issues to deal with on a daily basis, the actual management of policy issues often falls into the hands of the public servants in a line department or central agency, or to ministers' political aides. These government employees play a pivotal role in protecting the interests of their departments, analyzing relevant policy matters, and recommending action to their bosses (deputy ministers or ministers). Although one ministry may take a lead in developing a specific public policy, any policy has implications for many other ministries. To be effective in their roles, public policy developers need to explain policy matters clearly to these stakeholder groups, and must be careful and strategic listeners, so that these groups are not antagonized.

The variety of internal stakeholder groups that must be consulted regarding a draft public policy, combined with the inherent slowness of moving a draft from one group to another, highlights the need for effective consultation by public policy developers at the start of the process and ongoing regular consultation as the policy products are being developed, crafted, and completed. Consultations not only provide relevant and useful information, but they also create a sense of ownership of the policy-in-the-making. When a public policy is at the final stage of formation, everyone who has been involved in the process feels that he or she owns a piece of it. Although it may not be perfect, it is something all can live with.

SUMMARY
The federal and provincial governments have very similar structures of governance, despite their minor variations in organizational names, features, and processes. The Prime Minister's Office, premier's office, cabinet system, and central agencies have developed a system of translating ideas into public policies, while taking into consideration implications for financial resources and management. The last two decades have seen the federal and provincial governments neutralize the policy influence of the line departments and ministries by increasing the policy capacity of the political offices of ministers. This has resulted in an increase in consultations, negotiations, and compromises, leading to greater tension between politicians and bureaucrats. These factors have contributed to slowing the pace at which a public policy can be developed.

QUESTIONS FOR CRITICAL THINKING

1. The current development of a public policy involves many internal stakeholder groups (e.g., ministers, deputy ministers, directors) in different departments and central agencies. How do all of these groups shape the nature of a public policy?

2. How can public policy developers prepare themselves to work within an environment with so many active agents?

3. The federal and provincial governments' modes of public policy development are quite similar. They both exhibit similar trends in terms of the centralization and politicization of the process. Discuss the ramifications of these trends on the future of public policies.

PUBLIC POLICY PRODUCTS

INTRODUCTION

As the previous chapter illustrates, many groups participate in the development of a public policy. Spread throughout the government, each group—residing in line departments, central agencies, and the cabinet—has specific interests. To become acquainted with policy matters, members of these internal stakeholder groups must read or listen to the information provided by public policy developers, who create policy products in various formats for internal and external use. Internally, policy products are used to help ministers and government officials gain a more thorough understanding of policy issues and their implications for government positions and resources, and to make decisions. Externally, policy products may be used to inform the public of new directions the government is taking, or to begin a public dialogue. These products are reviewed and scrutinized by many involved parties at different stages of the public policy development process.

Policy products are documents written for the purpose of informing, documenting, planning, and generating ideas. They are highly customized and represent the numerous aspects of the public policy development process, although most centre on cabinet submissions. A cabinet submission is the most important policy product, as it outlines the various policy directions that a government can take and assists cabinet ministers to make a decision about which direction they will pursue. To get to the stage of policy decision-making, briefing notes, House book notes, and decision notes must be put in place to prepare the groundwork. When a cabinet submission is at its final stage, management board submissions are written to seek support from and make financial arrangements with the management board. These policy products help further the development process, with the end goal of gaining the approval of the cabinet ministers. Draft legislation and regulations, press releases, and policy statements are written after the cabinet submission has been approved.

Not all policy products are used exclusively for public policy development; some are modified to advance the development or attainment of funds for programs, services, or government activities that are indirectly linked to policy issues. Highly customized, policy products are chosen and tailored to suit specific purposes, audiences, and occasions. Some policy products have flexible formats, with no rigid requirements in terms of such items as headings and length, but many must adhere to standardized formats. The use of standardized formats ensures that public policy developers include all necessary and pertinent information in particular categories.

TYPES OF PUBLIC POLICY PRODUCTS

Policy products vary according to their context, purpose, audience, content, format, and method of communication. As classified below, some policy products are prepared specifically for internal use. They inform ministers and government officials, and help them to make decisions. These internal policy products usually have rigid requirements for formatting and presentation, presenting information in a clear, concise manner that makes it easy to read for individuals on a tight schedule. Other policy products are prepared for external use. These products are often more tactful in their approach, due to the nature of the audience and the sensitivity of some policy issues. The messages in these products must also be clear and concise to avoid creating misunderstandings or confusion among members of the public.

Products for Internal Use
- briefing notes
- House book notes
- decision notes
- research plans
- research papers
- discussion papers
- public consultation plans
- consultation highlights
- cabinet submissions

- cabinet presentation slides
- cabinet minutes
- management board submissions
- draft legislations and regulations
- program designs

Products for External Use

- correspondence
- public consultation papers
- stakeholder consultation papers
- policy statements
- press releases

TABLE 4.1: POLICY PRODUCTS AND THE PUBLIC POLICY DEVELOPMENT PROCESS

Pre-Cabinet Submission Phase	Cabinet Submission Phase	Post-Cabinet Submission Phase
Briefing notes		
House book notes		
Decision notes		
Correspondence		
Discussion papers	Cabinet submission	Draft legislation and regulations
Public consultation plan	Cabinet presentation slides	Program designs
Public consultation papers	Cabinet minutes	Press releases
Research plans		Policy statements
Research papers		
Stakeholder consultation papers		
Consultation highlights		
Management board submission		

OVERVIEW OF POLICY PRODUCTS

Correspondence

Strictly speaking, correspondence is not a policy product that public servants in public policy development usually produce. However, as the government is responsible for certain policy domains, members of the public, associations, institutions, and other groups write letters or emails to their ministers and inquire about jurisdictional policy matters or matters with policy implications. In response, ministers often ask public policy developers to prepare draft letters that respond to inquiries and/or provide general information on the status of policy matters. It is often difficult for the minister to say much about policy matters that have not been reviewed or approved by cabinet—in these circumstances, the information provided is usually quite general. If the questions posed by the public are specifically related to past accomplishments or records of government actions, then the answers must be specific and accurate. If the questions are not related to the jurisdictional responsibility of the government, public policy developers may refer the inquirer to the proper jurisdiction.

There are no restrictions on the number of pages or the format of written replies, but they are usually one or two pages, and their tone is diplomatic and courteous. Exercise 1, in part II, is provided to practice writing a reply letter.

Briefing Notes

Briefing notes, which are used to update deputy ministers and ministers on policy issues, are the most common policy product. Sometimes referred to as issue notes, briefing notes may provide background information on policy and program matters, including contentious or topical issues covered by media; evidence to clarify information or further issue comprehension; and updates of government action on specific policy issues. It is not uncommon for briefing notes to be spurred by media activity, the actions of public figures, press releases or allegations from stakeholder organizations, and publications and conference proceedings from think tanks or academic communities. Most briefing notes are short (one single-spaced page of about 500 words) as they are intended to be concise in their message. They are written in full sentences formatted as bullet points. Because some briefing notes are urgent, a public policy developer's preparation time may be only two or three hours, during which they must write quickly, clearly, and accurately. Ministers read these briefing notes before they appear in the legislature or parliament.

The headings that are used in briefing notes vary by government or individual ministry and are subject to change; however, it is common for briefing notes to be organized into the sections outlined below. Exercise 2, in part II, is provided to practice writing a briefing note.

Issue: This section highlights a single issue in the form of a question. Framing the issue as a question requires the public policy developer to write specific answers that enable politicians to respond easily when questioned by an opposition party. For example, an issue related to child care could be framed as one of the following questions: What is the status of the government's election promise of a child care subsidy? Does the current government provide a child care subsidy to parents? The answers and supporting evidence or data will vary, depending on the phrasing of the question. Other terms are also used for this section, including "Purpose," "Topic," or "Subject."

Background: This section summarizes pertinent information related to the issue, including government policies and programs, the government's current political platform, excerpts from the speech from the throne, and/or major historical patterns and trends. Background information may also include what, if any, public pressure has gained momentum and which stakeholder groups or organizations are vocal about the issue. Depending on the nature of the briefing note, "Status," "Facts," or "Current condition" may also be used as the heading for this section.

Current update: This section comprises the present position of the government and outlines related activities that are currently in progress. It may also raise unresolved issues that are being dealt with by the government. This section may alternately be labelled "Current status."

Summary: This section recapitulates the present position of the government in one or two bullet points. It may also be called "Recommendation," "Decision required," or "Advice required," based on the contents.

Do not disclose: This section is optional. Here, confidential information is provided. The advantage of this section is that public policy developers can provide the minister with sensitive information not for disclosure that is not suitable for announcement, such as internally collected statistical data and policies or programs in the making. No personal information or names of individuals should be included in this section.

House Book Notes

House book notes are usually put in a binder for ministers to use when the legislature or parliament is in process. It contains many notes to brief the minister, and each note addresses one policy or program matter. Ministers refer to them during question period; they are useful when addressing the media, public, or answering questions tabled by opposition parties.

The facts in these notes must be correct and up-to-date, and must come from reliable sources. They are sometimes produced for briefing purposes when a minister assumes a new position and is not familiar with the many policies and programs or current and future action items in his or her ministry. When parliament is in session and unanticipated events or media coverage on contentious issues arise, these House book notes are prepared under tight deadlines and are usually read in a hurry as the minister rushes to the House.

While there is a strict one-page rule for each note (approximately 500 words, single-spaced), each department is free to develop its own format. Use the information below as a template when constructing a House book note. Exercise 3, in part II, is provided to practice writing a House book note.

> *Issue:* State the issue in the form of a question. This question, if posed properly, will determine the evidence, facts, arguments, and recommendations that are to be presented.
>
> *Recommended response:* State the message with which the minister will respond publicly. The message must be simple and clear and should be appropriately framed. It usually denotes the public position of the ministry, which may include what the ministry has done and plans to do regarding the issue. Prior to writing this section, the public policy developer may need to consult with political aides to ensure that it aligns with the minister's political position.
>
> *Background:* Describe in a clear, concise, and objective manner why the issue has become contentious. Facts should be chronologically arranged so that the minister can easily follow the sequence of events. This section may also outline how the issue has affected the ministry, how stakeholder groups have reacted, and how the media has covered the issue.

Decision Notes

Decision notes are created when a minister is required to make a decision about a particular issue before the public policy development process can move forward. Usually one single-spaced page of approximately 500 words, they brief the minister on an issue, put forward items to consider, including benefits and risks, and recommend a course of action. Exercise 4, in part II, is provided to practice writing a decision note. The following information is usually included in a decision note:

Issue: State the problem that the minister has to resolve, in the form of a question.

Background: Sketch out the social and organizational context, as well as the magnitude and urgency of the problem. Also include the key stakeholder groups and what the government or other jurisdictions have done to address this issue.

Options: Provide a maximum of three options for the minister to consider that could resolve this problem. Under each option, list its pros (or benefits), and cons (or risks). These pros and cons may include political, economic, financial, and human considerations, from the perspective of the government, public, or stakeholder groups.

Recommendation: Consider the options outlined above, and make a recommendation of which one the minister should adopt. The recommendation must be one of the three options presented or, if they are consistent with each other, a combination of the options.

Research Plans

Public policy developers sometimes have to conduct research to gather relevant information. While major research projects are contracted out to external research firms or academic communities, there are occasions on which public policy developers must conduct research that may be too sensitive to be outsourced.

Prior to conducting research, it is crucial to prepare a plan that outlines the objectives, focus, methodology, budget and sources of funding, work schedule (with start and end dates), names of investigators, and anticipated deliverables of the impending research. Research that involves only documentary reviews of publications or internal documents is relatively straightforward; however, research that involves personal interviews or focus groups is more complicated. While there are no required formats for research plans, they usually encompass the eight standard sections listed below. Exercise 5, in part II, is provided to practice writing a research plan.

Research topic: Clearly state the research topic.

Research purposes: Explain how the proposed research will move forward the development of a public policy.

Methodology: Outline the core research questions, the research method(s) to be employed, indicators for measurement, types of information or data needed, and the sources of information that will be explored.

Researchers: Name all internal researchers and their roles.

Timetable: Record the start and prospective end date for the project, and identify the date that the research deliverable(s) will be submitted to senior management.

Budget: Prepare a research budget, including relevant expenses such as data computation, travel, accommodation costs, and incentives for focus group members.

Sources of funding: Identify the funding sources and state whether or not funding has been secured.

Deliverables: State the research deliverables, which may include a written report or a verbal presentation.

Research Papers

Research papers summarize findings, and are mainly intended for an audience of senior management or public policy developers in line departments; they are occasionally provided to the public. These papers are usually a prerequisite for public policy development because they contain pertinent information that helps the government understand the policy issue and prepare its position. The information presented in a research paper is typically an evaluation or an in-depth study of a specific policy or program issue. In some cases, a research paper is a literature review of jurisdictional responses to specific policy issues. Unlike an academic paper that focuses on testing a hypothesis, a research paper usually focuses on an existing or prospective policy issue.

Research papers are sometimes outsourced to external research firms or academic communities. If so, they may gain the value of being regarded as neutral, non-partisan, and academically robust. Public policy developers often work with external researchers to finalize the nature, scope, and methodology of the research. They may be required to hold regular briefings to keep the government abreast of the progress of the research, and preliminary or ongoing research findings. Research papers are submitted to the government by a mutually agreed-upon date.

There are no set formats for research papers, but they usually include the components listed below. To avoid overwhelming readers with research details, a section describing the methodology is usually set as an appendix, as are any complex statistical tables. Exercise 6, in part II, provides an opportunity to practice writing a research paper.

Executive summary: Summarize the nature and scope of the research, major findings, and analysis method used. Although it is placed at the beginning of the paper, this section is usually written after the paper is completed.

Introduction: Provide the context in which the research was done. The context may include a description of social and economic conditions and government priorities, or a rationale for the importance and urgency of the undertaking. State the core questions asked by the researcher and how the findings are presented in the paper.

Research focus: Specify the focus of the research by providing the questions asked at the outset of the project. Explain how the research was conducted in terms of time, geographic boundaries and jurisdictions, and the social domains involved.

Research findings: Articulate the research results and present an analysis of the evidence or data. The analysis should contribute to an understanding of the policy areas covered by the research. Research findings often give rise to additional policy questions, which necessitate additional research.

Conclusion: Raise the major themes on which the research findings are based and summarize their relevance to related policy issues.

Appendices: Include the details of the research methodology used, complex statistical tables, key resource materials, and list of organizations contacted.

Discussion Papers

Discussion papers are typically internal documents—though they are sometimes written for the public—geared toward public servants and ministers. Senior bureaucrats are especially interested in the content of discussion papers because they address imminent policy issues. Their purpose is to identify and discuss policy issues, the backgrounds of the problems at stake, the social and economic implications for the province or country, and the challenges and risks for the government with frankness and clarity. Research, utilizing primary or secondary sources, must be conducted prior to writing these papers.

Discussion papers have no page limits or format requirements. They are to be presented using simple language, but the positions expounded must be fully substantiated by statistics and evidence. Similar to most written presentations, they have an introduction, body, and conclusion. Major issues must be identified, delineated clearly and succinctly, and not too steeped in quantitative or technical information. If evidence and data are too technical or lengthy to be presented in the main text of the paper, they may be placed in footnotes, endnotes, or appendices. Exercise 7, in part II, is provided to practice writing a discussion paper.

Public Consultation Plans

Developing public policies often includes consulting the public, with the objective of soliciting viewpoints on specific policy issues. Conducting such a consultation is a time-consuming process, so if a tight schedule is set for public policy development it may not allow for consultation; in other cases, a minister may not see the need for a broad consultation. When a minister does decide to hold a public consultation on a policy issue, it is crucial that he or she have a public consultation plan to guide the process. The plan may be written by a public policy developer and then approved by senior management; alternatively, senior management may work with a public policy developer to create the plan. Other ministers can also use the plan as a helpful guide if a public consultation session headed up by another minister is being held in their constituency. Specific details regarding public consultations are discussed in chapter 7.

The information provided below is included in a typical public consultation plan, but there is some flexibility. Exercise 8, in part II, is provided to practice writing a public consultation plan.

Purpose of public consultation: Identify the purpose of the consultation, setting clear and achievable objectives. This will help to avoid wasting the public's time. Be sure that these objectives are communicated to participants prior to the consultation and focus all subsequent activities around these objectives.

Major topics for consultation: Narrow and specify the topics to be resolved and discussed to ensure that time is used effectively during the consultation and that the consultation is cost-effective. Make these topics known to the public at the start of any consultation activities so that the expectations of both members of the public and government officials are aligned to avoid misunderstandings.

Major stakeholder groups to be consulted: While the focus of public consultation is on the public, public policy developers may need to include key stakeholders (such as business associations) in consultation activities. In this section, describe special outreach endeavours to secure the involvement of these groups.

Consultation methods: Consultations can be executed in several ways. Common approaches are town hall meetings, focus groups, round table discussions, field surveys, phone interviews, and social media. Public policy developers must determine which methods are both cost-effective and appropriate for different segments of the population, and customize their chosen approach for each consultation.

Geographic locations of consultation: Locations have political implications; therefore, they must be deliberately selected to be sensitive to the target demographic. The public will judge the government on the location where it chooses to hold a consultation session. For example, to demonstrate its understanding of the geopolitical sensitivity of Canadians, the federal government cannot underestimate the importance of having public consultations in Quebec, and the Government of Ontario cannot ignore Northern Ontario during a public consultation process.

Schedule of consultation: This is largely determined by political factors (e.g., timing of political announcements), institutional factors (e.g., school breaks), cultural factors (e.g., festivities and religious holidays), and administrative factors (e.g., availability of politicians and facilities).

Format of public consultation: The success and effectiveness of a consultation may be determined by the agenda for the session. Facilitation, announcement of consultation rules and protocols, and the allocation of time for each item of consultation are all-important and should be spelled out and adhered to as closely as possible.

Coordination committee: If the consultation is extensive and complex in terms of scope, geographic spread, and number of participants, a coordination committee may be needed to oversee activities. Designated staff members may be made responsible for ensuring that the consultation covers areas of importance, and to monitor the progression of activities.

Major operational logistics: Operational logistics, if coordinated properly, can enhance the success of public consultation. If overlooked, small items—such as the lack of an extension cord or accessible washrooms—can embarrass the government and influence participants. An experienced logistics person can prevent important items from being overlooked.

Materials to be produced or printed for public distribution: Consultation papers, agendas, presentation slides, and other relevant materials may need to be produced and distributed to the public or participants. These materials are often scrutinized by the public and opposition parties and are best produced with the assistance of communication specialists, with the approval of the deputy minister or minister.

Communication strategy: A communication strategy is essential, especially when the topics for consultation are contentious. Depending on the government's political agenda, it is advised that the strategy include a public education component. Public education includes raising public awareness of particular policy issues, as well as the importance and benefits of sound public policy. It is also important to let the public know that their input is essential to the development of sound public policy. This education component is best completed before the public consultation sessions are launched.

Expected results and deliverables: Similar in importance to outlining objectives, public consultations should also have a clear set of anticipated results and deliverables; these could include gathering recommendations on policy issues from a broad spectrum of individuals from different segments of the community, and producing a synopsis of themes that emerged during the public consultation process that can be posted on a government website. Identifying these items contributes positively to the monitoring and evaluation process of the outcomes of the consultation.

Government representatives participating in consultation: The allocation of human resources is an important part of planning a consultation. Identify the staff members who are to be involved in the public consultation and clearly state their roles and responsibilities.

Budget: The allocation of financial resources determines a consultation's scope and quality. Operational costs, such as facility and equipment rental, travel and accommodation, and the preparation and printing of communication materials, should be determined up front for internal approval and to guide organization.

Public Consultation Papers

Prior to launching public consultations, the public policy developer usually writes a document for the public. This public consultation paper brings into focus the policy issues that will be addressed during the consultation so that the government will not be sidetracked by other issues. These papers can also be used to solicit ideas and suggestions from the public regarding how to resolve policy issues. Some public consultation papers put forward draft policy options for people to discuss; they can also be used as a springboard for additional comments or suggestions. The consultation papers give the public a glimpse of what policy issues the government is wrestling with, and indicate at what stage of public policy development the issue is at.

There are no set formats or page limitations for public consultation papers. However, the key is for the government to clarify the issue on which it wishes to consult, and to explain why it is doing so now. A public consultation paper may include the sections outlined below. Exercise 9, in part II, provides an opportunity to work on this kind of paper.

> *Letter from the minister:* A letter from the minister responsible for the public consultation prefaces the consultation paper and sets the tone of the document. The letter should be brief, but should inform the public about the policy matters, their background, and why the government is conducting this consultation now. The letter should explain what kind of input the government is looking for from the public, and encourage people to participate.

> *Executive summary:* Provide the key messages of the paper. This is usually written after the entire paper has been completed.

> *Background:* Briefly highlight the background of the policy matters, and describe the challenges for the government and Canadians.

> *Issues for consultation:* Outline the key policy issues for consultation and give reasons for why these issues were chosen. This section also outlines the questions and considerations on which the government would like to receive public opinion. It can be useful to describe a few likely approaches or options for the public to consider. For each policy

issue, provide its background, questions for consultation, factors to be considered, and possible approaches.

Conclusion: Inform the public about what the government intends to do with the consultation findings and point out the value of public input on these policy matters. The names and details of public consultation contacts should be included here.

Stakeholder Consultation Papers

Consultation papers for stakeholder groups can be modelled on public consultation papers. As stakeholder groups have specific interests, and the government has a history of working with them, the contents of the consultation can be quite specific and take into account previous encounters.

In a stakeholder consultation, the issues to be dealt with may be strategic or technical in nature. If there is no consensus on the strategic policy direction between the stakeholder groups and the government, then a set of policy direction issues may be brought forward by the public policy developer for consultation to solicit support from the stakeholder groups. However, if the stakeholder groups agree with the government's proposed policy direction, the government should consult with the groups with regards to more tactical or technical issues related to the implementation of the policy direction.

Consultation issues must be specific and focused; tentative options can be put forward by the government as a way to start the conversation. If the government has made up its mind on certain policy positions, they should be expressed firmly and clearly in the consultation papers so that stakeholder groups understand that they are non-negotiable. When describing consultation issues, the tone of communication must be flexible and open to discussion. Exercise 10, in part II, is provided to practice writing a stakeholder consultation paper.

Consultation Highlights

After consulting with the public or stakeholder groups, public policy developers usually complete an internal paper that outlines the issues raised during the consultation. The consultation highlights summarize the opinions, ideas, complaints, critiques, and suggestions of the people who attended the sessions. This public input is the basis for internal discussion and will be considered by ministers.

This paper may be short or lengthy, and there are no restrictions on the format. In some cases, it is worthwhile to separate key messages or arrange the highlights based on geographic location. Such categorization of information can provide insights into the interests and concerns of different parties. The following sections may be included in the consultation highlights:

> *Executive summary:* Summarize the major consultation findings in 100 to 200 words. Although it appears at the beginning of the paper, it is best to write this section last.

> *Background:* Provide background information on the consultation objectives, major consultation issues, and the time frame and locations in which the consultation took place.

> *Highlights:* Outline the issues and summarize the ideas and suggestions presented by the public. This information is usually categorized into themes and contentious points. It is best presented under the headings of separate issues, with related information listed under each in bullet form.

> *Conclusion:* List the issues raised and overarching observations made during the consultation. If ideas have been presented issue by issue in the "Highlights" section, it may be worthwhile to record the similarities of and differences between ideas presented in different geographic regions or by particular stakeholder groups. It is also valuable to identify recurring and polarizing issues.

Cabinet Submissions

Cabinet submissions, created for cabinet ministers, are one of the most important policy products. Their key purpose is to provide policy options and recommendations to be considered and potentially adopted by the cabinet. Under some circumstances, they are used for the additional purpose of updating cabinet on the status of policy issues and program delivery issues. Cabinet submissions contain a comprehensive analysis of key policy issues, put forward the pros and cons of various policy options, and recommend a course of action.

Public policy developers write cabinet submissions in consultation with the cabinet office, the deputy minister's office, and the minister's office. As the submissions usually have financial and management implications, it is advisable to consult with the treasury board, management board, and the ministry of finance at the start of the process. In some cases, endorsements from central agencies are needed prior to submission.

Advice from the cabinet office is usually relevant, as staff members are able to access an overview of policy activities from all line departments and integrate them into the submission in the best way possible. Working closely with the cabinet office and other central agencies can help guarantee a smooth process and potential acceptance of the recommendations, as it ensures their familiarity with the policy issue. The cabinet office and central agencies facilitate line departments' input and enable the prime minister or premier to give instructions with full knowledge of the policy direction.

Cabinet submissions follow very strict timelines, as they are tied to the government's political agenda. It is imperative that the public servants involved in producing the submission know these timelines in advance and follow them scrupulously. However, the nature of the process is quite fluid and timelines are subject to change, so it is also crucial that public policy developers go with the flow and adjust their schedules accordingly. The submission process follows strict protocols, and the format requirements (listed below) are quite rigid. Exercise 11, in part II, is provided to practice writing a cabinet submission.

Executive summary of submission: State the nature, rationale, impacts, and key facts or evidence of the proposal, the details of the government's commitment, cost of implementation to the government, and communication instruments in a few short sentences.

Summary of cabinet decisions: Summarize the object(s) of cabinet's approval, the government commitment to the issue, and rationale for immediate cabinet approval.

Recommendation to cabinet: Outline the key background information—events, issues, and consultations—that has led to the proposal, the policy recommendation, rationale or support for government priorities, and all anticipated major delivery issues. These may include, but are not limited to, delivery agents, timelines, expected outcomes,

management, and methods of monitoring, evaluation, and communication.

Options: Address major policy alternatives and their pros and cons,
and explain why they are not recommended.

Legislative and regulatory plan: Outline the legislative or regulatory
courses of action, if needed, to carry out the recommended option.

Financial analysis: Provide a cost estimate for the recommended
action, and its implications for revenue and human resources. This
section describes the potential impact on the operation of government services, such as labour relations, information technology, or
diversity. It also outlines the economic impact of the recommended
actions on economic growth, stakeholder groups, and geographic
regions.

Factors for consideration: Describe the potential risks to business,
finance, productivity, and the workforce associated with the recommended actions. This section provides a strategy to address
those risks, including how to deal with stakeholder group reactions. In addition, it summarizes consultations with other ministries, and the effect the recommended action may have on these
ministries. It also answers questions on jurisdictional alignment
by comparing the recommended action to what other jurisdictions
are doing. Finally, this section addresses any legal or constitutional
implications.

Communication: Outline the communication strategy for the proposed government action. This strategy may include how the government should position itself, what communication instruments will be
used, what the messages will be, and a timetable for implementing the
communication strategy.

Cabinet Presentation Slides
The cabinet submission may be presented to cabinet members and their aides by
the minister, deputy minister, senior management staff, or public policy develop-

ers. The purpose of this type of presentation is to allow the audience to understand the subject matter or decision issues, and facilitate the decision-making process.

In the past, hard copies of the presentation were provided to members of cabinet committees; today, a deck of PowerPoint slides usually accompanies a verbal presentation. The slides should capture the key points of the cabinet submission. As ministers are not expected to have expertise in the subject matter, language and terminology must be simple and user-friendly. Technical terms should be explained and key strategic points and issues clearly outlined on the slides.

There is no limit to the number of slides included in a presentation, but given the time constraints that often exist, 10 to 20 is usually optimal. Each slide should have no more than six lines and the font size should be large enough for the audience to see at a distance. Exercise 12, in part II, is provided to practice preparing a set of cabinet presentation slides. The following provides a brief overview of the contents of a typical slide presentation.

Slide 1—*Proposal:* Be very clear about what the ministry is seeking the cabinet's approval for. The request should be summarized in one sentence.

Slide 2—*Government commitment:* Explain what the government has committed to do for the public. Quote sources of the public commitment (such as throne speeches), including the date published or presented.

Slide 3—*Rationale for government actions:* Answer the question of why the government needs to take immediate action on the specific policy issue, and what the implications are if the government does not act now.

Slides 4 to 6—*Recommendations:* Outline the proposed recommendation(s) and the justification for the recommendations.

Slides 7 to 8—*Delivery:* Describe how the government will deliver the recommended actions. Outline the time frame, expected results, and breadth of impact, as well as the areas to be monitored, measured, and assessed.

Slides 9 and 10—*Assessment and mitigation of risks:* Identify the key risk factors for the government, their potential impacts, and how to address them.

Slide 11—*Additional options:* Outline the other major options that have been considered, their pros and cons—risks, outcomes, impacts, financial implications, anticipated stakeholder groups' reactions—and why these options are not recommended.

Slides 12 and 13—*Financial implications:* Identify the source and amount (broken down by capital and operational costs) of funding required if the government decides to approve the recommended actions. Identify any revenue implications, and include a cost-benefit analysis and a value-for-money analysis. In addition, identify the effects on the government workforce. In presenting these analyses, it is best to arrange them by year (as in Year 1, Year 2, and Year 3).

Slide 14—*Economic implications:* Identify the implications of the recommended actions for the economy, the business sector, competitiveness, productivity, and job creation.

Slides 15 and 16—*Communication:* Describe the communication strategy to be implemented. Include positioning, messaging, expected reactions from stakeholder groups and the public, and any projected impact on other government programs. Be sure to mention if any communication messages need to be targeted to specific audiences. These slides are best completed in collaboration with the government department in charge of communication.

Cabinet Minutes

Cabinet minutes can be either part of a cabinet submission or contained within a separate document. Cabinet minutes summarize the contents of a proposal and detail what the cabinet has approved. The minutes may include the time frame for the approved actions, responsibility centres (departments), and the communication or marketing strategy.

Management Board Submissions

The management board, which is run by cabinet ministers and is part of the cabinet system, is one of the central agencies in government. It has the huge responsibility of managing the operation of public services, and controls the allocation of money, labour, land, facilities, information, and technologies to all line departments, central agencies, programs, services, and initiatives over which the government has jurisdiction. Thus, when a draft public policy has implications for finance, labour, land, facilities, information, or technologies, the line department responsible for that policy has to request an endorsement and approval for the above resources from the management board. This request is made using a formal document called the management board submission. This submission is to be made prior to the cabinet submission, but under some circumstances it may be done after the cabinet submission has been approved.

There is a rigid time frame for processing the management board submission and submitting it to ministers, a strict limit on the number of pages, and a special format for the presentation of the request; these specifics will vary according to the government's preferences. The information required varies depending on the government, but submissions seeking approval for items related to management and funding usually require the information listed below. Exercise 13, in part II, explains how to construct a management board submission.

1. Nature of the Request
   Purpose of the request: Summarize the objective(s) in one sentence.

   Issue(s): Identify the issue(s) to be resolved, focusing on the impacts on stakeholder groups, jurisdictional and regional interests, industrial or economic impacts, implementation schedule, and the reason for requesting new funding.

2. Description of the Program
   Program description: Outline the purpose and target groups of the proposed program, and the legislative authority and its relationship to the ministry's approved plan.

   Policy support: Identify the cabinet committee's approval for the program, and the date of the approval.

   Background of request: Describe the contextual changes for the new or revised program, previous management board minutes, and past funding changes.

Substantiation for the request: Provide evidence, data, and trend analyses that can support the request.

3. Analysis of the Program

Business case for the request: Provide an assessment of various financial options, including cost-benefit analysis.

Impact on fiscal plan: Describe the impact of the request on the approved ministry expenditure over a period of years.

Options considered and proposed action: Describe the various options that have been considered, and the cost estimate, expected results, and multi-year financial implications of the chosen option. Discuss the expected achievements of the proposed action.

Performance measurement: Describe how the performance of the proposed program will be measured, in terms of the achievement of program objectives and the production of outcomes in both the long and short terms. Identify the standard that will be used for measurement.

Assessment of risks: Identify all potential risk factors—such as those related to demographics, the economy, and technology—and realistic assumptions and plans.

Implications: Identify and analyze the implications of the proposed program for other programs, stakeholder groups, ministries, and jurisdictions. Describe the consultations with and reactions of these parties.

Impacts: Determine the time frame for the management board to evaluate the program results to ensure their alignment with the approved plan; this includes legislation, workforce, labour relations, information technology, customer service, privacy, facilities, regions, and any other relevant factors.

Time frame: Outline the schedule for the implementation of the program from start to maturity or completion.

Approval sought: Provide the exact wording of the approval sought.

Communication plan: Outline the communication strategy for the proposed program and schedule of actions.

Draft Legislation

Draft legislations and regulations are usually executed by government lawyers, and they are intended for politicians in the legislature or parliament. Public policy developers must collaborate with government lawyers to draft bills and regulations. This collaboration includes written clarification of policy positions and comments on draft legislation to ensure that bills are true to their original intent, as approved by the cabinet. Very often, legislation comes in stages. While one cabinet submission may be the basis for a piece of law, another cabinet submission may be the foundation for a regulation. The collaboration of public policy developers with government lawyers in the drafting of bills is crucial—the subtlety of the wording, distinctions of concepts, sequences of components, scope of responsibilities, importance of government monitoring and enforcement, and roles of government are some of the many facets of legal clauses that must be comprehensively considered. These facets of public policy are to be put in a legislative framework and should be woven together for consistency, comprehensiveness, and seamlessness.

Policy Statements

After the cabinet submission has been approved and the cabinet minutes have been signed and dated by the minister and deputy minister, the next step may be writing the public policy, unless the policy is in the form of a piece of legislation. Not many public policies approved by the government are enshrined in a policy statement, but the few that are written up are done so for the purposes of public awareness or education. Public policy developers write these policy statements in collaboration with public servants in the cabinet office or the deputy minister's office. The minister's office approves these short statements; they are usually just a few sentences to half a page, but they must accurately reflect the cabinet minutes, what the cabinet has approved, or current legislation.

The format for a policy statement varies and there are no universal standards. It may outline the nature of the public policy or include its principles, objectives, key components, and benefits. Condensing and framing the policy position into a short statement of carefully selected terms is often quite difficult.

Program Designs

In addition to legislation and regulations, program designs are one of the end products of public policy development. Often when the cabinet approves certain public policies, it also approves programs that operationalize the policies. Program designs are important and require public policy developers to collaborate with program managers to ensure that they are in line with the objectives of the cabinet-approved public policies. With a better understanding of the policy objectives, program administrators, with their experience, can develop more effective programs to achieve the policy objectives.

Two of the most important elements of a public policy are the policy objectives and the target groups that the policy benefits. By working with program managers, public policy developers can ensure that policy objectives are fulfilled and the interests of target groups are central to the programs. For example, saving for retirement may be important to all Canadians, but it is especially vital for people in low-income categories. Currently, government incentives for people to save for retirement can be operationalized in such a way that they mainly benefit people in higher income brackets; as a result of the program design, the government policy on registered retirement savings is not as effective as it could be.

Program design is best carried out by public servants who have program management experience, in consultation with frontline program people; public policy developers are there to make sure that the policy intent remains intact. The following topics should be considered when constructing a program design:

> *Program description:* Describe in general terms how the program should work to fulfill the government's mandate.

> *Objectives:* Specify the aims and intended accomplishments of the program.

> *Eligibility of target groups to be served:* Specify the characteristics of the target groups that will be served by this program. Define clearly the eligibility criteria for these groups.

> *Eligibility of funding recipients:* Specify the qualifications required of organizations that may receive funding to run the program.

Operation mechanics: Describe the administrative structure and operational processes of the program, including time frame, milestones, and infrastructure.

Marketing and communication: Describe the strategy behind communicating and marketing the program.

Accountability measures: Outline the reporting mechanism, and expected sets of data that will be submitted to the government.

Funding formula: Specify the funding arrangement.

Program review and evaluation: Describe the timetable and mechanisms for review and evaluation of the program through individual funding recipients, organizations, and target groups.

Press Releases

Press releases from the government are public announcements of public policies, programs, services, initiatives, and any other information that the government deems important for the public to know. They are usually prepared when the government sees the timing of such a release as beneficial. A press release is usually one page and has a very clear message, relating the what, where, when, why, and how of a new policy or program. In collaboration with public servants in communication, public policy developers can help prepare these press releases by providing the intent of a relevant public policy or program.

SUMMARY

Public policy products are related to the different components of public policy development. Most are for internal use only. They vary in purpose, content, audience, and format, but all must contain accurate and up-to-date information. The length and format requirements for some policy products are quite strict; such rigidity is normal for documents that will be presented to ministers and the cabinet. Some policy products are written to inform and prompt decisions at a high level, while others are written to generate discussion and support, and still others are created as follow-ups. Policy products are routinely created in response to external or internal requests.

Public policy developers play key, though not always lead, roles in producing these products; these roles may be supportive, advisory, consultative, or collaborative. As the range and content of policy products suggest, the key aspect of public policy developers' work is analytical and creative within the confines of a government bureaucracy.

QUESTIONS FOR CRITICAL THINKING

1. Why should most policy products be written in simple, user-friendly language?
2. Why do many policy products have a rigid format, length, and timeline for development?
3. Unlike most policy products, public consultation papers are written for the public or stakeholder groups. What makes these consultation papers challenging to write?

PRINCIPLES OF GOOD PUBLIC POLICY

INTRODUCTION

With the right knowledge and skills, an awareness of government structures and processes, and an understanding of policy products, public policy developers are in an excellent position to formulate good public policies. But what exactly constitutes good public policy? This chapter outlines six principles used to determine whether a specific public policy is "good" or "bad." As is true of the very definition of public policy, these principles are not universally agreed upon; however, they enable one to assess the positives and negatives of a specific public policy.

WHY ISN'T THERE CONSENSUS ON THE DEFINITION OF "GOOD" PUBLIC POLICY?

There are several reasons why people do not agree about what constitutes good public policy. First, worldviews and values differ among individuals. People have their own ideas of how the world should evolve, how people should lead their lives, and how the government should be run. They refer to their own beliefs when judging public policies, and differences in these beliefs may mean a difference of opinion with regards to how good or bad a public policy is deemed to be. Second, stakeholders have a vested interest in protecting or furthering their own beliefs, resources, and lifestyles. They may assess public policies on the basis of how they either enhance or threaten their interests. Third, public policies can be assessed according to various criteria, from individual to international impacts, to short- to long-term benefits or risks. When people use different criteria to assess a public policy, they are likely to come to different conclusions about the value of that policy. Fourth, some people may not value a particular public policy on its own merits, but may instead see it as crowding out or displacing other policies that they feel are more important. In this sense, some policies are viewed negatively in comparison to others, not because they are intrinsically bad, but because they are secondary in priority. Finally, some view government policy as an unwelcome intervention. A public policy may be perceived as bad solely because it is a manifestation of formal government interference in the individual's life.

PRINCIPLES OF GOOD PUBLIC POLICY

Knowing the principles of good public policy enhances the public policy development process, as these standards become the benchmarks that all policies should meet. These principles guide the government in determining which policy options or frameworks it should adopt. More importantly, when public policy developers wrestle with public problems and draft public policies to address them, keeping these principles in mind enables them to develop public policies that embody the notion of the "public good." This is the fundamental reason why democratic governments exist.

What distinguishes a good public policy from a bad one? A good public policy provides the greatest benefits to the broadest spectrum of the population—in other words, it bolsters the public good. How can we determine what is good for the public? A good public policy factors in these six principles: (a) balance of public interests, (b) accountability, (c) impact, (d) cost-effectiveness, (e) justice, and (f) balance of short- and long-term considerations. Many public policies cannot be evaluated until they have been implemented and a reasonable period of time has elapsed. Developing public policies that adhere to a combination of these principles—the greater the number, the better—ensures that they will be effective.

Balance of Public Interests

A good public policy must be an accurate representation of public interests, which refers to the well-being of citizens; however, many segments of the population have different and competing interests. Competing and conflicting interests appear throughout our society—between businesses and labour unions, farmers and land developers, landlords and tenants, sellers and buyers, mining companies and environmentalists, and so on. This makes it difficult for politicians to determine which interests should be preserved and promoted for the public's benefit, and for the government to create public policy that balances all of the interests of different groups of people. If each of the various interests is important, how should they be balanced? As Chandler and Chandler (1979, pp. 133–135) noted, there are just too many interests to find common ground.

One of the most effective ways to deal with the issue of interest representation is to appease stakeholder groups by favouring their interests in one element of a public policy if they are being forced to sacrifice in another. In this manner, their interests are being traded off based on their priorities in relation to a specific issue. For example, in the area of employment equity, one contentious issue for the business sector is the increased cost of implementing employment equity programs. To appease businesses, a public policy may require them to complete and submit less paperwork to the government, thus lowering costs. In return, the government may require these businesses to make reasonable efforts to consult their employees or labour unions when completing their employment equity tasks. The same public policy may allow labour unions to retain seniority rights even though they place women and other groups at a disadvantage. In return, the public policy may require unions to communicate and consult with their members, as well as collaborate with employers, on employment equity matters. In other words, there is an element of give-and-take for each stakeholder group and trade-offs among them. As a stakeholder group, the government may have to sacrifice some information or data due to the reduction in paperwork that was negotiated to get employers to buy into the policy.

The above example illustrates the negotiations and effort necessary to strike a balance among the interests of employers, labour unions, and the government. The ability of the government to accomplish a fair compromise among various interests depends largely on extensive consultation and collaboration with the stakeholder groups.

Accountability

While accountability is one of the most cited principles in public policies, it is also the one that is most often neglected. Accountability is the responsibility of the government to ensure that the public policy is well researched, and properly resourced, implemented, managed, monitored, evaluated, and readjusted according to evaluation findings. In other words, answerability is an integral part of public policies.

Answerability means that politicians and government bureaucrats are able to explain their decisions to the public and the legislature or parliament. To ensure this, some public policies, especially those embodied in legislation, have built in a higher degree of monitoring, enforcement, evaluation, and readjustments. The law and its execution are reviewed regularly—once every three to five years—by a legislative or parliamentary committee. Committee members examine whether or not it is fulfilling its policy goals; if not, adjustments can be expected. Other laws may not have been written with clauses on monitoring and reviewing, but they may have a certain degree of built-in tracking (including submission of reports) and enforcement mechanisms (including entry of premises, seizure of documents, laying charges, and penalties).

When public policies are translated into programs or services that are funded by the government, the monitoring and evaluation requirements are often more lenient, as there may not be enough pertinent data or information in the program or service reports. This usually results when the components of monitoring and evaluation are not explicitly stated when public policies are drafted in the cabinet submission. After the policy is approved by cabinet and ratified in the legislature or parliament, the bureaucrats translating the policies into operation (as concrete programs or services) may not include the components of observation and evaluation. This can occur as a result of the urgency imparted to implement programs or services, or the pressure ministers are under to get the new programs or services under way.

A common trend that undermines the principle of accountability is the creation of independent agencies by cabinet ministers to implement public policies. Because of pressure on the government to look small—by reducing the number of public servants, lowering the cost of facilities for ministerial operation, cutting down on annual deficits and debts, and giving the appearance of impartiality in operation—arm's length agencies or, in some cases, public-private partnerships are established to manage government-funded programs or services.

With these independent agencies or public-private partnerships, the accountability question is, who is responsible for spending taxpayers' money? When these agencies are set up—to make the arrangement attractive to the private sector or to appear impartial—some aspects of monitoring and evaluation may be abandoned by the government. It is paradoxical for the government to maintain the arm's length model and, at the same time, legislate or determine the management structures and processes for these agencies in an effort to oversee their daily operations. Furthermore, it is up for debate how much discretionary power the government should give to the management of these agencies. The more management control the government gives away, the weaker its accountability. In such a case, it is clear that in the final analysis of the public policy's development, the issue of accountability has not been carefully thought through.

Public-private partnerships are problematic because, in spite of the requirements of a public-private legal contract, specifics of how the joint organization
will run, who will be responsible for what, and at what point the government
can take over cannot be anticipated during the public policy development
stage. This may lead to gaps or faults in the organization design and process.
If public policy developers and public servants are not able to foresee all of
the management issues that may arise, and the circumstances in which decisions will have to be made, it is unlikely that these issues and circumstances
will be placed in the public-private contract. As a result, there are ambiguous
areas in the contract where obligations and responsibilities are not spelled out
clearly. This is especially the case when the policy fields (e.g., transportation,
infrastructure, recreation, health care) involved are inherently different from
each other, and there are no public-private models that the government can
adopt as a best practice. Even if formal, well-defined administrative policies
and procedures are adopted up front, the government is still accountable to the
public. It is extremely difficult, and not in the interest of the public good, for
the government to negate its responsibilities.

Because many public domains are complex in nature, public policy developers and politicians must be thorough when evaluating evidence-based data and
meticulous when assessing research, so that they can develop comprehensive
public policies that are seamless when put into operation. Such high standards
prioritize accountability as a signature feature of good public policy.

Impact

Every public policy is intended to solve a specific issue (or issues), which has been
defined as problematic by the public or segments of the public. The government is
usually concerned with how particular public policies affect people, institutions,
or society, either directly or indirectly. Because bureaucrats contribute to policy
development, and government funds are allocated for policy implementation,
the government must justify the use of these human and financial resources. If
a public policy does not have the expected impact after implementation (or yield
the benefits it was supposed to), many would suggest that the policy has failed.
A good public policy produces its expected impacts after being approved by the
cabinet, ratified in the legislature, and put into operation.

Public policies that are not properly developed lack formal, explicit, clear, and
consistent objectives. This happens more often than one would expect. At times,
cabinet submissions and related treasury board submissions or management board

submissions may not have clear and consistent statements of their policy objectives. Equally problematic are slight variations in the wording, and sometimes content, of policy objectives in different government documents and communications. As a result of these differences, the evaluation of public policies is not as systematic or comprehensive as it should be. Without clear and consistent objectives, it is difficult for government bureaucrats to operationalize them effectively in programs or services, and to measure the impact they had. Good public policies must have clear and consistent objectives so their impacts can be monitored and measured.

Related to the above problem in public policy development is the lack of thought that sometimes goes into linking the problems defined by the public and the resultant policy expectations. This linkage, in which the public policies are the intervening variable between the public problems and the expected impacts, is called an impact model. The public policies (or intervening variables) are intended to reduce or eliminate the public problem. A lack of an explicit description of this process—the connection between the public policy and public problems on one hand, and between the public policy and its impacts on the other—in writing often leads to the absence of a clear understanding of the expected impact; in other cases, a description may be provided, but be vague, or worse, ambiguous. Including an impact model in a cabinet submission, even in a summarized form, helps clarify the logic behind the public policy. Figure 5.1 uses the example of youth unemployment to show the links between the various elements of an impact model.

FIGURE 5.1: IMPACT MODEL

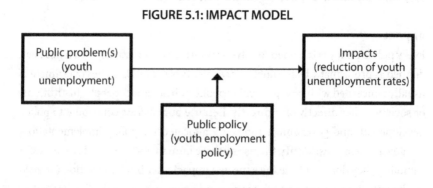

Another common mistake in public policy development is the confusion of outcomes and impacts. Outcomes are the output or tangible deliverables of a public policy. Examples of outcomes include the number of users contacted or participants involved, material items produced, phone calls made, and workshops conducted. These outcomes do not indicate whether a public policy is meeting its objectives and producing the benefits (or impacts) as planned. A policy may have satisfactory outcomes, but still not have the intended impacts that were outlined in the policy objectives. For example, a public policy on youth unemployment may be operationalized in youth employment counselling centres. The outcomes (for example, the number of centres or the number of youth participants in counselling workshops) do not indicate whether the policy is having the intended impact or effect; this can only be demonstrated when a reduction in the youth unemployment rate is shown to be directly related to the implementation of the public policy. Clearly distinguishing between these two terms and what they represent makes public policies better—both outcomes and impacts should be stated clearly in a cabinet submission.

Cost-Effectiveness

There are usually capital and operational costs associated with public policies. If a public policy can be implemented using minimal funding and the same level of impact can be expected, it makes financial sense to use the lower-cost option, provided the risk factors are manageable. During the public policy development stage, a realistic estimate of the amount of funds required to implement a public policy helps politicians make better decisions. Public policy developers need to provide realistic cost options based on different operational models. This can be done by controlling the type of policy instrument (or form of government intervention) used, or securing reliable information from other jurisdictions that have policies of a similar nature.

While it is highly desirable to have the principle of cost-effectiveness built in at the public policy development stage, this is usually easier said than done. Some public policies tackle uncharted policy fields; to determine the costs of something new, public policy developers must crunch numbers based on unverifiable assumptions. Even if financial data is available from other jurisdictions that have implemented similar public policies, it may not be applicable for a variety of reasons, such as the breadth of the unknown variables, lack of knowledge of the institutional arrangement, or unfamiliar terminology. Public policy developers can also formulate cost estimates for new public policies by borrowing financial information from different programs and using data collection methods to assemble it, while taking into account their own assumptions about the new policy. Any method used to estimate costs is bound to have shortcomings, and may be unreliable.

When a new public policy is ratified in the legislature or parliament, in the form of a piece of law or estimate for a program, funding is usually attached to its implementation costs. If the cost estimate is not accurate, the new program or service will encounter financial difficulty. Finding shortcuts in the operations of the program or lowering the level of projected deliverables usually solves this problem, although in some cases policy impacts are compromised. The principle of cost-effectiveness in good public policy development is crucial to maximizing a public policy's benefits.

Justice

Social justice is a central component of our society, and should therefore be integrated into good public policy. Distributive justice denotes fairness in the distribution of resources in a society; these resources cover a broad range of properties (e.g., facilities, equipment, technology, natural resources) and opportunities (e.g., knowledge, skills, services, consumption, housing, health care). John Rawls' three principles of social justice (Wolff, 2008, pp. 17–31; Craig, Burchardt, and Gordon, 2008, pp. 4, 18) maintain the following: (1) each person is entitled to the most extensive set of basic liberties compatible with the same liberty for all (liberty principle); (2) all positions of public responsibility or private advantage should be open to all on the basis of fair equality of opportunity (fair opportunity principle); and (3) any inequality in the distribution of resources for a good life is permissible only insofar as it is to the advantage of the worst-off group in society (difference principle). Incorporating these principles of justice into public policy makes the policy fair, more inclusive, and equitable.

In a country such as Canada, which prides itself on being a land of opportunity, one would expect such justice principles to be integrated into public policies. Some social policies (such as income supports, housing, and education) do incorporate these principles; however, when policy goes beyond the traditional social policy fields (in departments responsible for such areas as economic or environmental policies), the justice principles are seldom considered. This is largely due to the fact that public policy development has a tendency to be compartmentalized; this causes a silo effect in many government departments, which means that employees in one department may not be aware of what those in another department are doing and that there is little cross-fertilization of ideas among departments. The cabinet also demarcates public policy development into different cabinet committees that specialize in justice, social, economic, and environmental policy matters. This may be why past public policies on the environment, natural resources, agriculture, consumer relations, international relations, and other traditionally non-justice domains are generally devoid of justice principles. In the last few decades, research on social justice has permeated all aspects of human activity, even those that have not been traditionally linked with the concept of justice. The ascendency of notions of environmental, consumer, food, economic, and global justice give public policy developers a sense of the overarching importance of justice.

The concepts of equality and equity are an integral part of the justice principles. Equality rights in citizenship are guaranteed under the Charter of Rights and Freedoms. While abstract in meaning and idealistic in nature, these concepts should be translated into public policies in more concrete terms. Good public policies should embody an equality of opportunities (with no barriers for anyone to access a good life) and the concept of an equality of conditions (which removes disadvantaged conditions in which people are raised, educated, nurtured, and trained). Public policies should build in an equity component (such as supportive measures, accommodation, and additional financial assistance) so that people, irrespective of their diverse backgrounds, are able to successfully access (without barriers) the opportunities available to all, whether these opportunities are in the areas of education, employment, training, or resource acquisition.

Balance of Short- and Long-Term Considerations

A good public policy must be both present and future oriented. Its objectives should be formulated to meet short-term needs and achieve long-term gains by resolving current public problems and enriching the future. Without taking into consideration the ramifications public policies will have in the future, we may be building a society that achieves short-term gain, but also experiences long-term pain. There are many examples that make clear the significance of achieving this balancing act; our current consumption of natural resources (for short-term gain) and lack of care for the environment raise serious questions about environmental sustainability and degradation in the future (long-term pain) (Barry, 2005; Capeheart and Milovanovic, 2007; Margai, 2010). Another example is in the area of health and health care. Our current public policies on medical care, public health, sanitation, and living conditions have a greater negative impact on the most vulnerable members of our society. The next generation will inherit responsibility for the ill health, high stress, and premature mortality of their disadvantaged parents (Barry, 2005, pp. 70–94). This is more than an issue of justice; it extends to the well-being of future generations and the longevity of humankind.

Similarly, our current accumulation of national debt and annual deficits, and continual borrowing from the future to pay for the past, raise serious questions about how well we can sustain our current expenditure without endangering the well-being of future generations. Will the standard of living have to be downgraded for our children and grandchildren? Will their financial situation worsen and their life expectancy be jeopardized due to a lack of financial resources and a decline in economic growth? Once again, this is an issue of societal longevity and survival. It demonstrates the importance of striking a balance between gain in the short term and pain in the long term.

Public policies cannot be short-sighted. They may be intended to solve current problems, but the long-term effects may not be worth it. It has been observed that due to the rise of neo-liberalism and growing concern about debts and deficits, the new public management (NPM) movement in the private sector model of public policy development is growing in popularity, and this growing demand for fiscal constraint is driving public policies. As a result, the long-term value of environmental sustainability, water quality, public safety, education, and health care is being undermined.

BALANCING PRINCIPLES

To make a public policy as good as possible, public policy developers should ask themselves the following questions:

- Are the interests of stakeholder groups well balanced?
- Is an accountability framework well articulated?
- Are the objectives and expected impacts of the public policy explicitly stated?
- Is the public policy the most cost-effective way to resolve the problem(s)?
- Is the public policy just to everyone affected by its implementation?
- Does the public policy balance both short- and long-term considerations?

When public policy developers can answer these questions adequately and conclude that the public policy in development adheres to these six principles, then the policy may be considered good. However, the extent to which these six principles are being followed is contingent on many factors, many of which are beyond the control of the public policy developers, such as political context, public opinion, stakeholder pressure, economic conditions, international relations, culture, and ideology. These factors are likely to influence the final form and content of a public policy, which may deviate from the principles.

FIGURE 5.2: BALANCING THE SIX PRINCIPLES OF GOOD PUBLIC POLICY

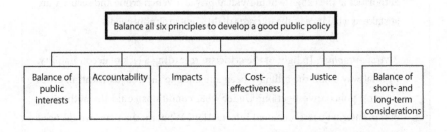

BILL C-30: *PROTECTING CHILDREN FROM INTERNET PREDATORS ACT*
Bill C-30 was introduced by Federal Public Safety Minister Vic Toews in 2012 with the stated intention of requiring telecommunications service providers to develop and maintain certain capabilities that would facilitate the lawful interception of information transmitted by telecommunications, and to provide basic information about their subscribers to the Royal Canadian Mounted Police, the Canadian Security Intelligence Service, the Commissioner of Competition, and any provincial police services.

The bill sparked criticism from many people, including legal experts and privacy commissioners, who viewed it as intrusive. It was nicknamed the "snooping bill," as it allegedly gave power to policing authorities to monitor Internet users in Canada and to obtain personal information—real names, home addresses, email addresses, and Internet Protocol addresses—from service providers without a warrant. Bill C-30 went through first reading on February 14, 2012, and was reviewed by the Committee on Justice and Human Rights for amendment prior to the second reading. During the review process, the federal Conservative government came to the conclusion that the bill had to be withdrawn in light of the strong public opposition. On February 11, 2013, Federal Justice Minister Rob Nicholson announced the end of Bill C-30.

Bill C-30 is a good example of how a proposed public policy could have been better assessed using the six principles of good public policy:

1. *Balance of public interests:* Numerous stakeholder groups had a vested interest in the bill: Conservative politicians and their constituents, opposition parties, police services, the RCMP, victims of crime and their families, Internet service providers, civil rights groups, labour unions, and any individuals who use the Internet. The following questions should have been asked while the policy was in development: Is the policy too skewed in favour of the policing authorities at the expense of individual privacy? When crime and security are at stake, is a balance of the interests of different groups needed?

2. *Accountability:* In light of the criticism regarding a lack of accountability, in what way could the bill have been amended to include justification criteria for a police investigation? Under what conditions could the authorities obtain Internet users' personal information? What mechanisms would need to be put in place for the government to oversee the policing authorities and their compliance with proper protocols, standards, and procedures? What checks and balances should be explicitly stated in the bill? For this bill to be determined a good public policy, answers to these questions and many more related to accountability would have to be provided.

3. *Impact:* The expected impact of Bill C-30 is the investigation and prevention of potential criminal communication through electronic means to protect children from Internet predators. Those developing the policy should have considered the following questions with regard to its impact: Is this bill the most effective way to protect children from sex offenders or human trafficking? Is monitoring Internet communication and obtaining the personal information of all Canadian Internet users the most effective way to prevent children from being exploited? Does this bill have a hidden agenda to strengthen police power? How clear is the impact model in justifying Bill C-30 as resolution to the sexual exploitation of children?

4. *Cost-effectiveness:* If the bill had passed, implementing it would have required realistic costing for capital and operations, including human resources, facilities, equipment, and administration. The cost for Internet service providers to upgrade their server systems would have been cost-effective from the government's perspective, but these costs may have been passed down to consumers. Public policy developers need to explore all alternatives and determine which means are the most cost-effective.

5. *Justice:* The justice issues associated with this bill are related to police power and the perceived powerlessness of ordinary citizens. In this case, the degree of state intervention over the private sector in the name of the public good was a very contentious issue. Public policy developers needed to consider the justice principle in relation to the various stakeholder groups and assess how this bill furthered the principle.

6. *Balance of short- and long-term considerations:* In relation to Bill C-30, the short-term issues included the ability of policing authorities to monitor and control criminal behaviour and protect the vulnerable. The long-term issues that needed to be considered included the possibility that criminal behaviour would be driven further underground, the erosion of privacy and individual rights, the balance of state and business, and the financial sustainability of the policy implementation.

It is unlikely that all of these principles will be perfectly adhered to in the final version of a bill, but any serious attempts to ensure that these principles are addressed in a proposed bill can be a step forward in making a public policy better. In reality, public policy developers and politicians must often trade off one principle for another or address each principle in a diluted form to balance all six principles. When a bill becomes law, these principles have to be balanced by public policy developers and politicians, who must decide which of the principles will be adhered to, sacrificed, or diluted for public good.

SUMMARY

It is almost impossible to achieve consensus on whether a public policy is good or not because people have different worldviews, values, vested interests, and assessment criteria, or they may disagree with the level of government intervention. The six principles of good public policy—balance of public interests, accountability, impact, cost-effectiveness, justice, and balance of short- and long-term considerations—put forward in this chapter can be used to determine how good a public policy is. While most public policies do not adhere to all of these principles equally, it is important that each is considered during the development process, and integrated into the policy in a well-balanced manner.

QUESTIONS FOR CRITICAL THINKING

1. This chapter outlines six principles of good public policy—balance of public interests, accountability, impact, cost-effectiveness, justice, and balance of short- and long-term considerations. Think of two additional principles that could contribute to the development of good public policy.

2. Should balancing these six principles be a mandatory requirement or an optional consideration in public policy development?

3. The six principles of good public policy often compete with each other. How should a public policy developer determine which principles have a higher priority, and how the principles can be balanced?

IDENTIFYING PUBLIC POLICY ISSUES

INTRODUCTION

The process of public policy development begins with the identification of public policy issues. Because many issues are perceived to be problematic in our society, it is difficult for public policy developers to sort out and identify which issues the government should tackle. Issues that have not been identified as worthy of further pursuit by the government are not public policy issues.

The process through which a policy issue is identified is fluid and constantly evolving. Many factors have to be considered during this process and many players are involved. Public policy developers may identify issues using a number of approaches, depending on extrinsic and intrinsic factors, which will be discussed in this chapter. Because issue identification is the first component to be addressed in public policy development, any errors in judgment at this stage can have a compounded negative effect on the rest of the process. These negative effects include misdirecting or wasting research efforts and resources, constructing irrelevant policy options, putting forth inappropriate recommendations, and making ill-advised political decisions.

GENESIS OF POLICY IDEAS

Policy ideas are abstract and vague concepts of how a certain aspect of society or human behaviour can be changed. Policy issue identification is a process that makes these ideas more concrete. Policy ideas can arise for a number of different reasons, including global and social change and public or organizational pressure, and from various sources, including stakeholder groups, consulting firms, think tanks, published research findings and investigative journalism, media coverage, government bureaucrats, and politicians.

Globalization, with its rapid movement of people, goods, services, and ideas among interconnected nations and marketplaces, may increase the urgency of formulating public policies and finding solutions to policy problems. Some policy ideas arise as a result of international events and trends; evolving political, economic, and technological conditions; changing social norms and values; emerging worldviews; or natural disasters. This larger social context sets the stage for the emergence of new ideas about how to manage the country and provinces. Traditional ways of resolving issues and planning for the future have been challenged by an increasingly interconnected global population. When people have ideas about how to do things better, they may form or join groups that can exert pressure on the government to adopt their solutions. These include lobby groups, community organizations, non-profit alliances, professional and business associations, and trade unions.

Newly released information, either internal or external to the government, may also spur new policy proposals. Research findings presented in government reports, such as those issued by royal commissions, committees, task forces, and the Office of the Auditor General, provide evidence of the ineffectiveness, inefficiency, or inappropriateness of public policies, programs, or services, or misuse of funds, and thus may recommend new solutions to problems or innovative ways of doing things. Research results from think tanks and consulting firms may also stimulate new ideas or solutions to lingering problems. The media, through their own investigations, may unearth illegitimate or illegal activities. Academic and professional researchers may discover a new and challenging issue that could benefit from the government's involvement. These findings and revelations can act as a catalyst for new policy ideas, because they suggest that something has to be changed.

Government officials—including public policy developers—can put forward ideas for ministers to consider. While some ideas are merely extensions of the political ideology of those in power, without much empirical evidence to support them, external groups play an important role in bringing forward policy ideas. Since the 1980s, the federal government has relied on think tanks and private consulting firms, valued for their political or independent advice, and their assistance in helping senior executives in the federal government to fulfill their agendas. Their services are utilized to formulate or analyze public policies in fields such as education, social justice, and health. These firms are beginning to shape public policies in the same manner that they have shaped the private sector (Speers, 2007, pp. 399–400). This trend may be in line with the new public management (NPM) model of operation. This model is manifested in the attempts of the federal and provincial governments to redefine core business and streamline government functions under the auspices of budgetary restraints and expenditure reduction. With this model as a lens, government sees itself as a business organization focused on steering jurisdictions without having to row. As the policy capacity within government bureaucracy is being hollowed out, navigating public policy development now means that the government adopts policy ideas generated by think tanks or private consulting firms, and places these policy ideas on their political agenda.

PRIVATE VERSUS PUBLIC PROBLEMS

There are an infinite number of potentially problematic issues that individuals can identify and demand that the government attend to. Why do individuals perceive some issues as problematic? Pal (1992, pp. 133–134) maintains that an issue is often defined as problematic because it creates a barrier to our "desired actions or ends," or violates our sense of what is right, just, fair, or proper. Recognition of a problem is based on a combination of objective facts and subjective interpretations. There is also a distinction between a private and a public problem; unless a substantial segment of the public has shifted its view of a problem from private to public, it will not be viewed as warranting government intervention. This shift, if it occurs at all, takes time.

Stakeholder groups use pressure tactics—including lobbying, protests, letter campaigns, media exposure, and releasing research reports—to change politicians' perceptions of problems from private to public in an effort to have them put on the government's agenda. These pressure tactics are most effective during the early stages of public policy development, and are effective only when a critical mass of people is affected by the problem and has organized to make their demands known. Sometimes when mass mobilization occurs, groups with competing or conflicting viewpoints become polarized. This creates a situation that is difficult for politicians to manage, as it can deteriorate into open conflicts and destabilize society. To contain this instability and prevent it from becoming unmanageable, the government must define the problem as public and start looking for solutions.

The ability of a critical mass of people to cause politicians to change their opinions regarding the nature of a problem—instigating a shift from private to public—is subject to debate. In some instances—such as the federal government's policy to eliminate the mandatory long-form census questionnaire in

2011 (see the text box below)—the government adopts policies that go against the will of a substantial segment of the population. This negation of the validity of public opinion suggests that political ideology is often a factor to be reckoned with, especially in the realm of formulating new public policies. At times, there has been a need for the political party in power to consolidate the base of its traditional constituency. The elimination of the mandatory long-form census is an example of the federal Conservative government's efforts to adhere to its political ideology of a smaller government that interferes less in individuals' lives. Such efforts may make the party more appealing to its traditional political base. The controversy over the removal of the long-form census questionnaire illustrates how a new policy idea can be adopted despite opposition from a substantial segment of the population.

MANDATORY LONG-FORM CENSUS QUESTIONNAIRE REPLACED BY VOLUNTARY NATIONAL HOUSEHOLD SURVEY

In 2006, the Canada census was composed of two forms: (1) a short-form census questionnaire consisting of 10 questions that all Canadians were required by law to complete and return, and (2) a long-form census questionnaire consisting of many more questions that was sent to only 20 percent of Canadian households, which were legally required to complete and return their responses. Citing complaints about the threat of the long-form census to individual privacy and the coercive power of the state in jailing those who refused to complete it, the federal government (with the support of the National Citizens Coalition and the Fraser Institute) decided to eliminate this form on June 17, 2010, issuing a press release to announce its decision on July 13, 2010. For the 2011 census, the mandatory long-form census questionnaire was replaced by the voluntary National Household Survey.

Opponents of the federal decision to cancel the long-form census were concerned about the expected lower rate of return of the National Household Survey questionnaire, as its completion is voluntary, not mandatory. As a result, they anticipated that the reliability of the census data would be compromised. In addition, the response rate of marginalized people was expected to be particularly low, making data on this segment of the population even more unreliable and under-reported. Historically, government and many institutions have relied heavily on the data generated from the long form for analyses, projections, and, ultimately, organizational decisions. Data unreliability increases the likelihood of miscalculated decisions.

For these reasons, many opponents of the federal decision mounted massive protests. This included a broad spectrum of institutions and organizations representing municipalities; provincial and national economic councils; universities; religious groups; professional groups such as medical doctors, statisticians, nurses, economists, planners, public policy developers, and professors; immigrant groups; housing groups; labour unions; non-profit organizations; research companies; business associations; and others. Munir Sheikh, then Statistics Canada's chief statistician, resigned over this issue on July 21, 2010. In the end, the combination of these concerted efforts was not strong enough to overturn the federal decision.

The House of Commons' Standing Committee on Industry, Science, and Technology revealed in July 2010 that there were only 166 complaints about the long-form census out of 12 million forms completed in 2006. Jack Layton, then leader of the national New Democratic Party, noted that in the entire history of Canadian censuses, the federal government had not jailed one single person for not completing the census. As these facts suggest, the two reasons for eliminating the long-form census cited by Minister of Industry Tony Clement—lack of individual privacy and the imprisonment of those who do not complete the long form—were largely exaggerated, and the substantial segment of the population that supported the continuation of the long-form census was largely ignored.

The response rate to the National Household Survey, released in May 2013, showed that 69 percent of those who received the survey forms responded, compared to the 94 percent response rate to the mandatory questionnaire used in previous censuses, a difference of 25 percentage points (Chase and Grant, 2013; Ditchburn, 2013; Statistics Canada, 2012). The release of the census data on Aboriginal peoples also suggested that there is a higher potential of non-response errors in the data, which has implications for the data reliability, especially for smaller communities (Statistics Canada, 2011).

This is one example of how a public policy can be implemented without consulting the public, and how demands from a substantial segment of the population may not change the nature of a public policy.

External stakeholder groups with different political inclinations and vested interests may identify the same problem in a very different manner; in fact, their views may be diametrically opposed or in competition with each other. The government often views these conflicting or competing concepts of the problem as difficult to manage. Politicians in power would like to reduce such issues to something that is manageable (based on resources) and palatable (based on political ideology); they seek to avoid having the problem escalate to the point of polarizing stakeholder groups or the public.

FIGURE 6.1: SHIFTING PROBLEMS FROM PRIVATE TO PUBLIC

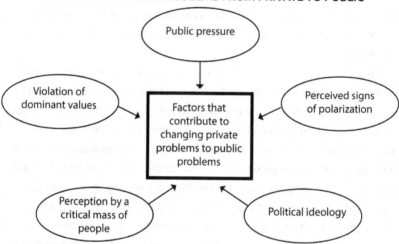

PRIORITY SETTING IN GOVERNMENT

Both the federal and provincial governments have some form of planning and priorities board that classifies which problems politicians in power must deal with. These planning and priorities boards, which are part of the cabinet system, prioritize tasks and plan for the cabinet by soliciting items from line ministers who have identified what issues should be prioritized. Ministers, deputy ministers, political aides (political offices), and public policy developers usually work on this stage of identification. Public policy developers may compile a list of policy issues and submit it to the deputy ministers. When the ministers have a public policy issue that requires additional action, political aides usually work with public policy developers to see how the policy issue can be further developed and sometimes informally communicate with the planning and priorities board.

While the general public or stakeholder groups may be keen to define and publicize problems as they see them, the government takes a more neutral approach to the defining process, attempting to frame policy issues without value judgment. Issue identification is the first and most important step in public policy development. If a problem is not properly identified, and forwarded to the planning and priorities board through the line ministers and the cabinet committees, it will not graduate to the next level to become a potential issue for development. As not all issues are worthy of cabinet's consideration, line ministers, in consultation with their colleagues and the premier (or prime minister), examine propositions before finalizing their submission list. This stage of issue identification can be routine, as it is with regards to renewing annual funding for existing programs for which no additional research on policy issues needs to be conducted, or creative, as it is when formulating new policy issues for the next fiscal year. Public policy developers do not work in isolation when determining issues; ministers and deputy ministers of line departments—with their knowledge of the big picture—often instruct public policy developers to add items the priority list.

Taking into consideration the platform of the party in power, and/or direction from the premier or prime minister, the planning and priorities board distills the items submitted by the line departments and arranges them into bundles—usually from highest to lowest in terms of priority—and schedules time for cabinet discussion. The cabinet reviews these items and decides whether or not to select them for additional action, including public announcements as highlighted in the throne speech or estimates. The cabinet's determination of priority issues has implications for the government's political agenda, which should be flexible enough to incorporate new agenda items as circumstances require.

Setting a political agenda demonstrates what the government plans to accomplish during its term of governance or within a specific time frame. When making public announcements regarding its agenda, the government highlights themes to illustrate its priorities, which can range from economic development to early childhood education, from health care to energy consumption. Items included in the agenda are at an early stage of development, and are usually just vague ideas. Public policy developers must adhere to and articulate policy issues based on these ideas.

FIGURE 6.2: PROBLEMS, POLICY IDEAS, AND POLICY ISSUES

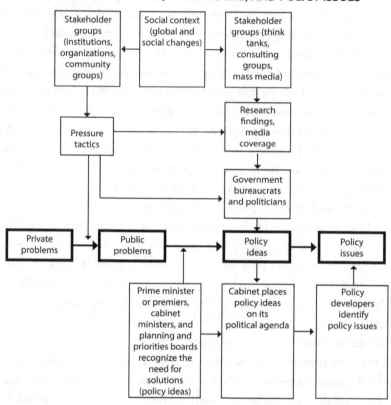

EXPLANATIONS FOR POLITICAL AGENDA SETTING

As discussed above, there is an abundant supply of policy ideas that come from different sources, and it is the planning and priorities board's mandate to sort and rank them. How are these policy ideas sorted, ranked, and placed on the political agenda? The answer to this question varies, depending on the approach taken; these include the historical and structural approaches, the value-oriented approach, and the intermediate approach.

Historical and structural approaches emphasize the stages and levels of economic development (e.g., an early stage of industrialization necessitates labour and work conditions on a political agenda), type of economic structure (e.g., with the flow of capital being central to capitalism, it places banking issues on a political agenda), and the outcomes of economic development (e.g., working class and urbanization issues take priority on a political agenda as more people move from rural areas to cities). Key political and government activities also determine the government's agenda, including elections, budgets or estimates, parliamentary sessions, and the release of government reports. Political parties have their own schedule of events and this, combined with leadership reviews and policy conferences, shapes the political platform and government agenda (Pal, 1992, pp. 123–124). A variation on this viewpoint is the issue-attention cycle, which is the period of time during which the specific issues become the focus of public attention. Some would argue that issues that catch the attention of the public stand a better chance of being pushed toward government action. Such public attention is usually short-lived, unless the issues are tied to routine government events (such as a throne speech or budget announcement), which usually sustain media interest for a long period of time (Howlett, Ramesh, and Perl, 2009, pp. 100–101).

There are other persistent socio-political and economic factors that affect government priorities. Such factors may linger on for years or decades; examples include English-French relations, the US-Canada trade arrangement, and the capitalist system and its inherent class conflicts. Increasingly, as a result of globalization and the interconnectedness of countries around the world, national priorities are influenced and even controlled by other countries or international bodies, such as the International Monetary Fund and the World Health Organization (Capeheart and Milovanovic, 2007, pp. 78, 81–87; Cramme and Diamond, 2009, pp. 3–22). Transnational forces exert persistent structural pressure on government policies. Since the federal government occasionally places structural issues on the political agenda, some of these issues flare and catch the attention of politicians, who believe that they must be tackled at the policy level. In all cases, these structural issues will be placed on the political agenda only if politicians interpret them as problematic (Pal, 1992, pp. 121–123).

With a value-oriented approach, a politician's worldview affects the nature of a policy idea. Perspective is crucial in setting a political agenda, whether a politician believes in self-regulation of the market (Adam Smith's metaphor of the invisible hand), or sees the government as economic regulator (interventionist) (Howlett, Ramesh, and Perl, 2009, pp. 93–96). When the values of external stakeholder groups interact with those of politicians, a policy idea may favour the special interest groups with values that align with those held by the politicians; for instance, gun control may favour the police services and not hunters or gun lobbyists, and capital punishment may favour those who support strong law-and-order deterrents and not those who support the rehabilitation of criminals (Howlett, Ramesh, and Perl, 2009, pp. 96–99).

Somewhere between the historical and structural approaches and the value-oriented approach is the intermediate approach. The increasing influence of this approach is predicated on the roles of stakeholder groups in political agenda setting. Stakeholder groups that know how the political system works—specifically the agenda-setting process within the government—and are aware of the limited opportunities available to influence the political agenda are in a position to monopolize these policy windows, regardless of how brief they are. They seek to control the perception of a policy idea by defining it in a particular manner, and trying to prevent other presentations of the same problem from emerging. Those who oppose the presentation of a policy idea must work hard to change public opinion, and to dismantle the idea as it has been constructed by their opponents. This is done in an effort to gain a position of influence, which can be used to not only reconstruct the image of a particular policy idea, but also to restructure the agenda (Howlett, Ramesh, and Perl, 2009, pp. 106–107).

As Wu and colleagues (2010, p. 13) have noted, the agenda-setting process is often fluid, non-linear in progression, political in nature, and a synergy of both social and political factors. This process reflects the conflicting interests of various political (elected officials) and non-political stakeholder groups (interest groups, research foundations, think tanks, labour unions, and business associations), the ideological and institutional elements (political beliefs and values, and the institutional resources mobilized) within these conflicts, and the undefined course of action influenced by changing circumstances (including media exposition of controversial issues or sudden unexpected events).

When these three approaches—historical and structural, value-oriented, and intermediate—are considered, the way in which policy ideas are added to the political agenda can be explained using the funnel of causality model. This model views the development of public policies as the result of various contributing factors that are intertwined in a nested pattern of interaction. This model begins with the macroscopic, which are the socio-economic, political, and cultural frameworks that establish the context for emerging issues. When policy issues are aligned with these frameworks, they are then filtered through intermediate factors, such as the organizational and decision-making mechanisms of government. When these policy issues are aligned with intermediate factors, they are filtered through the agenda-setting process of the government and considered by cabinet ministers. This viewpoint does not necessarily explain why one factor may be more influential than another in terms of whether or not a policy issue is placed on a political agenda (Howlett, Ramesh, and Perl, 2009, pp. 99–100).

Historical and structural factors (such as economic development or the aging population) and persistent public perception of issues (such as Canada's heavy reliance on the United States as a trading partner) may place pressure on the government, but seldom define policy issues. When social institutions and administrative mechanisms become the status quo and are unable to address large structural issues that are a source of discontent for stakeholder groups, these groups push the government to develop new public policies to eliminate these problems. When they exert enough pressure on the government, policy ideas related to the elimination of the problems end up on the political agenda (if they align with the ideology of the political party in power).

INITIAL FACTORS TO CONSIDER IN ISSUE IDENTIFICATION

Public policy developers do not have much autonomy to decide which public policies advance to the cabinet; as public servants, they are typically instructed to identify policy issues by deputy ministers or ministers. If a problem has been identified by an external group, ministers or deputy ministers may ask public policy developers to develop a policy idea to solve this problem, or to identify new and related policy issues.

Prior to plunging into policy issue identification, public policy developers need to ask several questions related to jurisdiction, legality, government direction, issue urgency, and anticipated impact, *in this order*. If the government does not have the jurisdictional mandate to deal with the policy idea, there is no need for public policy developers to continue identifying policy issues related to this idea. Legal issues related to the policy idea need to be clarified and examined by lawyers to define the boundaries of the policy idea prior to beginning policy work. When a policy idea is not consistent or compatible with the government direction, the cabinet may not have the appetite for these policy ideas, and policy efforts could go to waste. The urgency of a policy idea depends largely on the magnitude and intensity of the problem, and the timetables of both the government and stakeholder groups. A lack of urgency from ministers may indicate a wait-and-see position. If the anticipated impact of not developing a public policy in relation to a particular issue is negative or damaging, public policy developers may need to advise the ministers of the urgency of the issue—as expressed by stakeholder groups—and encourage them to take the matter seriously.

FIGURE 6.3: FIVE INITIAL QUESTIONS FOR IDENTIFYING ISSUES

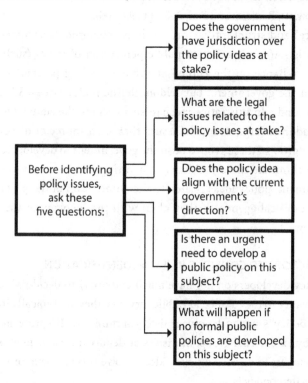

Jurisdiction: Does the government have the jurisdictional mandate to work on the policy idea?

Jurisdictional issues are paramount in any public policy development work, especially during the early stage of issue identification. Canada is a confederation of provinces and territories, and the legal boundaries of governments are described in the *British North American Act* (1867) and the *Canada Act* (1982). There are legal demarcations of federal and provincial responsibilities in many domains, such as housing, education, employment, training, and health care.

Although there are grey areas within jurisdictional issues, knowledge of the jurisdictional boundaries and general responsibilities of each area is imperative for issue identification. It is a waste for public policy developers to spend time and effort identifying policy issues that are not part of their government's jurisdictional mandate.

Legality: What are the legal issues related to the policy idea?

The legal dimensions of a problem are best reviewed or analyzed by lawyers; however, knowing the major legal issues connected to a problem is quite useful for public policy developers, as it allows them to determine if an issue must be resolved through legal means or can be translated into a piece of legislation, an amendment, or a regulation. Looking at a problem from a legal angle enables public policy developers to pose a range of questions that may have legal implications. To view a problem from a legal perspective, public policy developers must have a detailed understanding of the underlying principles of the idea, target groups, actions and outcomes, monitoring and review processes, legislative enforcement, appeal process, and penalties for non-compliance. Identifying policy issues through these legal aspects increases the comprehensiveness of the identification process.

Government direction: Does the policy idea align with the current government's direction?

Every government has a political platform. Speeches from the throne are often good indicators of where the government intends to go. Public policy developers must tune into the direction of a government. If the policy ideas identified do not align with the government's direction, they will have a difficult time moving the public policy issues from the line departments to cabinet for consideration. Identifying policy ideas that can be framed to align with the government's direction increases the likelihood that they will be approved by cabinet. Policy ideas that are at odds with the government's direction are usually non-starters that will not be recognized unless there is a drastic change of circumstance.

Issue urgency: Is there an urgency to develop a public policy on this subject?

The timetables of the political agenda and specific stakeholder groups or the general public may not correspond to each other, but a sense of urgency on both sides affects the speed at which a public policy is developed.

Public policy developers can become familiar with these timetables by maintaining close contact with related stakeholder groups, monitoring conventional and social media coverage, and paying close attention to news from the ministers' and cabinet's offices. When a public matter becomes urgent, there is a need to identify policy issues that are relevant to the matter, specific, and manageable. As time is of the essence in such situations, there is no room for errors or misidentification of an issue; therefore, public policy developers must be able to quickly analyze material related to such issues.

Anticipated impacts: What will happen if no formal public policies are developed on this subject matter?

When identifying policy issues, public policy developers may question what would happen if no action were taken. This allows them to get a sense of the possible consequences the problems may have on the public, institutions, the environment, or any other societal domain, and provides insight into how broad or deep the anticipated impact of an alleged problem may be. This question also forces public policy developers to examine how the problem is connected to other ministries. This broad lens helps them to approach the issue from different perspectives, and may enable them to identify the most wide-ranging policy issues that will affect the greatest number of people.

ISSUE IDENTIFICATION AND GOOD PUBLIC POLICY

Political agendas are broad overviews of political activities that every party institutes prior to coming into power. The policy ideas contained in political agendas are usually generic and vague concepts used to galvanize political support. If and when a political party forms the government, ministers may instruct their political aides and public servants to concretize existing policy ideas and start identifying policy issues connected to these, or they may seek new policy ideas as new situations arise even after the political agenda has been set. A search for new policy ideas can be broadly understood as an attempt to find new solutions to evolving problems under new circumstances.

To remain focused, it is fruitful for public policy developers to translate policy ideas into specific policy issues by posing them in the form of a question, rather than just identifying a topic. For example, the political party in power may have identified pension reform as a policy idea. If the term *pension reform* (which is generic and vague) is used as a topic for further research, public policy developers could go in many different directions, as this broad topic encompasses a multitude of issues. If these issues are not narrowed, public policy development efforts may become unwieldy, and resources and efforts may be diffused without tangible progress. When a clear direction on the policy idea of pension reform is given, public policy developers can then put the policy idea into question form, which helps make the issue explicit and focused enough to solicit specific answers.

As the core objective of identifying policy issues is the development of good public policy, the way a policy issue is set up is instrumental to solving the problem according to the principles outlined in chapter 5. One starting point for formulating policy issues is to ask questions that take public interests, accountability, impacts, cost-effectiveness, justice, and short- and long-term factors into consideration.

PENSION REFORM

Asking some pointed questions can help public policy developers identify policy issues. Using the example of pension reform, we will look at examples of such questions. The questions listed here are just a sample of the many questions public policy developers may pose. They illustrate how a policy idea can be narrowed down into different concrete inquiries, the answers to which will bring the idea of pension reform into focus. The answers to these policy questions often give rise to additional questions. When public policy developers begin seeking the answers to these questions through research, the development process is under way. It continues until satisfactory answers are obtained or the time for issue identification runs out. Public policy developers addressing the policy idea of pension reform could ask the following questions:

- What are the public problems that pension reform can solve?
- What are the anticipated impacts on each of the stakeholder groups when pension reform is carried out?
- Which aspects of the Canadian Pension Plan (CPP) require modifications and which need radical changes to ensure the expected impacts when resolved?
- Do CPP and Old Age Security (OAS) need to be harmonized into one program?
- What new programs need to be put into place if the current pension programs are eliminated?
- What roles will the federal government, provincial governments,

employers, insurance companies, and individuals play in pension reform planning?

- What accountability framework is needed to ensure that there are checks and balances, transparency, integrity, public answerability, reviews, and enforcement when stakeholder groups are participating in new or reformed pension programs?
- What monitoring and measurement mechanisms are needed to ensure new or reformed pension programs are run in a cost-effective manner?
- What justice components must be built into the new or reformed pension programs to ensure that pensions are fairly and equitably allocated to their recipients?
- What short- and long-term factors should be considered when developing new or reformed pension programs?

APPROACHES TO ISSUE IDENTIFICATION

Policy issues can be defined narrowly, specifically, broadly, or generically, depending on the approach that public policy developers take in identifying the issue. There are four approaches to policy issue identification: academic, partisan, generic, and specific. These approaches are not mutually exclusive. In general, direction from the minister sets the path for issue identification. Ministers can be particular about the kind of public policies that they want to see, and usually prefer either a partisan or a specific approach. If the minister is open to a wide spectrum of public policies, he or she may provide autonomy for public policy developers to adopt a broad (generic or academic) approach to issue identification. The availability of resources often determines the approach—more resources (people, time, and money) are needed to adopt a generic or academic method. Academic and partisan approaches are methodological in orientation, while generic and specific approaches deal with the scope of inquiry. An academic or a partisan approach could be either generic or specific in scope and a specific or broad approach could either be academic or partisan in methodological orientation.

Academic Approach

Public policy developers may identify policy issues in an academic tradition by posing a series of questions that demand evidence-based, scientific, and non-partisan answers. These questions can only be answered by using a sound research methodology. The recommended solutions must be rational and address the underlying sources of the identified problems. Using this approach, policy issues are likely to be comprehensive and objective, but the process may take longer and utilize more resources.

Public policy developers use this approach only when the time frame is not constrained, resources are adequately allocated, and the politicians in power are not ideologically driven. This can be illustrated using the hypothetical example that Canada's tourism industry is in decline. If Canadian businesses note that fewer American tourists have come to Canada in recent years, they have identified this decline as an economic issue—fewer American tourists means fewer customers, and fewer customers means reduced revenues. If the exchange rate is identified as a contributing factor, the issue could be seen as related to currency. If public policy developers do not exercise due diligence, they may accept this rationale and pose policy issues around currency or economic factors. This tendency precludes the government from debunking these factors and, more importantly, from discovering the actual state of Canadian tourism and determining the true source of its decline.

The academic approach would treat the framing of this issue by the business sector as merely one possible perspective; it does not assume that the cause of the tourism decline is either financial or economic. The academic approach discourages public policy developers from jumping to conclusions; rather, it encourages them to ask a series of questions (examples of which are provided below) with the objective of determining an accurate explanation for the perceived decline in tourism. Posing these questions constitutes the first round of issue identification; finding the answers requires research:

- In which provinces, cities, or other geographic locations is tourism in decline?
- Which stakeholder groups are involved?
- What are the indicators and evidence of the decline in Canadian tourism, as claimed by the business sector?
- Are these indicators valid and is the data reliable?
- What do the statistics on tourists indicate?
- If a decline is indicated, how serious is it?

- If data shows that fewer American tourists are coming to Canada, what are the possible causes?
- Historically, has the exchange rate played a role in the decline of tourists?
- How effective are current marketing and promotion efforts for tourism programs?
- What do other countries with booming tourism industries have that Canada may not?
- What changes are occurring in the socio-economic and political conditions in the United States and Canada? How might these conditions affect the tourism industry?
- What are some additional factors in the tourism industry that the government should be aware of?

These are a few of the many questions that public policy developers may pose if they follow an academic approach. One characteristic of this approach is the posing of open-ended questions, which allow public policy developers to formulate hypotheses; they can then work from those hypotheses to review existing literature and research in the field and consult experts in the area. This approach strives to avoid blind spots or tunnel vision of the subject matter, which can result from the pressure exerted by external and internal stakeholder groups. The academic approach is acceptable if the identified policy issues have not been posed in a biased manner, as the solutions that emerge may or may not align with a minister's political inclinations. Posing the policy issues in an academic manner allows one to examine them through a scientific lens— policy questions are posed as neutrally as possible and are not biased in favour of any one stakeholder group and the issues are value-added.

Answers to the above questions can help public policy developers understand the nuances of a problem, which may lead to posing more meaningful policy questions and, ultimately, a more in-depth and rigorous analysis of the issue. Policy issues that are formulated using an academic approach present a neutral front to all external stakeholder groups, and should therefore be able to withstand the scrutiny of the media, which may criticize how the government frames the policy idea. This often depends on whether or not the media organization supports a particular stakeholder group or the government itself.

FIGURE 6.4: ACADEMIC APPROACH TO ISSUE IDENTIFICATION

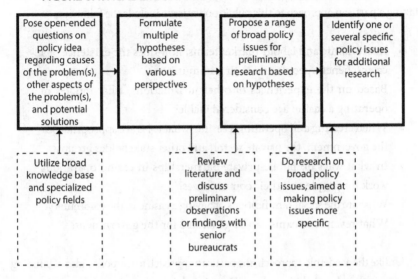

Partisan Approach

Not all policy issues are tackled in a neutral, academic manner. Ministers may direct public policy developers to take a partisan approach on a policy idea. In this case, there is not much interest in understanding the problem objectively or comprehensively. This approach reflects the tendency for the political side (politicians) to control the bureaucratic side (public servants) of government. This approach saves time and is efficient in terms of resource use because comprehensive research is curtailed. In some cases, this approach even precludes consultations with the public or stakeholder groups, allowing policy issues to be identified and resolved quickly.

The following example uses a hypothetical casino development to illustrate the nature of the partisan approach. Politicians in power may believe that establishing a casino in a community with a sluggish economy will stimulate economic growth and employment. This belief may be considered partisan, especially if the policy idea of building casinos has not been thoroughly studied and the social and economic ramifications of already established casinos have not been comprehensively reviewed.

When the minister in charge of the tourism portfolio instructs public policy developers to identify policy issues based on this partisan idea, several policy issues may emerge, none of which are based on an academic line of inquiry, such as asking critical questions and conducting research prior to the identification of policy issues. In this case, the partisan view is that the casino will lower unemployment and lead to economic growth. Questions that could be asked by public policy developers when taking a partisan approach to this public policy issue include the following:

- In economic and labour market terms, how does the existence of a casino benefit people and their communities?
- Based on the experiences of other jurisdictions, what models of operating a casino are considered viable?
- When creating and operating a casino, what roles are appropriate for the government, the private sector, and other stakeholder groups?
- In what ways do public-private partnerships in casino operations work for people and their communities?
- What are the social ramifications of having a casino in the community?
- What revenue streams can be generated for the government?

Unlike the academic approach, the partisan approach to the policy idea of building a casino is closed-ended, since the minister has defined it as the only way to increase economic growth and employment at the outset. Finding alternative methods to produce economic growth and increase employment has been prohibited. Public policy developers cannot identify policy issues that challenge or go beyond the primacy of the idea that a casino lowers unemployment and leads to economic growth. As is visible in the nature of the above questions, the policy issues are limited to how to make the policy idea happen and what the anticipated impacts will be. The questions do not challenge the policy idea of building the casino.

In contrast, the following questions are framed by a less partisan approach; they are more open-ended, and their answers may cast doubt on the viability of establishing a casino:

- What mechanisms, besides casinos, has the government put in place to stimulate economic growth and employment in communities?
- What are the benefits and risks for residents in communities with casinos compared to those in communities without casinos?
- Casinos in towns on both sides of the Canada-US border compete with each other. Is that type of competition good for the provinces and Canada?
- Besides building casinos, what additional programs could be put in place to stimulate economic growth and improve employment in local economies?

The partisan approach to issue identification does not generate critical think-ing or openness in public policy development and is limited in its scope of research. However, such an approach is common in the federal and provincial governments because it ensures that policy issues are consistent with the pol-itical ideology of the party in power, saves time and resources, and the public policies that result from it are likely to be approved by the cabinet. This trend of politicization and centralization of public policy development, in which political offices take control of the process, is discussed in greater detail in chapter 3.

FIGURE 6.5: PARTISAN APPROACH TO ISSUE IDENTIFICATION

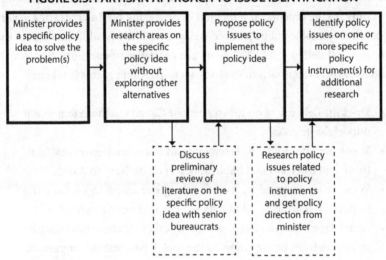

Generic Approach

When policy issues are identified in a generic manner, issues must be defined broadly. Such an approach presents a relatively wide range of issues for public policy developers to work on. It allows for flexibility to explore various pos-sibilities without being boxed in by any one avenue of inquiry; this is in direct contrast to the partisan approach. In spite of its broadness, this approach does lead to the narrow identification of specific issues; the identification process evolves through different stages, each of which is narrower and more specific than the previous one. It is similar to a funnel effect, as issue identification starts broadly and narrows as issues are further specified.

This approach is usually used in governments that afford a certain degree of autonomy to their public policy developers to explore different aspects of a problem. The time frame for the development of a particular policy idea under this approach is more flexible. The ministers involved do not have a partisan view on the subject matter; rather, they may be interested in finding out more about the nature of the problem. Unlike the academic approach, the generic approach does not necessarily utilize a scientific methodology to examine every aspect of the subject matter and it does not require many resources or a lot of time. Unlike the partisan approach, it is not confined to a specific ideological perspective. Essentially, it is pragmatic in approach and tries to build in flexibility.

Take, for example, the policy idea of building a pipeline to deliver oil to Asia from Alberta. If this idea were approached in a partisan manner, it would focus only on the pipeline as a method of delivering oil. In contrast, a generic approach may enable public policy developers to identify additional issues that go beyond oil delivery. The following are examples of questions that may be asked if a generic approach to the issue identification process is taken:

- Does the delivery of oil to Asia benefit Canada to the extent that it outweighs its risks?
- What are the political, economic, military, environmental, cultural, and international implications of oil delivery to Asia?
- What criteria should be used for the government to evaluate the impacts of delivering oil to Asia with or without a pipeline?
- Apart from the economy, are there other relationship-building infrastructures or programs in the social, educational, or cultural domains that Canada could put in place to further its relationship with Asian countries?
- Apart from pipeline delivery, what other mechanisms could Canada put in place to further the growth of its natural resource sector?

The generic approach focuses not only on the environment or the economy, but also on many other fronts.

If the generic approach is adopted, the tendency is for public policy developers to narrow the issues as quickly as possible to accelerate the issue identification process. If and when the issue is narrowly identified as an environmental one, it automatically restricts the boundaries of the policy idea. Defined as an environmental issue, this situation may capture the interest of a number of external stakeholder groups, including environmentalists, community members, farmers, tourism operators, and First Nations communities. However, if the issue is identified not only as an environmental issue, but broadened to include issues concerning international relations, business, economic development, cultural heritage, national security, health, ecology, and poverty, many more stakeholder groups will be involved. It follows that the scope of policy inquiry and research will be broadened. This may support the idea that the federal government is a government with a broad vision that is capable of taking into consideration many different interests.

Identifying policy issues in a generic and broad way is a win-win-win situation for external stakeholder groups, government bureaucrats, and politicians at the earliest stage of public policy development. This is because it gives the appearance that the government is attempting to address the interests of a broad segment of the population. As the government begins to narrow its vision, some stakeholder groups may perceive that their interests are no longer being prioritized. By that time, public sentiment and the concerns of stakeholder groups have become more entrenched. Some of these groups may have had high hopes of promoting their vested interests, but end up being disappointed—some may even claim that the government has misled them. As a result, such generic and broad approaches, while beneficial to public policy development at an early stage, may backfire, as the government could be perceived as playing a diversion game to shift public opinion, or perhaps employing a divide-and-conquer tactic to dealing with policy issues.

FIGURE 6.6: GENERIC APPROACH TO ISSUE IDENTIFICATION

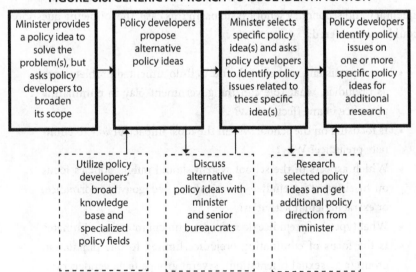

Specific Approach

When a problem is presented in an all-encompassing manner, it can be broken down into specific components. If a policy idea is too broad, it will be difficult for public policy developers to focus on finding solutions; therefore, some public policy developers opt for a specific approach by considerably narrowing down the policy idea up front. A narrow scope of policy issues, similar to those identified using the partisan approach, is characteristic of this approach. The exception is that policy issues identified under the specific approach are not ideologically driven and do not come from the minister's office. The minister usually welcomes this approach from the bureaucratic side (that is, public servants) because it is pragmatic and allows the emerging policy issues to be managed within a specific time frame. From the public policy developer's perspective, this approach is focused and likely non-partisan.

Take, for example, the problem of prejudice in Canadian society; perceived prejudice is found in many domains of our society, such as housing, employment, media, education, and health care. The term *prejudice* has a broad and imprecise meaning. If eliminating prejudice is posed as a policy idea, public policy developers must narrow it down so that government can focus its attention and resources to resolve the issue. One way to focus is to be as specific as possible about the areas policy issues can cover. For example, the policy idea of eliminating prejudice could be narrowed down to the elementary and secondary school systems; in this case, the following questions could be considered:

- For a persistent, widespread, and well-documented problem such as prejudice, what role can the government play in eliminating prejudice in an effective way?
- Is focusing on the school system the most impactful way to eliminate prejudice? Why?
- Which aspects of the school system should public policies focus on to eliminate prejudice—curriculum, pedagogy, performance, or extracurricular activities?
- What type(s) of prejudice does the government intend to eliminate?
- Is the focus of eliminating prejudice limited to one population group (e.g., sexual orientation), several groups (e.g., gender, race, ethnicity, and religion), or all people?

- Who are the target groups of this policy idea—teachers, administrators, or students?

As there are numerous aspects of the idea of eliminating prejudice, narrowing the scope is the first step. After conducting additional research to address the questions listed above, a public policy developer may ask which aspects of the school system public policies need to focus on to work towards eliminating prejudice. If the answer indicates that curriculum and pedagogy are the two areas in which results can be seen faster and will last longer, policy issues related to these two areas could be narrowed down further. The following questions could be used to further reduce the scope of the issue:

- Should the policy focus narrowly on curriculum and pedagogy without tackling the sources of the problem, which may lie in the way in which teachers are educated and hired and in the composition of the school board members?
- Should prejudice be framed as a policy of human rights, diversity competency, personal security and safety, or education and learning?
- Should the policy on the elimination of prejudice be based on individual voluntarism, the decisions of individual school boards, or legislative requirements for all school boards?

To move the public policy development process forward when there are multiple ideas of how best to tackle a problem, policy issues need to be narrowed and specified. When a minister is unable to narrow down the policy idea by him or herself, he or she depends on research conducted by public policy developers. Instead of following the academic approach, which is comprehensive but time-consuming, specifying policy issues based on existing information is a faster way of setting priorities in terms of what the government can do about the policy idea. This approach is usually used in consultation with stakeholder groups and experts. Given the time frame of a government, its political agenda, and its election schedule, a specific approach is an effective way to develop public policies in a timely manner.

FIGURE 6.7: SPECIFIC APPROACH TO ISSUE IDENTIFICATION

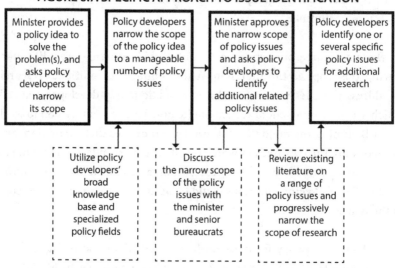

POLICY WINDOWS AND STAKEHOLDER GROUPS

No matter what approach—academic, partisan, generic, or specific—public policy developers take, they have to be cognizant of the roles that stakeholder groups play, the nature of their interests, their definition of the problem, the pressure tactics they use, and what they want the government to do. Paying attention to stakeholder groups can enable public policy developers to identify policy issues more effectively, especially when they have competing or conflicting perspectives of particular policy ideas.

As politicians are interested in expanding and maintaining their constituency of support, they are prepared to listen to the perspectives of stakeholder groups. Historically, groups that have been effective in lobbying issues position themselves closer to the centre of power, and have knowledge of how the system works. They understand the development process in government on the political and bureaucratic sides, and how these two sides are connected; the general routines and schedules of the government; the decision-making processes; the key political players; and where the access points in the system are, and when and how they can use them to influence the process. It is therefore common to see members of external stakeholder groups participating in public consultations and arranging meetings with ministers, political aides, deputy ministers, and other senior bureaucrats. This allows them to share their views of the problems and proposed solutions, and, at the same time, get to know the politicians and government officials, and the status of their problems on the government agenda.

Policy windows are opportunities for people to promote their policy ideas and influence the government to adopt their ideas. In addition to utilizing routine policy windows, such as the budgetary cycles and reading periods (Wu et al., 2010, pp. 18–19), stakeholder groups also often use non-routine policy windows, such as unforeseen international political events, political scandals, natural disasters, and leaks of sensitive information, to connect their causes with public policies. There are also situations in which one policy issue is drawn into the debates of another related issue, and external stakeholder groups may make use of this opportunity to lobby their policy ideas with timely renewed pressure. These windows may be brief and hard to come by, and may emerge unpredictably.

When politicians in power appear uninterested in the perceived problems of external stakeholder groups, some of these groups may escalate pressure on the government by mobilizing the public to write letters and sign petitions, or by organizing boycotts, protests, and demonstrations. Mass media may also intensify pressure on the government by writing comments on editorial pages or covering the activities of external stakeholder groups and their viewpoints. As problems receive more media attention, opposition parties intensify their pressure on the government by raising questions in the legislature or parliament, or during interviews with the media. A one-day increase in media coverage or attention during question period may not be enough to pressure politicians to adopt the viewpoint of stakeholder groups; however, when these three forces—stakeholder group pressure tactics, media coverage, and questions from opposition parties—converge to exert pressure on the government to solve a problem, policy shifts may occur at the ministerial and cabinet levels. Such shifts may be gradual and smoulder in the government for some time as the pressure intensifies. During this time, public policy developers may broaden their range of policy issues as ministers start to incorporate the suggestions from the stakeholder groups and develop their own policy ideas.

When external stakeholder groups make use of policy windows to put forth their opinions, there is added pressure on public policy developers to incorporate their positions in policy issues. As a consequence, policy developers may pay less attention to the positions of stakeholder groups that seldom use (or do not know how to use) these windows to make themselves heard. Under these circumstances, public policy developers have a tendency to gravitate to the policy ideas of active stakeholder groups, and may fail to perform due diligence on the problem at stake. The active stakeholder groups may crowd out other policy ideas. As a result, the issue identification process may be skewed in favour of the active stakeholder groups. To avoid this pitfall, public policy developers are advised to stay up to date on the various views of problems by reaching out to less active stakeholder groups. Balancing the interests of stakeholder groups is one of the principles of good public policy, and such outreach will help public policy developers to properly identify policy issues.

Fluidity in Public Policy Development

As a result of the factors outlined above—closeness to the circle of power, knowledge of lobbying, windows of opportunity, and government's reactions to pressure and crises—policy issues are defined and redefined as circumstances unfold, which creates challenges for public policy developers. This fluidity creates constant change, and not only necessitates a constant demand of human resources and time, but also requires an ongoing analysis of the configuration and reconfiguration of the issue at stake. This is why public policy developers need to have a strategy for updating their knowledge, networking, and filing information, as discussed in chapter 2.

Because the public policy development process is fluid, policy issues often change too, sometimes moving in the opposite direction from where they began. Issue identification might start off with a partisan approach, with the resultant policy issues constrained to a partisan perspective; however, these policy issues may change drastically when stakeholder groups come up against one another in a public arena, or exert immense pressure on the government. Issue identification that began with a partisan or academic approach may adopt a more generic or specific approach as external pressure mounts. Academic thoroughness may have to be sacrificed in favour of an approach that narrows policy issues. As illustrated in the diagram below, the issue identification process is influenced by stakeholder groups, mass media, opposition parties, and ministers.

FIGURE 6.8: FACTORS THAT INFLUENCE THE ISSUE IDENTIFICATION PROCESS

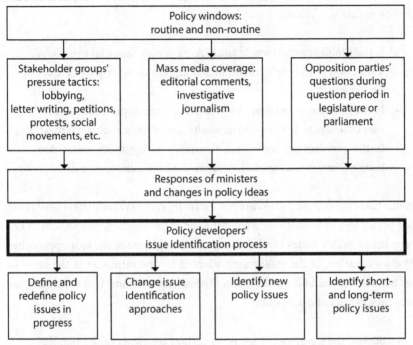

POLITICIZATION OF POLICY ISSUES

Configurations of historical and structural factors and value orientations influence whether or not particular kinds of policy ideas are placed on a political agenda. The pressure tactics used by external stakeholder groups, mass media, and opposition parties, and their use of policy windows, also shape the issue identification process in the government. This process, from vague policy ideas to concrete policy issues, is loaded with political elements, as illustrated in the following example.

When people find it increasingly difficult to make ends meet, and have trouble paying rent, buying groceries, nurturing children, purchasing homes, or paying bills, they may demand that the government do something. Stakeholder groups, such as tenants, parents, unemployed persons, anti-poverty groups, and taxpayer associations, may exert pressure on the government to acknowledge these problems and find solutions. In response to the pressure from these groups, the government may develop a policy idea to address these problems. What kind of policy idea this will be is the question that ministers and public policy developers must answer. In this case, at least three types of policy ideas—economic, social justice, and individual responsibility—could be identified. Public policy developers may begin the process of issue identification by asking the following questions:

- Is the problem an economic issue? Are people's financial situations a function of unemployment, inflation, recession, or part of market cycles?
- Is the problem a social justice issue? Are their experiences a function of unequal distribution of wealth and other structural issues?
- Is the problem an individual financial management issue? Are their experiences a function of individual financial responsibility?

While these three policy ideas are not mutually exclusive, ministers may select one policy idea to work on, or a combination of the three. When a decision has been made, policy issues can be identified through one of the four approaches discussed earlier. If the policy idea adopted by the ministers is the issue of individual responsibility, policy issues (posed as questions) that centre on this idea may include the following:

- Should the government focus on certain segments of the population or the population as a whole in its efforts to cultivate skills in financial planning?
- How should the government help individuals to be responsible for their financial situation?
- What have other jurisdictions done that has proven to be effective in motivating individuals to be responsible for their financial futures? Should the government model its response on the actions taken in other jurisdictions?
- Should the government focus on instigating a change in the values or habits of the population to strengthen individual financial responsibility?
- Should the government use incentives and disincentives to foster the value and habit of effective individual financial planning and management?
- If the individual responsibility approach adopted by the government is found to be too limited in its effects or too slow to yield results, should it be augmented by other approaches to resolve the problems associated with financial difficulties?

The decision of which policy issues are selected as priorities is based on several factors. The political factors include pressure from stakeholder groups, public opinion, and the ideology or political direction of the party in power. The non-political factors include the knowledge levels of the public policy developers, the evidence available on the subject matter, the effectiveness of current mechanisms, and the experiences of this and other jurisdictions with similar problems. Based on observation and experience, these factors do not carry equal weight. Of the factors listed here, the most important is the political direction of the party in power. As Wu and colleagues (2010, pp. 16–17) noted, policy issue identification is not just an academic exercise of finding truth, it is the crafting of an image for the political party in power. This image crystallizes the naming, claiming, blaming, and framing of a public policy by a political party: naming defines the boundary of the problem (in this example, financial difficulty); claiming defines the credit of the political party in power (the efforts made by the current government); blaming labels those who are responsible for the problem (opposing parties or groups that have contributed to the depressed financial situation); and framing defines the positioning of the government in relation to specific problems (the government, in this example, reinforces the value of individualism and individual ownership of their past, present, and future).

In this context, policy issue identification is more of a political act than an academic exercise. Politicians in power have to determine the political value of a policy issue by evaluating the political benefits and risks if it is adopted. As such, the political element is always inherent in the issue identification process, even if public policy developers are trying to be as academic, scientific, neutral, objective, or non-partisan as possible. However, there are situations in the public policy development process in which politics plays a more pivotal role in shaping policy issues. The tension between the political (politicians) and bureaucratic (public servants) sides of government is not often conducive to furthering the professionalism of the public policy developers. There is a saying that ministers come and go, but public servants stay on. As public servants, public policy developers usually have a longer lifespan in government than elected officials. For this reason, they usually have longer institutional memory. From an administrative viewpoint, they are in a better position to assess the applicability and administration of policy ideas that come from external stakeholder groups or politicians. Some policy ideas might have been discussed in the past and some may have been tried before; public policy developers can informally evaluate their chance of succeeding with a certain degree of confidence. If they speak truth to power, that is, dare to speak honestly to the politicians in power, they may brief their ministers regarding the lessons learned in the past, and the pros and cons of putting these policy ideas forward for cabinet consideration.

However, professional advantages associated with institutional memory often work against public policy developers, especially if and when their briefing notes are interpreted by ministers as showing resistance to new ideas or as creating an obstacle. In this context, a minister may delegitimize and disregard the public policy developer's view. Once this suspicion has germinated and become ingrained in a minister's mind, his or her political aides will take over the public policy development process, and the ministers will drive the political agenda forward without much consultation with public policy developers. As noted earlier, there have been attempts by politicians in power to increase the policy capacity of their political aides—almost to the point of running a parallel policy shop in their offices. In this situation, public policy developers' ability to identify policy issues is very much diluted.

SUMMARY

A government cannot solve all of society's problems at one time—it must set priorities. This priority-setting process is part of the larger political agenda. There are several reasons that some policy ideas are on the political agenda and some are not. On the macro level, economic structure and development are often cited as a contributing factor; on a micro level, people's worldviews, beliefs, and ideas are often determinants. A combination of these factors, along with some intermediate factors (such as stakeholder groups), contributes to establishing the political agenda.

Political agenda setting is a fluid process in which multiple variables are at work. Policy ideas and the identification of issues for public policy development are constantly in flux. The interplay between factors means that issue identification may be scientific at one time and political at another, with external stakeholder groups, mass media, and opposition parties playing influential roles. External stakeholder groups have a tendency to utilize policy windows to shape public policies. The ministers and public policy developers respond to these players.

Issue identification is the first step in public policy development. It concretizes vague policy ideas. Prior to beginning this process, public policy developers are advised to consider five factors—jurisdiction, legality, government direction, urgency, and anticipated impacts. They will then adopt one of the four approaches to issue identification—academic (non-partisan), partisan, generic, or specific. During the issue identification process, the approach that is used will vary depending on pressure exerted by stakeholder groups and shifting direction from politicians, as well as changing circumstances (both internal and external).

QUESTIONS FOR CRITICAL THINKING

1. Identification of policy issues is largely a political act. Discuss.
2. Policy issue identification is a process in which many players are involved. What roles does a policy developer play in this process?
3. There are four major approaches in issue identification. What factors are at work in determining the approach that public policy developers take?

CONDUCTING RESEARCH AND ANALYZING INFORMATION

INTRODUCTION

Once a policy issue has been identified and framed as a question, public policy developers proceed to determine the answers to that question. Answers are based on research that is intended to assess the nature, magnitude, costs, risks, and impact of an identified policy issue, as well as to evaluate the environment in which the issue is located and provide insight into stakeholder groups (Bardach, 2009, p. 11). Research is not completed until the public policy enters the decision-making process at the cabinet level or the ratification process in the legislature or parliament. Research is an integral component of public policy development, because sound and thorough solutions cannot be determined without accurate and reliable information. Any errors in research negatively impact research outcomes, analyses, and conclusions, and the resultant solutions to the problems. In other words, improper research leads to flawed public policies.

RESEARCH PLAN

Conducting research on policy issues requires a research plan. This plan sets focused objectives, acknowledges time constraints, takes available resources into consideration, and establishes a structure for research activities. Additionally, research plans make public policy developers accountable, and provide their departments with the necessary information for synchronizing other activities for progress report purposes. As research activities at the department level must be aligned with those of the entire government, a research plan appeases internal stakeholder groups, especially when it includes public or stakeholder consultations. Because any outside contact by public policy developers has ramifications for government communication, relevant ministers expect to know before these consultations take place so they can be prepared if their constituents contact them regarding policy matters or planned consultations. A research plan addresses the following questions:

- How are research questions framed?
- What information will be needed?
- Where is information to be found?
- What research methods will be employed?
- How will information be collected?
- How will research findings be analyzed?
- What is the time frame for these research activities?
- What are the anticipated costs of the research?
- How will the research activities be managed?

HOW ARE RESEARCH QUESTIONS FRAMED?

When public policy developers frame a policy issue in the form of a question, the question defines the nature and scope of the inquiry, as well as the direction of the research. These policy issues become policy questions for research. The framing of a policy research question is defined by the policy idea provided by the minister. If policy ideas are not provided, public policy developers may follow an academic approach to identify policy issues to pose as research questions. If the research questions are broad, public policy developers create subsets of research questions. A public policy will never have only one policy issue; because there are many aspects of any given subject, any public policy will include more than one policy issue. Ideally, public policy developers state as many of these policy issues and research questions as possible at the beginning of the policy development process, although at that stage, they can only outline the major and immediate ones. The subsets of these issues will be added as they are triggered by the research findings; this is why issue identification can be a lengthy process.

Developing a public policy is not a linear process. Public policy developers do not have much control over the scope or timeline of a policy issue. Political circumstances change and the personal inclinations of politicians shift over time; as minds change, new impressions are formed about what areas should be researched and in which direction policies should be heading. When instructions for a new course of action come from a higher level of government, public policy developers must follow them. Under these circumstances, research activities may have to be shelved so that public policy developers can start working on new policy issues.

FIGURE 7.1: FROM POLICY ISSUES TO RESEARCH QUESTIONS

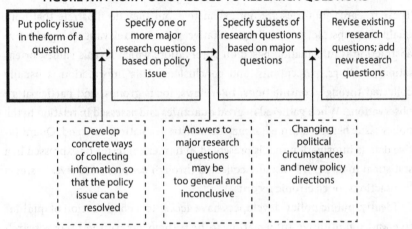

WHAT INFORMATION WILL BE NEEDED?

When the research questions have been established, public policy developers need to determine the type of information needed to answer the questions. Identifying indicators and measurements can help to answer these research questions. Indicators are signs that point out the existence of phenomena to be researched. Measurements are degrees of phenomena as they are expressed in quantitative units. For example, a policy idea on youth employment may ask if youth unemployment, especially among racial minorities or youths with immigrant backgrounds, is the result of poor job-searching skills. To answer this inquiry, a public policy developer may look for indicators by pursuing the following types of information:

- unemployment rates of Canadians, including a breakdown of rates for racial minorities and immigrants, for comparison to white and non-immigrant youth
- observations and research findings on the causes of youth unemployment from the perspectives of employers, job counsellors, employment agencies, and a broad range of Canadian youth, including racial minorities and immigrants

- findings on the success of job-search skills from administrators of current and past youth employment or youth counselling programs, as well as from youth with different backgrounds and from multiple jurisdictions

These research inquiries are not exhaustive, but they do illustrate that both qualitative abstractions and quantitative data are relevant. A qualitative abstraction is information based on observation, which reveals values, orientations, feelings, perceptions, and conclusions. This information is usually collected through consultations, interviews, focus groups, and participatory observations. When gathered in great quantities and assessed in relation to the policy issue being examined, it may demonstrate a pattern or trend. Quantitative data is information that is presented in numerical terms or expressed in a statistical manner; it is usually collected through censuses, surveys, business transactions, or electronic records.

Ideally, public policy developers have access to a combination of qualitative and quantitative information to help them determine their research questions. However, this information may not be readily available, or it may be incomplete, outdated, or only vaguely relevant to the issue. Under these circumstances, proxy information may have to be used. Proxy information is an approximation of the required information; it does not provide valid measurement of what public policy developers are looking for, but it may provide some insight. When developing major public policies that have immense jurisdictional or societal implications, proxy information is not an acceptable type of information for politicians to rely on, as there are too many risks associated with basing decisions on potentially incorrect information. Equally important is that proxy information cannot be legitimately used as a justification to introduce new public policies, as it will not withstand stakeholder scrutiny. When major research work is necessary, financial and human resources are allocated to ensure factual accuracy and legitimacy.

As previously mentioned, a lack of funds, labour, and time prevent public policy developers from conducting their own primary research. Time and resources determine how much and from which sources information is to be gathered. The success of the balancing act between conducting primary research and acquiring tangentially related secondary data depends on the public policy developer's experience in research and policy work.

In general, such balancing acts always carry a certain degree of risk; it is therefore important for public policy developers to qualify their policy work with explicit written statements addressing the limitations of their information.

Bardach (2009, pp. 12–13) advocates for the value of an educated guess, or guesstimate, to save the unjustifiable cost and time of doing additional research or locating new information. Obviously, there are risks that come with such tactics, including the reputation of the public policy developers who did the guessing, and the potential embarrassment such guesstimates may bring to ministers when the media or stakeholder groups question them about the sources of their information. For these reasons, public policy developers must make judgment calls regarding these risks prior to using guesswork as a basis for developing public policies.

FIGURE 7.2: FROM RESEARCH QUESTIONS TO THE IDENTIFICATION OF NEEDED INFORMATION

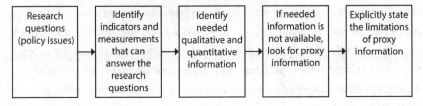

WHERE IS INFORMATION FOUND?

There are two main sources of information in public policy development: people and existing documents. Information from people is usually based on primary research, while information from existing documents is based on secondary research. Existing documents include conference papers, published journal articles, reports and books, government reports and briefing notes, magazines and newspapers, websites, audiovisual materials (film and video), and other electronically transmitted images and words. Community organizations, advocacy groups, and professional associations often produce documentation, which is sometimes available on their websites—these can be great sources of information.

There is an abundance of available information, but it is not all useful for public policy development. Some sources (for example, the Internet or some advocacy organizations) may merely circulate information without ensuring its authenticity or present selective data, which may be skewed. In general, organizations with a reputation for professionalism have a greater likelihood of making valid information available on their websites and in their published material.

Public policy developers may conduct primary research or evaluate the applicability of existing information to the policy issues under research. Financial resources, time frames, and political factors determine which method is used. If and when the government needs to conduct primary research, it is usually outsourced to external organizations such as academic institutions, think tanks, research firms, and consulting companies; sometimes, the government creates a commission or task force to conduct research. Public policy developers may acquire information from the public, stakeholder groups, or field experts through primary research. Some segments of the public—such as those living within a particular neighbourhood, or included in a certain income or age group—may provide information that is pertinent to certain public policies. Their knowledge and experiences are valuable because they offer information at the ground level. Stakeholder groups may be divided into external and internal groups. External stakeholder groups are groups of people outside of the government who have vested interests in the subject matter of related public policies; they may work or invest in a related industry. Internal stakeholders are people with a vested interest in the subject matter who work within the same government, but in different departments. Field experts are those who have extensive work experience, comprehensive knowledge, and a deep understanding of the policy issues that public policy developers are working on. In circumstances when information—such as the financial costs of running specific programs, or the environmental and health impacts of specific toxic spills—is difficult to gather, and collecting primary information is too costly or time-consuming, these expert opinions (while still costly) are invaluable.

For the above example of youth unemployment, information could be gathered through statistics on youth unemployment (custom-sourced from Statistics Canada), and published documents from other jurisdictions. Public policy developers could acquire information on the success of job-search skills by interviewing young people who have engaged with these programs, or by requesting data from the people who run these job-search skill training programs.

FIGURE 7.3: FROM IDENTIFYING NEEDED INFORMATION TO IDENTIFYING ITS SOURCES

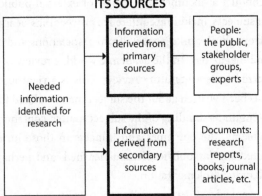

WHAT RESEARCH METHODS WILL BE EMPLOYED?

There are three commonly used research methods in public policy development: documentary reviews, focus groups, and consultations. Public policy developers rely primarily on reviewing documents to find background and policy-related information. When this groundwork has been completed, the next logical step is to form focus groups or conduct consultations. Both focus groups and consultations are very policy-specific in content, and the resultant information is customized to the needs of those conducting the inquiry, and compared with existing data. Consultation is considered to be the core research method used to find answers to specific policy questions.

Documentary Reviews

Reviewing documentary material is the most common research method used in public policy development. It consists of reading and analyzing existing information or data (published or unpublished) related to the policy issues in question, beginning with internal government documents and followed by external documents. Documents are available internally within the government or externally in college and university libraries and archives, through business associations, and on the Internet. Internal government documents—such as working papers, memoranda, briefing notes, previous cabinet submissions, and minutes—are usually reviewed to gain an understanding of the history of a particular policy and specific details on previous, existing, or related policies and programs, as well as the specifics of decisions made by the government.

After policy issues and research questions have been specified, it is routine procedure to conduct a documentary review of external publications on the same or similar subjects, including conference proceedings, academic journals, policy papers from think tanks, reports from associations and organizations, newspapers, and magazines. In the academic world, a review of documentary material is referred to as a literature review. This is a rigorous way of determining what has been written about the subject matter related to the potential policy, the current understanding of the subject matter, contentious issues and unresolved problems, the outcomes and impacts in those jurisdictions that have implemented similar policies, lessons learned, and perhaps issues that arose as a result of its implementation.

Not all retrievable documents are directly relevant, so public policy developers must evaluate their usefulness and applicability. Because certain policies in other jurisdictions may have developed in a different political culture, institutional arrangement, industrial composition, or demographic profile, the documented experience of these jurisdictions may only be used as a proxy to resolve the policy matters under research.

Focus Groups

Focus group discussions are advantageous because they allow investigators to discuss policy matters comprehensively with people. The synergy that may develop when people sit down together in a group can produce a broad range of ideas; this is seldom accomplished in individual interviews. Focus groups, usually organized by public policy developers, can include a wide range of participants—members of business associations, labour unions, community organizations, colleges and universities, professional administrations, or members of the public—depending on the subject matter and the policy issues at stake.

Focus groups are often used at the end stage of development. When public policy developers have a clear sense of what needs to be done, conducting a round of focus groups can help them refine their policy options. For example, if a public policy on old age support has been under development, a focus group of internal government officials may be organized to determine the pros and cons of the policy proposal before it is finalized as a recommendation to the minister. On other occasions, public policy developers may invite representatives of stakeholder groups with competing demands to participate in a focus group in an effort to reach a compromise. Rather than reviewing a written draft of the policy framework on their own, these representatives review key components of the draft as a group during the session and share their opinions.

Organizing focus groups for internal government officials and external stakeholder groups requires the permission of senior bureaucrats and sometimes ministers, because some policy framework issues are too sensitive to be publicized. It is common for all of the elements of a focus group—potential participants, facilitators, discussion topics, and documents for distribution—to be reviewed and approved by high-level officials. Due to the sensitivity of internal policy work, preparations must be made, protocols followed, and the cabinet office made aware of the meeting.

To prepare for holding a focus group, public policy developers formulate a set of open-ended questions to be raised and probed during the discussion. These questions cannot be rigidly sequenced; it is best when they flow together to deepen group engagement. Due to the complexity of some policy matters, a focus group may become a negotiation session in which people with different perspectives debate the issues, and public policy developers attempt to find out whether compromise among these perspectives is possible. For example, a focus group could be composed of people from the business sector and labour unions, who often have polarized views on specific matters. Some public policy developers use these group discussions as testing grounds—they may put forward several options or scenarios for the two opposing factions to discuss, and move forward on only the most accepted recommendations. If compromises cannot be reached during the focus group session, at least the different perspectives expounded during the discussion provide public policy developers with a sense of the priorities of the competing groups.

External research firms may be contracted by the government to conduct focus groups. In these situations, the government is usually seeking neutrality and robustness. Public policy developers present at these discussions are there to observe, not facilitate.

Consultations

Consultation is a balanced and democratic way to address policy issues, and has increasingly become mandatory in the public policy development process (McArthur, 2007, pp. 256–257). A consultation is a formally arranged conversation between public policy developers and other government officials, and stakeholder groups or field experts. The conversation can be of any duration and can reoccur as often as public policy developers need. Most consultations take place in a government environment, on the premises of stakeholder groups, or on neutral ground (such as at a hotel).

Consultations are usually focused on select topics, but the people involved have ample flexibility when asking and answering questions. Some consultations are more structured than others, which means that there is a specific set of questions that must be answered. Public policy developers can optimize the value of a consultation by preparing participant-specific questions after establishing a list of who will be attending. When conducting consultations, public policy developers should be cognizant of participants' busy schedules, ensuring that sessions are well organized and fairly short. Based on the target group, there are five different types of consultations:

- internal consultations within the government
- cross-jurisdictional consultations
- consultations with experts
- consultations with stakeholder groups
- public consultations

The government's approach must take into account and be sensitive to the nature of the subject matter, the scope of the issue, the persons being consulted, the types of questions seeking solutions, and the timing of the consultation. Due to their sensitive nature, many consultations must be approved prior to their execution.

Internal Consultations within the Government

Most policy issues affect multiple areas of society. An example is the development of a public policy on privacy of information, which covers personal information collected by doctors and hospitals, banks, merchants, academia, and for marketing or clinical research. The development of a privacy policy must be in sync with the operation of other parts of government administration. For this reason, consultations are conducted with internal government officials. Consultation with officials from central agencies is useful because they have a broad knowledge of the public ideas and policy ideas from different line departments, and ongoing relationships with other central agencies. Consultation with other line departments also has its benefits. Each government department, in accordance with its mandate and nature of work, has its own external stakeholder groups, and the public policy developers in these departments know them well. Thus, internal consultations may bring to light the potential impacts of policy issues on these external stakeholder groups. These internal consultations extend the breadth of understanding, and are pivotal in creating a public policy with internal consistency and external applicability.

Internal consultations with government officials are usually conducted during the early and final stages of public policy development. Public policy developers engage in these consultations at the beginning of issue identification or after policy issues have been identified. Towards the end of policy development, consultation is required again; at this time, colleagues from other departments mediate proposed policy options and recommendations. If there are great variations in feedback among departments, efforts should be made to resolve them. If the consultation meetings are of prime importance, verbal briefings or written briefing notes must be prepared after each consultation for senior bureaucrats. Internal consultations are usually mandatory because outstanding issues on a particular public policy-in-the-making among departments have to be resolved prior to its submission to cabinet. It is easier for cabinet members to approve a cabinet submission if they know that outstanding issues between line departments have been resolved.

Cross-Jurisdictional Consultations

Cross-jurisdictional consultations provide public policy developers with information about the experiences of other provinces, territories, or countries before implementing policies, operational models, business processes, and resource requirements. The lessons learned from various administrations (via consultation with their public policy developers, program managers, or other government officials) enrich the public policy development process. This kind of consultation is usually conducted during the early stages of public policy development. For example, a provincial government may be considering the social and economic consequences of differing levels of minimum wage. By consulting with other provinces, public policy developers can find information that may assist them to develop better public policies; there are lessons to be learned from other jurisdictions regarding how their business and labour sectors observe the minimum wage, and how this affects household income, quality of life, consumption patterns, and the economy across the country.

Public policy developers can conduct cross-jurisdictional consultations through telephone, email, mail, or in-person meetings. The consultation method is determined by the informational needs. Occasionally, it is necessary to make an on-site visit to see how public policies are put into operation, or to build rapport with those involved. As the cost of field visits is a determining factor in whether or not they will be approved, this kind of consultation must have demonstrable benefits. Telephone and email consultations are both less costly and less formal.

Consultations with Experts

Consultations with experts can yield insight into specialized policy fields. Experts include professors, professionals, tradespeople, business executives, former ambassadors, and international delegates. These people have deep and broad knowledge of their fields, and a great deal of hands-on experience. Experts may disagree with each other, but their differences of opinion often illustrate the complexity of a particular subject, and the resulting difficulty of developing good public policy. Experts may provide their observations in areas where little or no research has been done; as a result, their years of experience add exceptional value to the development process. Take, for example, amnesty for refugee claimants. Experts who have done research in this field and practitioners (lawyers) who work with refugee claimants can provide useful information about the demographics of refugee claimants, past experiences within amnesty programs, issues of settlement or deportation, the mechanics of amnesty, humanitarian implications, and implications for the politics and economy of the host country. They can provide public policy developers with a deeper understanding of the nature of amnesty, enabling the formulation of better-informed public policies.

Consultation with experts can be carried out in several ways, the most common of which are formal face-to-face meetings and written correspondence. To maintain formality, it is best for public policy developers to request meetings in writing, and clearly inform the expert of the types of questions they have in mind. This gives the expert time to prepare. It doesn't necessarily mean that the policy developer cannot pose additional questions during a meeting; however, this type of consultation is usually limited to a few crucial questions that only an expert can answer. These questions should ascertain information not generally available in publications. Like external consultants, experts are remunerated for their contributions.

TABLE 7.1: COMPARISON OF CONSULTATION TYPES

	Internal Consultation	Cross-Jurisdictional Consultation	Consultation with Experts	Consultation with Stakeholder Groups	Public Consultation
Who is to be consulted?	Officials from central agencies and line departments	Public policy developers, program managers	Experts with specialized knowledge and experiences	People with a vested interest	Anyone
What will be discussed?	Policy issues, policy options, recommendations	Operational models, experiences	Specialized policy fields	Stakeholders' concerns and suggestions	Broad or narrow range of policy topics
Why is consultation beneficial to public policy developers?	Policy priority, policy focus, areas for improvement, integration with other policies, internal consistency, external applicability	Variety of models, business processes, resource requirements, policy lessons	Unique knowledge of complex policy issues	Policy relevance, balancing of interests, democratic appearance, sense of ownership	Range and intensity of public opinion, degree of polarization
When does consultation take place?	Early and final stages of public policy development	Early stage of public policy development	When no published research findings are available or when time is limited	Middle stage of public policy development (after public policy developers have done their homework)	Middle and final stages of public policy development
Where does consultation take place?	Government offices	Government offices	Anywhere	Government offices, stakeholders' premises, or neutral site	Neutral premises
How is consultation conducted?	Office conversations	Electronic communication, letters, on-site visits	Public policy developers provide policy questions and experts answer them in writing, face-to-face meetings	Face-to-face meetings	Town-hall style meeting, round table discussion, social media

Consultations with Stakeholder Groups

Stakeholder groups have a vested interest in specific subjects. Public policies related to these matters affect them in both direct and indirect ways. Currently, public policy development has a tendency to favour stakeholder groups backed by a critical mass, or those that place a significant amount of pressure on the government. Knowing the positions of stakeholder groups helps the government develop public policies and make them more relevant. Consulting with stakeholder groups makes the process more democratic, or at least presents the illusion of democracy. Being involved in consultation creates a sense of ownership among stakeholder groups. For example, the key stakeholder groups in the development of a youth employment policy would include youth, employers, agencies that assist youth, community organizations, parent groups, justice-seeking groups, schools, colleges, and universities. Most of these stakeholder groups have youth as constituents and have experience working with them. They often have insight into why some youth have problems getting or keeping jobs, the difficulties they may experience during the transition from school to the job market, problems with the design and delivery of programs or services for youth, and what employers can do to help youth. In addition to their perspectives on the sources of youth unemployment, they may be able to provide suggestions for how to improve the system in ways that will lead to a lower unemployment rate among young people. These stakeholder groups are able to outline the constraints in which they are working and offer ideas of how best to deal with these constraints.

Public policy developers who consult with stakeholder groups must be prepared to address the potential difficulties that can arise when the various groups have competing or conflicting perspectives on policy issues. Prior to consultation, public policy developers must determine each stakeholder's general position, organization, leadership, power base, government-related history, common pressure tactics, and their connection to other stakeholder groups. The government cannot be seen as playing favourites with stakeholder groups, but, in reality, public policy developers may not have time to consult with all interested groups. Under these circumstances, it is important to balance the range and regional distribution of the groups that are consulted. Governments have a tendency to consult more moderate groups. When the government does not see any value in consulting with radical groups, it simply avoids meeting with them face-to-face, but will create openings for them to voice their opinions though emails and letters.

Every consultation should be specifically designed to gather the desired information. Public policy developers may find it helpful to prepare a list of questions prior to each consultation. As stakeholders view these consultations as an opportunity to get up-to-date on the latest policy issues in development, public policy developers must decide how much information they wish to share. Regarding prospective consultation venues, there are advantages to either inviting stakeholder groups to meet in government buildings or for consultations to take place on the premises of a stakeholder group. The latter symbolizes the government's willingness to go the extra mile.

Public Consultations

Public consultation sessions are open to anyone and everyone. These sessions provide an opportunity for people to voice their opinions and engage in the process of public policy development. People who attend usually have relatively strong opinions about the policy issues that the government is working on, meaning that they either have something very positive or very negative to say about the subject matter. Exposure to these intense sentiments gives the government a sense of the polarizing issues within a community, the magnitude of differences, and the nature of concerns. Public consultations are usually conducted during the middle or final stages of public policy development, after public policy developers have done most of their research and have a good comprehension of the policy issues and what they wish to learn during the consultation. Depending on the policy development stage at which the consultation occurs, some public consultations are broad in scope, while others are narrow and specific. A consultative session on heritage preservation, for example, may be selective or open in content and scope. The public policy developers who conduct these sessions can expect to hear feedback on the adequacy or inadequacy of government effort related to heritage funding, administration, monitoring, and enforcement. A broad range of opinions and suggestions from the public puts the government in a better position to develop adequate public policies in the field. Public consultations can be conducted in a town-hall style, in which people make deputations and raise questions. If the number of people participating is manageable, consultations can also be carried out in round table format. Alternately, they can be conducted using social media. If public consultations are conducted face to face, they are best carried out in a neutral environment, rather than a government building.

There are three phases of public consultations. In the first phase, the preconsultation phase, a consultation paper outlining the policy issues is prepared and provided to the public. The paper defines the focus and boundary of the public consultation. During this phase, public policy developers prepare a list of locations in which public consultations will take place; the locations should demonstrate a balance of jurisdictions, regions, and stakeholder groups, and should be accessible and accommodating for persons with disabilities. During the second phase, the consultation period, public policy developers must establish the rules of consultation. These should be announced at the beginning of the meeting so that the participants know exactly what to expect. The consultation meeting should be used as an opportunity for public policy developers to update the audience on policy developments. During the consultation, public policy developers should focus on the information that is shared by participants. During the third phase, the post-consultation period, public policy developers compile and code the notes taken during the consultation, start the review of the consultation results, and provide alternative opportunities or methods for more people to voice their opinions.

FIGURE 7.4: FROM IDENTIFYING INFORMATION SOURCES TO CONDUCTING RESEARCH

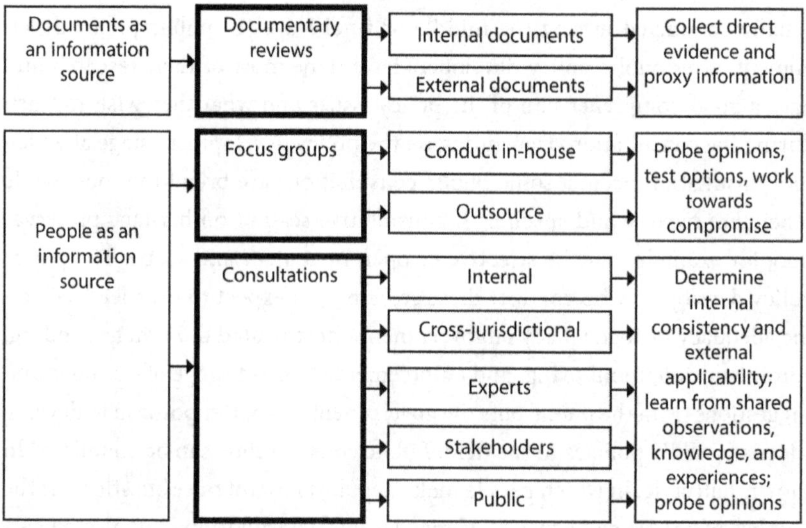

Documents as an information source	Documentary reviews	Internal documents	Collect direct evidence and proxy information
		External documents	

People as an information source	Focus groups	Conduct in-house	Probe opinions, test options, work towards compromise
		Outsource	
	Consultations	Internal	Determine internal consistency and external applicability; learn from shared observations, knowledge, and experiences; probe opinions
		Cross-jurisdictional	
		Experts	
		Stakeholders	
		Public	

HOW TO COLLECT INFORMATION

Given the time constraints under which public policy developers tend to work, a focus on core policy issues, as opposed to peripheral material, is imperative. To maintain this focus, it is useful to refer back to the research questions of the core policy issues regularly, and to have a framework for collecting information. This framework should consist of an inventory of research questions that need to be answered, and the type or range of information that needs to be collected. Any relevant information should be collected and placed under the specific research question that it seeks to answer. To manage their time and keep track of information—in an effort to avoid collecting too much or too little data—public policy developers must be disciplined and diligent. They must determine if information gathered through documentary reviews, focus groups, or consultations—whether factual evidence or proxy content related to the research questions—will enable better analysis. They must especially focus on the validity and reliability of this information.

There are occasions when customized statistical data—business, labour market, and demographic data—is needed. This customized data can be acquired from Statistics Canada at a cost, and cross-tabulated with other variables as required to determine the extent of possible usefulness. Since policy research does not follow a linear progression, ministers and senior bureaucrats often suggest new areas of inquiry throughout the public policy development process. To ensure that new requests do not jeopardize research work that is under way, as they often do, it is helpful for public policy developers to record additional work needed to supplement current research as reminders and for reference. In public policy development, issues sometimes go through different phases in terms of prioritization and importance. Some partially researched issues may lose momentum for a period of time, then re-emerge somewhere down the road. Such shifts are often the result of political changes in ministerial or cabinet priorities. Public policy developers need an organized filing system to store and find the information they have collected over time with ease; this accommodates a fast-paced work environment, and allows them to revisit any outstanding policy issues in the future.

The task of collecting relevant information is challenging for a number of reasons, including the following:

- Research questions may not be clearly stated at the beginning of the process. As a result, some collected information may not be relevant to the policy issue upon further review.
- Some published information and data are geographically specific or industry specific, and cannot be generalized to answer new research questions.
- Though information obtained during consultations and focus groups can be specific and relevant to research questions, due

to the potential biases of the stakeholders involved, public policy developers need to be aware of its limitations before utilizing this information.

FIGURE 7.5: FROM RESEARCH QUESTIONS TO COLLECTING INFORMATION

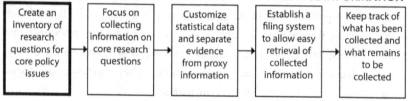

| Create an inventory of research questions for core policy issues | Focus on collecting information on core research questions | Customize statistical data and separate evidence from proxy information | Establish a filing system to allow easy retrieval of collected information | Keep track of what has been collected and what remains to be collected |

HOW TO ANALYZE RESEARCH FINDINGS

If a documentary review is the main source of collected data, public policy developers may find that some proxy information will not answer the core policy questions. Under these circumstances, public policy developers have to judge whether such information can be used as evidence to support or reject their policy positions. For example, if a jurisdiction has implemented a specific public policy for a number of years, and the policy has yielded all of the expected results, it is likely that such a public policy will deliver similar results if applied in another jurisdiction. This proxy information can potentially be used as supporting evidence.

Some proxy information may not be as clear-cut. In these cases, public policy developers must examine the political culture, economic conditions, and institutional arrangement under which the policy was carried out to determine whether implementation might have the anticipated results in another jurisdiction. As discussed earlier, the use of proxy information carries a certain degree of risk. If public policy developers have to use proxy information to support or reject a policy position, it is best to explicitly outline its limitations and qualifying conditions so that ministers and senior managers are cognizant of them.

Consultations and focus groups usually provide information pertinent to the policy questions, because the questions asked during these sessions are more direct and specific. Participants—people living within relevant jurisdictions—are motivated sources; however, they do not provide watertight evidence to support or reject the policy options. Additional analysis is still required to determine whether additional variables are at work. Public policy developers need to be careful about the validity and reliability of information provided by stakeholder groups, because their interests may predetermine their conclusions. Stakeholder information sources may need to be verified for authenticity. Comparing and analyzing information provided by different stakeholder groups is useful; these different viewpoints, placed in the context of other jurisdictional findings and historical periods, can produce a wider perspective for public policy developers to work with.

Analysis of information collected during consultations and focus groups is enhanced when it is categorized by theme. Categorizing is a useful way to identify themes, patterns, and hot-button issues that are prevalent across regions, stakeholder groups, or segments of the population. Organizing information in this way may show that there is polarization along regional lines or among stakeholder groups.

Often required in public policy development is the estimation of proposed program costs. Available information based on other similar programs may help, but that information cannot be mechanically applied to just any context. Cost estimation is based on assumptions about numerous factors, including the workforce, facilities, equipment, management infrastructure, and organizational readiness. Public policy developers have to examine these assumptions and assess whether or not they are can be confidently applied in a particular situation.

Statistical data, and its applicability to the identified policy issues, is another area that requires analytical caution. While most statistical data collected by Statistics Canada is of high quality, censuses and surveys always have their own definitions of terms and data limitations. When using statistics quoted in research papers, public policy developers must also be cognizant of how concepts and terms are defined, as well as the limitations of the research methodologies used to generate that data. One must be cautious of the risks involved when statistical data from one research project is compared to that of another, due to project-specific assumptions, samples, measurement indicators, and a host of other variables. In addition, demographic data is not to be treated as if it is the manifestation of human behaviour. There are a number of variables between demographic data and the actual behaviour of human beings. Policies on homelessness and shelters are a good example of this disconnect. It cannot be assumed that because there are homeless people in a specific geographic location (information that can be acquired through the analysis of demographic data), they will all go live in shelters (assumed human behaviour) once these shelters are built and made available. There are a number of intervening variables that determine whether a person will choose to utilize a shelter, and determining these intervening variables may require additional information or research beyond gathering statistics.

Public policy developers may find that the data required to address some research questions is not readily available for analysis because the subject matter is so new that no jurisdictions have yet established related public policies. In such cases, they must find closely related subject matter to use as a reference point. For example, digital privacy and piracy, genetic engineering, and the commercialization of human eggs are all relatively new topics; therefore, it is difficult to find solid and related references on which to base further research. Proxy research findings may have to be generalized to be useful. In new areas in which no policies have ever been formulated, the lack of pertinent or direct evidence may limit the use of proxy information; in this case, it is advisable to consult experts or experienced government officials regarding how best to handle this situation. Sometimes, when information is scarce or when all available sources of information have been exhausted, developing public policies is a gamble. The politicians in power will have to decide whether or not to take the risk, provided they are aware of the limitations, benefits, and negative consequences of doing so.

FIGURE 7.6: FROM COLLECTING INFORMATION TO ANALYZING RESEARCH FINDINGS

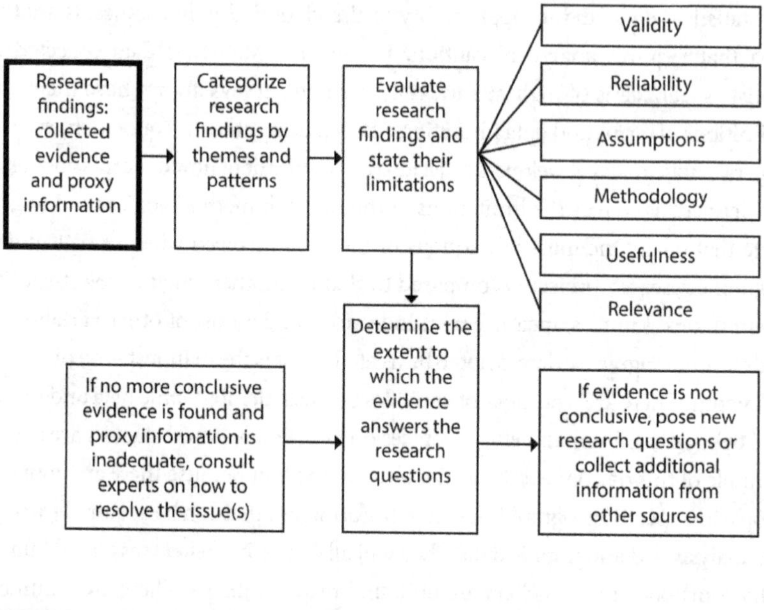

RESEARCH ACTIVITY SCHEDULING

Generally, the time frame for developing a public policy depends largely on the prime minister (or the premier) and the cabinet, and it is likely to change as the project progresses. This is because the government does not deal with only one public policy at a time, and it must respond to a variety of factors that can affect policy development, including political urgency or expediency, natural disasters, human accidents, emergency situations, media exposure, allegations, scandals, stakeholders, and public pressure.

For public policies that will have a major impact on society as a whole or on a significant segment of the population, as well as those that are contentious and polarizing, the timetable for research activities is usually longer, if the political pressure to implement the policy is not strong. However, when there is a strong will at the cabinet level to quickly develop a specific public policy, the timetable for research could be compressed. In fact, some public policies are approved at the cabinet level with hardly any research conducted at the bureaucratic level. This suggests that politics sometimes takes precedence over comprehensive research.

The amount of time designated for research depends on the magnitude, complexity, and type of research activities required. It is also contingent on how much money is available, how prepared the organization is, and whether needed information is readily available. When the subject matter demands that policy developers seek input from other jurisdictions, and involves many stakeholder groups or requires public consultation, research work can be expected to take a long time, as consultation papers need to be distributed, logistics ironed out, post-consultation summarizations prepared, and briefing processes conducted.

FIGURE 7.7: TIMETABLE FOR RESEARCH ACTIVITIES

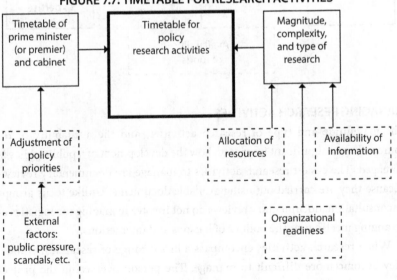

THE COSTS OF RESEARCH

The allocation of funds for a research project depends on its magnitude, type, and urgency, as well as the nature of the research methodology. With the exception of large-scale commissions, task-force projects, or outsourced research projects, most internal research conducted in the government consists of documentary reviews, consultation or focus groups, and field research. These undertakings depend largely on the efforts of public policy developers; however, time constraints and lack of internal expertise in specific policy areas may push line departments to outsource research components to external organizations.

The three common research methods discussed earlier—documentary reviews, focus groups, and consultations—do not cost much. The money used to carry out these activities usually comes from the operational line of a departmental budget. These costs cover the logistics of organizing events, travel and accommodation, printing materials, and communication.

FIGURE 7.8: RESEARCH COSTS

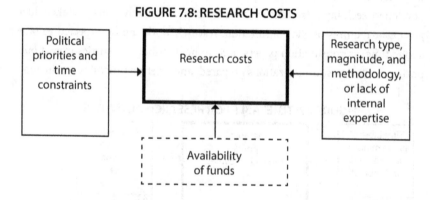

MANAGING RESEARCH ACTIVITIES

The magnitude and type of research activities, and the availability of resources, have a significant impact on how the development of a public policy is managed. The easiest research activities to manage are documentary reviews because they are carried out using available documents. Unlike focus groups or consultation, documentary reviews do not involve managing the logistics of arranging meetings or the politics of liaisons and interactions.

When research activities encompass a broad range of research methods, they become more difficult to manage. The person overseeing the project must synchronize the activities and deal with the political components of the research. The politics of managing focus groups and consultations is a factor that public policy developers must consider. The following is a list of management principles that are important for public policy developers to keep in mind:

Strike a balance among stakeholder groups—socially, geographically, and demographically diverse people should be selected as participants in consultations and focus groups. Managing the expectations of people who wish to participate in research activities is crucial. If not handled properly, consultations and focus groups can develop into politically explosive situations in which media may be used to publicize perceived unfairness and the curtailment of public participation. Managing this research process must include preparing alternative ways for people to voice their opinions on policy matters if they cannot attend consultation meetings or focus groups.

Allow sufficient time for people to study the policy issues and respond accordingly—when the research process is perceived as being rushed, people may feel that the government has a hidden agenda, undermining the democratic process. When arranging consultations or focus groups, begin contacting people early to give plenty of advance notice. Short notice may signal desperation on behalf of the government.

Build flexibility into the schedule for and arrangement of research activities—since the process of public policy development usually includes some twists and turns, public policy developers have to be able to change course midstream to adapt to new circumstances or new direction from the top. Some research activities may have to be sped up, while others may have to be shelved in spite of many hours spent working on them.

Communicate with and update senior bureaucrats and cabinet ministers on a regular basis—it is essential that those who make decisions about public policies are aware of the status of research activities, especially when the public and external stakeholder groups are part of the public policy development process.

FIGURE 7.9: RESEARCH MANAGEMENT

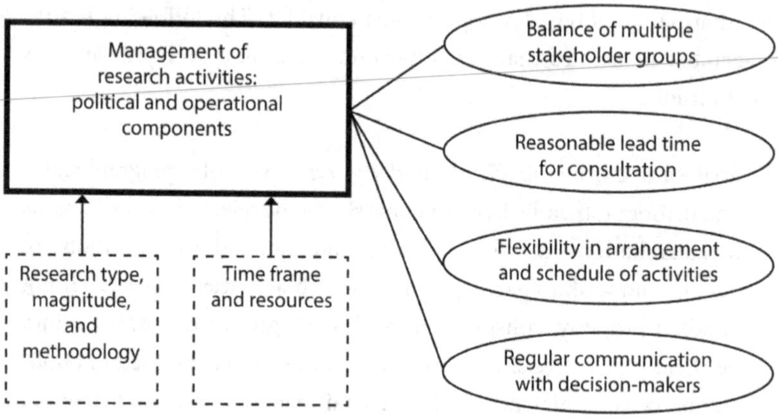

SUMMARY

Research is an important component of public policy development. The process begins with a research plan that identifies the types of qualitative and quantitative information needed, sources of information, and research methods and the processes to carry them out. As consultation has become an integral part of public policy development, this chapter has particularly focused on how public and stakeholder consultations can be coordinated.

Compiling relevant information requires some discipline on the part of public policy developers. Information must be categorized, and common themes identified. Policy developers must make judgment calls when proxy information is used and additional variables need consideration. Timetables and costs for research activities depend on many factors; therefore, public policy developers must be flexible when scheduling research work.

Managing research activities is largely a political act because it must take into consideration political factors. Public policy developers who are managing research projects must take the following management principles into consideration: balancing the representation of different groups of people, providing sufficient time for research, building flexible schedules and arrangements, and maintaining continuous communication with senior bureaucrats and cabinet ministers.

QUESTIONS FOR CRITICAL THINKING

1. To what extent can public policy developers determine their research methods?
2. Are public and stakeholder consultations research activities or merely symbolic acts?
3. Using a recent public policy issue as an example, discuss why the public policy development process can be lengthy.

FORMULATING POLICY OPTIONS AND RECOMMENDATIONS

INTRODUCTION

An analysis of research findings will provide some, if not all, of the answers to the research questions raised at the start of the public policy development process. However, public policy developers seldom have the luxury of collecting a great amount of information for their research projects due to time constraints— as unexpected emergencies or crises, shifts in public sentiment, and emerging social pressure take precedent over research. These circumstances often truncate the research process. As a result, government decisions are generally made, and action required, in short order. Public policy developers must analyze whatever information they have and formulate options under strict deadlines.

There are political restraints as well. Each political party has its own ideologies that influence decisions. As public policy developers are officially non-partisan, they have an obligation to put forth policy options that are in line with their research findings. However, because policy options are provided to the cabinet, public policy developers must include elements from cabinet members' wish lists if they want their recommendations to be tabled and discussed. Under these circumstances, public policy developers must include some partisan elements in the options they present to cabinet, even if there is a lack of research to support them.

WHAT ARE POLICY OPTIONS?

Policy options are the directions or ways of carrying out government activities. When people define particular issues as problems, and the government decides to recognize these perceived problems as public problems, they are framed accordingly and a new question is posed about what should be done to address them.

If the government is uncertain that a problem constitutes a public problem and is therefore unprepared to move forward to address it, it will take a wait-and-see position. The government may choose not to move forward for political or financial reasons, or because it simply does not see itself as responsible for the issue at hand. Declining to take action is a policy option in itself. If the government decides to take action, then the process to consider the variety of ways the problem may be resolved begins.

HOW TO DEVELOP POLICY OPTIONS

The development of policy options requires the creativity and imagination of public policy developers. After they analyze the available information, public policy developers must formulate viable and realistic policy options for their ministers to consider. Public policy developers must keep the six principles of a good public policy in mind—balance of public interests, accountability, impact, cost-effectiveness, justice, and the balance of short- and long-term considerations—when developing policy options. Several additional factors should also be considered: research findings, dominant values, public sentiment, stakeholder sensitivity, political climate, economic environment and trends, the government's fiscal situation, the cabinet's political inclinations, as well as international and jurisdictional factors that may emerge at the time of development.

FIGURE 8.1: FACTORS TO CONSIDER WHEN DEVELOPING POLICY OPTIONS

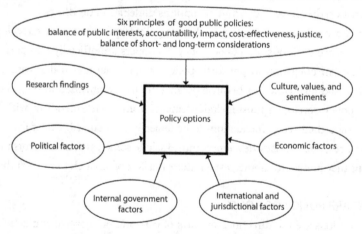

When policy options are being developed, cabinet ministers are only interested in reviewing the few most practical options. As such, public policy developers are expected to put forward three to five options for consideration. This practice of formulating and providing policy options is valuable, as it makes the analyses of research results obvious to the ministers. Considering the suggestions outlined below can make the process of formulating policy options easier.

Major Headings (Topics)

Prior to listing policy options, it is critical that public policy developers determine the major headings under which these options fall. These headings are topics or subjects under which research has been conducted, and they can be used to organize the presentation of policy options. Public policy developers usually develop these major headings in consultation with senior bureaucrats (such as deputy ministers or those in the cabinet office) before undertaking research, and they must be approved and finalized by ministers. Major headings for policy options may be changed, added, or deleted over time.

Major headings are essential areas that the government must consider when resolving public problems, and they are the areas under which the cabinet must make decisions. Depending on the nature of the public policy, these major headings may include any aspect of the target groups (or institutions) at which the anticipated public policy is aimed, their roles and obligations, the roles of the government, the type and scope of activities required to resolve the problems, the deliverables (end products) of these activities, the monitoring and enforcement mechanisms and the rewards and penalties associated with the performance of these activities. Usually, the more intensely a government wishes to directly manage a particular policy area, the more extensive the major headings are, and the more policy options ministers have to consider. Take, for example the major headings (topics) under which policy options could be formulated if the federal government were interested in developing a national child care policy:

- scope of child care services
- standards of child care services
- age eligibility criteria for children
- income eligibility criteria for families
- models of child care funding—private and public sectors
- models of child care funding—federal and provincial jurisdictions
- models of operation
- phase-in schedules
- monitoring mechanisms
- enforcement mechanisms

Guidelines

Once these major headings are determined, public policy developers' formulation of policy options is easier because the scope of the issue has been narrowed. However, each major heading necessitates at least one set of policy options and, very often, despite the narrowing of topics, there is still a plethora of policy options that public policy developers can formulate. Policy options are not merely different directions or actions that the government can take; they reflect a variety of compromises that it has made in relation to resource requirements, structural constraints, expected impacts, political expediency, public perception, and government priorities. The following factors should be considered when developing policy options:

Viability: Viability means that a policy option is feasible and workable. To determine the viability of policy options, public policy developers have to consider whether they will be politically and culturally acceptable to stakeholder groups and the public, if there are adequate resources (financial and human) to carry out the options, the readiness of institutional arrangements, and the social conditions under which these options are carried out.

Impact: Policy options should have measurable and positive effects. Because public policies are established with the intention of solving problems, they must fulfill their objectives to be considered successful. In other words, upon implementation, these policy options must have produced their anticipated impact. Therefore, rigorous research must be conducted and ample evidence or data must be collected. It is never recommended for a public policy developer to suggest inaction as an option for ministers.

Distinctiveness: Policy options are to be distinguished from one another by substance and degree. Each policy option must be noticeably different from the others in terms of content, extent, scope, amount, frequency, and magnitude of action. Such perceivable differences usually result in differences in anticipated behaviour, effort, resource usage, or impact. If the anticipated end result is minimal, then these policy options are not viable choices. Options are not necessarily mutually exclusive, and different options can be combined.

Balance: Public policies are established to ameliorate public problems. Where multiple stakeholders are concerned, the interests, needs, and demands of the public will vary, and policy options must reflect the interests of all involved in a balanced manner. To achieve this, policy options are to be judged based on their various combinations under all major headings, not individually. Only when presented as a bundle can cabinet ministers evaluate the balance of policy options, taking into consideration the trade-offs and the reciprocities among them. Some policy options include ways to eliminate or neutralize the sources of a problem; however, the sources of problems are often intertwined and a problem is seldom determined by a single source. In this case, public policy developers may develop policy options to address these various sources. If policy options provide simple solutions to problems, they may run the risk of being ineffective and limited upon implementation. If policy options provide complex solutions, cabinet ministers may find them difficult to comprehend, or to convince stakeholders to embrace, as they may appear cumbersome. Public policy developers have to balance the risks of these two extremes and propose both effective and acceptable policy options.

Starting Points

Public policy developers are advised to consider the following before beginning to develop policy options:

Consider existing options or recommendations proposed by political parties, think tanks, experts, and community members. Compare these suggestions with research findings to determine whether or not there are justifications for their inclusion as options in modified forms. Some of these options may be grouped together.

Review how other jurisdictions have framed their policies on similar topics. These policy options can be customized if applicable. It is important to validate and express the similarities and differences between jurisdictions—this comparison should provide an indication of whether or not the solution would work well in a different environment.

Put forward "best practices" as policy options. Best practices are those that have proven effective when used by other organizations or in other jurisdictions. It is important to recognize that practices that have been successful for other organizations or in other jurisdictions may not actually work as well when transplanted from one environment to another. Best practices are often derived from the private sector; there is a risk when applying these practices in the public sector without due diligence, as they may not be the best fit or even applicable in this environment. It is important to be critical when practices based on profits (the private sector) are being considered for adoption in a sector that is based on public good (the public sector).

Apply international standards as recommendations. International bodies such as the World Health Organization (WHO) and the Organisation for Economic Co-operation and Development (OECD) have established international standards from studying the experiences of numerous countries. These standards can be used as a starting point in developing policy options.

FIGURE 8.2: FACTORS TO CONSIDER WHEN DEVELOPING MAJOR HEADINGS AND POLICY OPTIONS

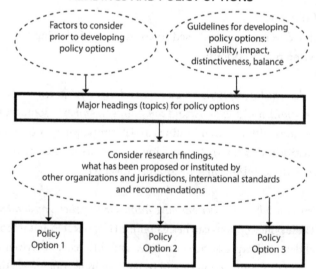

Policy Instruments

One of the major items that must be addressed for any policy option is the policy instrument that will be used. Under this heading, cabinet ministers must decide what means they intend to use in their efforts to alter people's behaviour or the performance of institutions. According to Pal (1992, pp. 138–139), *policy instruments* are "means whereby policy goals and policy problems are bridged"; they are the "concrete manifestation" of government policy.

A policy instrument may also be a policy option. Policy instruments can be broad and generic at an early stage of public policy development, as the policy moves towards legislative drafting or program design. In broad terms, policy instruments may include public spending (grants, loans, or subsidies), tax expenditure (incentives), public awareness and education (advertising or guidelines), taxation (on incomes, sales, and properties), legislation and regulations, public ownership (state-run operations or arm's length agencies), and coercive and intrusive means (police or military action). These policy instruments range from influencing to coercing behaviour and performance.

There are several other policy instruments that cabinet ministers may consider, such as allowing people or organizations to act autonomously without state interference, delaying policy decisions by creating a task force or commission to study the matter, or organizing a conference to encourage further public discourse. These policy instruments amount to non-actions, passive actions, or symbolisms on the part of the government. Whether or not they have any impact on the problems can only be speculated.

While policy instruments may be useful policy options for cabinet ministers to consider, they are usually quite broad. They may need to be broken down further once ministers have made a decision about their appropriateness in the current environment.

FIGURE 8.3: TYPOLOGY OF POLICY INSTRUMENTS

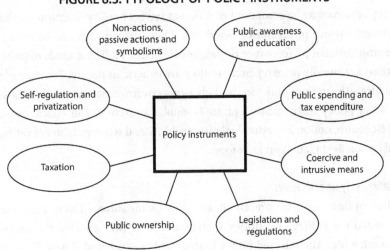

Distinguishing Primary and Secondary Policy Options

When developing policy options, public policy developers must be cognizant of the limited time that politicians will have to review these options. Accordingly, it is advisable to distinguish policy options into two types: primary and secondary. Primary policy options are fundamental to public problems, and secondary policy options are derived from these. Primary options define the broad directions that cabinet ministers wish to take. Secondary policy options may detail the specifics of the primary options. For example, if cabinet ministers are interested in limiting the harm caused by smoking cigarettes, public policy developers may put forward a public education campaign as a primary policy option for ministers to adopt. Once this primary policy option is adopted, public policy developers may propose more specific forms of public education, such as printing warning messages on cigarette packages, as secondary policy options for ministers to adopt.

The distinction between primary and secondary policy options enables cabinet ministers to examine options by beginning with the big picture and moving to the details of how the policy can be implemented. Such a distinction also enables public policy developers to summarize the public policy in one or two sentences, which will make the public policy direction clear to both politicians, and, later, the public, if the policy option is approved by the cabinet.

Policy Options as Variations or Gradations

Variations in Policy Instruments

Policy options may be composed of different types of policy instruments that represent various incentives or deterrents. These instruments can be used to alter institutional performance or individual behaviour. These kinds of policy options are usually primary because they are generic in nature. For example, to address the issue of junk food and obesity, a government may consider three different policy instruments: option 1—public awareness and education on public health; option 2—individual responsibility and self-regulation of eating; and option 3—taxation on junk food.

Variations in Types of Measures

Policy options may be presented as types of measures. These measures are usually a subset of a policy instrument, and they specify the means through which the selected policy instrument is expressed. These kinds of policy options can be considered primary or secondary, depending on how extensively a government is willing to intervene and how comprehensively it anticipates managing the policy direction. If the type of measure is considered a primary option, then it is expected that some secondary options are to follow for government intervention. For example, variations in types of measures may be found in the types of junk food that the government wishes to regulate. If taxation is used as a policy instrument, and three policy options on measures are to be formulated under this policy instrument, option 1 could be higher taxes on sugary drinks, option 2 could be higher taxes on fatty foods, and option 3 could be higher taxes on salty foods. These three measures can be put forward as individual options as they are distinct enough for demarcation, or they may be combined to constitute a single public policy.

Gradation in Criteria

Policy options may be based on gradations in criteria. Criteria cover the standards or principles upon which certain activities are to be demarcated. They may cover different aspects of human and organizational activities, such as applications to programs or awards, food safety, and entry of immigrants to the country. For example, if the government were considering the age eligibility criteria for the Canadian Pension Plan, the options for who is eligible to apply could be outlined as follows: option 1—age 67, option 2—age 70, and option 3—age 72. This illustrates the gradation in age eligibility criteria.

Gradation in Content

Gradation in content refers to the different degrees of intensity or magnitude of activities that institutions or individuals must undertake to comply with a new policy or legislation. Consider the reports that employers must submit to the government on an annual basis to comply with employment equity legislation. If a new regulation were under consideration, the following three options could be put forward: option 1—a report on the company's workforce profile only; option 2—a workforce profile and a hiring data report; and option 3—a workforce profile, a hiring and promotion data report, and an employment equity plan. These options place different demands on employers with regards to their documentation and reporting obligations to the government.

FIGURE 8.4: DIFFERENT FORMS OF POLICY OPTIONS

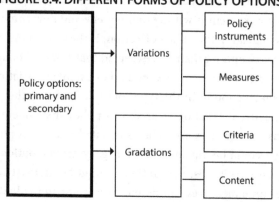

Publicizing Policy Options

Public policy developers sometimes have to formulate draft policy options for consultation purposes for the public or stakeholder groups. Under these circumstances, they face different challenges in the wording of policy options. Draft policy options that appear to be final give people the impression that the government has already decided on its policy direction, which may inspire resentment. However, when the draft policy options are too generic, they give the impression that the options are incomplete and not anchored in research. Some people may perceive these options as too tentative and not worthy of comment. Draft policy options that are too broad may be vulnerable to clamouring stakeholder groups, who would like to see their interests represented in the options. In this scenario, whichever group has the greatest influence on decision-makers is likely to have its interests embodied in these options. Public policy developers must strike a balance between these two extremes and craft options that are conducive to fruitful consultation.

Policy Options as Program Modifications

Public policy developers are sometimes required to examine existing publicly funded programs or operational arrangements to see how they can be modified to align with the government's policy direction. The task is similar to redesigning programs or operations; however, the objective is not related to administration, but to positioning policy direction.

At the request of politicians, public policy developers may review the funding arrangements of current programs, their organizational set-ups, eligibility criteria of target program users, service types and durations, performance measurements, and monitoring and enforcement mechanisms. Cabinet ministers will consider the resource requirements of each one of these options, to ensure the configuration of some of these options will follow the new policy direction they wish to take. The key word here is configuration. When the components of programs or operations change, they must be aligned properly so that they work seamlessly, and align with the government's broad policy direction. This means aligning program components such as target user groups, eligibility criteria, funding formula, reporting mechanisms, and other relevant operational details. Public policy developers need to be cautious when creating policy options, because these options must work within an existing institutional arrangement. These proposed options for modification are not just policy options, but possibilities for organizational change.

Policy Options as New Programs

Some policy options signify the introduction of new programs. These programs are not modifications of existing ones, but brand new sets of activities with new goals, objectives, foci, target groups, eligibility criteria, funding, and institutional arrangements. Sometimes, a new piece of legislation will have to be introduced and passed in the legislature or parliament to legalize and legitimize the policy and related funding for a new program. These policy options also imply that the government has to "sunset" or remove previous programs that represent old ways of doing things. While the new policy options do not usually focus on these implications, they should address the pros and cons of moving forward with a new program.

Policy Options as Legislative Changes

A separate new piece of legislation may or may not be required when existing programs are modified or new ones are created; however, in both cases, if money is needed for the program, separate estimate items must be tabled in the legislature for ratification. New programs, with new names, contents, and funds, usually need separate new legislation. The development of policy options that affect existing legislation or may result in the creation of new regulations often involve additional government funds. When presenting policy options of this nature, public policy developers must be familiar with existing laws, and must attempt to find some legal means to rectify a situation that was not envisioned when the existing laws were drafted. Such policy options have to ensure legal consistency across different pieces of legislation, institutional arrangements, and administrative procedures. An amendment to one piece of law sometimes necessitates amendments to others. Similarly, new regulations being considered under various policy options have to be consistent and compatible with existing regulations. Public policy developers have to work with legal counsel to find the correct way to address legal issues and craft the proper documents for amendments. In this consultation and collaboration process, the political, financial, social, organizational, and administrative implications of policy options must be considered and balanced. For example, when considering an amendment to the legal obligations of employers, policy developers need to address the following: the acceptability of such obligations to those employers (who now have additional responsibilities); the financial costs for employers (to carry out the responsibilities), as well as the government (to monitor or audit employers and enforce the new legislation); other stakeholder groups' perceptions of such obligations; the division of labour among government departments (that are responsible for the different legislations under review); and the administrative procedures (that may need to change to accommodate such legal requirements). Policy options with legal content usually have far-reaching and significant effects.

WHAT ARE THE PROS AND CONS OF POLICY OPTIONS?

The development of viable policy options is dependent on research and careful consideration to determine the pros and cons of a policy option. The pros are any benefits that the option will provide upon implementation, such as economic growth, social stability, community well-being, environmental sustainability, educational accessibility, health care benefits, or industrial expansion. Cons are any risk or harm that may accompany the option, such as social injustice, gender inequality, destabilization of international relations, loss of investment, environmental degradation, public illness, neighbourhood deterioration, job loss, and political chaos.

The following example of the provincial government's decision to implement mandatory daily physical activity for all primary and secondary public school students to improve the well-being of young Canadians illustrates how pros and cons are identified during the public policy development process.

TABLE 8.1: IDENTIFYING PROS AND CONS OF POLICY OPTIONS
Policy option:
Thirty minutes of daily physical activity is to be made mandatory for all primary and secondary school students.

Pros	Cons
Students will become physically healthier.	Current supply of physical education teachers will not meet the demand created by this new public policy, if it is to be implemented immediately.
The school curriculum will become more balanced in terms of physical and mental development.	Most school facilities are not capable of handling the increased volume of students doing physical exercises at one time.
Provincial education standards will improve, as will students' academic standing.	Resistance is expected from some teachers, students, and parents. Some may oppose the new public policy on religious grounds.

There are several factors that public policy developers should consider when identifying the pros and cons of policy options:

Political factors: Because policy options are usually framed in a non-partisan manner, political factors are seldom explicitly outlined as pros and cons; however, when these factors are expressed in a non-partisan manner, they are crucial for cabinet ministers to consider. Political factors to consider may include the following: Is the policy option aligned with the ruling party's political platform? Are regional and stakeholder interests balanced in the policy option? What political risks must the government take to adopt the policy option?

Stakeholder and public acceptability: This may be difficult to achieve because stakeholder groups often have dissimilar, and occasionally irreconcilable, interests. Therefore, one stakeholder group may view a particular item as a positive, but another may see the same item as a negative. Public policy developers may be able to anticipate the reactions of stakeholder groups by knowing the history of their reactions to similar issues. To put the issue of stakeholder acceptability in perspective, it must be framed in the context of public opinion and the prevailing values and beliefs at that historical juncture.

Financial costs: Costs may be expenses for the government, the broader public sector, the private sector, or individuals. The exact costs are seldom worked out at the policy development stage, but an estimate is usually provided so cabinet ministers have a sense of the potential financial burden of the policy.

Organizational constraints: Constraints are manifested in terms of additional demands on human resources, changes in organizational structure within the government, institutional changes outside the government, and increased capabilities (knowledge and skills) for those involved in implementing the policy option. Internal resistance to change should be expected.

Legislative changes: When a policy option requires a new piece of law or an amendment to an existing law, it can be interpreted as either a pro or a con. If it is viewed positively, it can be assumed that the embodiment of the policy option in law makes the public policy stronger and more sustainable. It may be viewed negatively if immense change is needed to put the policy into action, or if it must undergo the parliamentary process, during which the legislation will be debated, go through three readings in the legislature, and may be subject to intense media scrutiny.

Expected impacts: Different policy options produce different impacts. Based on their research, public policy developers are in a position to estimate the potential impact of each option. The difference in impact may be a matter of degree, but it is still worthy of cabinet consideration. In this situation, a pro may imply that the policy option has a greater chance of positive effects, whereas a con may mean that it has less. The quantification of anticipated results is one way to determine the magnitude of the impact of a policy option, especially if public policy developers have reliable statistics to draw on. When public policy developers quantify the estimated impact of a policy option, it is advisable that they keep a record of how the numbers have been calculated, what assumptions were made when doing so, and what indicators were used, as they may be asked to justify their findings.

FIGURE 8.5: POLICY OPTION PROS AND CONS—FACTORS TO CONSIDER

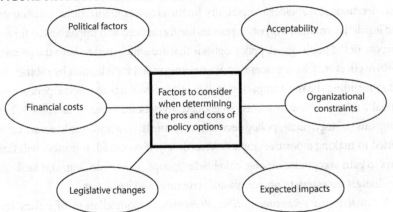

HOW TO MAKE RECOMMENDATIONS

In a cabinet submission, three to five policy options are usually provided under each major heading. After listing these policy options and their respective pros and cons, public policy developers are expected to put forward their recommendations. Determining the superior policy option, based on research and analysis, is sometimes the most difficult task. After assessing the potential positive and negative elements, it is often the case that some policy options are strong according to one or two criteria, but are weak according to others. For example, one option may be quite significant in its impact, but expensive to carry out or expected to spur backlash from certain segments of the population. Meanwhile, another option's impact may be unclear, but it is likely to be acceptable to the public and cost-effective. These variations in strengths and weaknesses make it difficult for politicians to choose between options.

Strategies for Presenting Recommendations

To make decisions easier for ministers, public policy developers use one of four strategies to frame their recommendation: good public policy, impact-based, constellated, or enveloped.

1. *Good public policy recommendation:* This strategy follows the six principles of good public policies described in chapter 5—balance of public interests, accountability, impact, cost-effectiveness, justice, and balance of short- and long-term considerations. Public policy developers evaluate each policy option based on these six principles and determine the best option for recommendation.

2. *Impact-based recommendation:* Public policy developers may recommend an

option based on its expected impact, and ignore any risks associated with political considerations, stakeholder acceptability, financial costs, organizational constraints, and legislative changes. As public policies are formulated and implemented for the purpose of the public good, policy options that are anticipated to have the greatest positive effect may be the ones that are recommended for adoption by cabinet. By recommending the most impactful policy option, public policy developers are essentially asking cabinet ministers to endorse an option in spite of its risks. When using this strategy, public policy developers assume that cabinet ministers are committed to making a positive impact. Accordingly, if espoused, ministers will find ways to gain acceptance among stakeholder groups, secure funding, and facilitate the changes necessary to organizational structures and legislation.

3. *Constellated recommendation:* Presenting a constellation of policy options is sometimes an optimal strategy. Here, all policy options under all major headings are reviewed and the options that have the best chance of being accepted by cabinet ministers are selected and bundled for potential adoption. This constellated mix of policy options that will get the most support from the cabinet ministers, based on financial costs, stakeholder acceptability, and expected impacts, creates a combination and balance of options. Each option may not be the best under its heading, but when combined with others, the mix of options becomes an ideal package for adoption. Using this strategy, public policy developers should present each recommendation under its own individual major heading, and, in conclusion, state the constellated mix of selected policy options as the recommendation.

OPTIMIZED DISABILITY SERVICES: AN EXAMPLE OF A CONSTELLATED RECOMMENDATION

The provincial government is considering new legislation intended to optimize services for persons with disabilities. To simplify this example, only three major headings (topics) are provided for consideration: employer coverage, effective date, and disability coverage. Each heading has four options. Each option would have several pros and cons; for simplicity, they will not be outlined in this example.

(A) Employer coverage

Option 1: Legislation covers employers with 10 or more employees in the public and broader public sector, and employers with 500 employees in the private sector.

Option 2: Legislation covers employers with 500 or more employees in the public and broader public sector, and employers with 2,500 employees in the private sector.

Option 3: Legislation covers employers with 2,500 or more employees in the public, broader public, and private sectors.

Option 4: Legislation covers only public sector employers with 10 or more employees.

(B) Effective date

Option 1: Legislation becomes effective one year after its proclamation, irrespective of the number of employees.

Option 2: Legislation becomes effective two years after its proclamation, irrespective of the number of employees.

Option 3: Legislation becomes effective three years after its proclamation, irrespective of the number of employees.

Option 4: Legislation becomes effective one year after its proclamation for employers with 2,500 or more employees, two years after its proclamation for employers with 500 or more employees, and three years after its proclamation for employers with 10 or more employees.

(C) Disability coverage

Option 1: Legislation covers only persons with physical disabilities.

Option 2: Legislation covers only persons with developmental disabilities.

Option 3: Legislation covers persons with physical and developmental disabilities.

Option 4: Legislation covers persons with disabilities of all kinds.

After reviewing the major headings and policy options and their pros and cons, a public policy developer may choose one option from each major heading. In this case, a singular policy option may not be the best, but when combined and constellated together, they may constitute the best recommendation for the proposed new legislation.

In this scenario, a public policy developer may choose the following policy options for a constellated recommendation:

Employer coverage—Option 1: Legislation covers employers with 10 or more employees in the public and broader public sector, and employers with 500 employees in the private sector. In terms of expected impact, this has the broadest coverage of employers in the province, and it is therefore the best option under this heading.

Effective date—Option 3: Legislation becomes effective three years after its proclamation, irrespective of the number of employees. In terms of expected impact, this policy option is the least impactful as it delays the implementation of this legislation for at least two years; during this period, if a new government is elected, this legislation may be repealed as there is no legislative entrenchment among employers. But, as the effective date is three years away, it maximizes acceptability among employers, as it gives them time to prepare or influence the government, if implementation details need to be worked on.

Disability coverage—Option 3: Legislation covers persons with physical and developmental disabilities. This policy option is not the most impactful, as it covers only a portion of all persons with disabilities. Persons with other disabilities beyond physical and developmental disabilities are not covered, so the selection of this option includes the risk of protests from those communities. Despite this, limiting disability coverage reduces costs to employers for service delivery, and this may increase the chances of acceptability.

A combination of the three policy options outlined above will not please every stakeholder group, but it may strike a balance of interests, impacts, and costs among stakeholder groups. In the recommendation section of a cabinet submission for this proposed new legislation, a public policy developer may write: It is therefore recommended that employer coverage option 1, effective date option 3, and disability coverage option 3 be adopted by the cabinet.

4. *Enveloped recommendation:* This strategy sees public policy developers create several envelopes of policy options and provide a summary of the benefits and risks of each. Similar to a constellation of policy options, envelopes contain different combinations of policy options, each of which has its own strengths and weaknesses. Unlike constellated recommendations, an enveloped recommendation strategy does not present policy options under major headings. These envelopes are presented to the cabinet for consideration and only one will be put forward as a recommendation. For policy recommendations to be supported by cabinet members, public policy developers have to consider the points of contention related to the issues. The recommendations that address these contentious issues are more likely to garner support from the cabinet.

OPTIMIZED DISABILITY SERVICES: AN EXAMPLE OF AN ENVELOPED RECOMMENDATION

Consider once again the example used in our discussion of a constellated recommendation: The provincial government is considering new legislation intended to optimize services for persons with disabilities. Cabinet ministers are expected to determine its major components in an effort to construct a comprehensive and accommodating service package. Unlike constellated recommendations, an enveloped recommendation strategy does not present policy options under major headings; instead, they are presented in several envelopes, consisting of various groups of policy options.

Envelope A: Optimal Package

Employer coverage—Option 1: Legislation covers employers with 10 or more employees in the public and broader public sector, and employers with 500 employees in the private sector.

Effective date—Option 4: Legislation becomes effective one year after its proclamation for employers with 2,500 or more employees, two years after its proclamation for employers with 500 or more employees, and three years after its proclamation for employers with 10 or more employees.

Disability coverage—Option 4: Legislation covers persons with disabilities of all kinds.

Envelope B: Moderate Package

> *Employer coverage—Option 2:* Legislation covers employers with 500 or more employees in the public and broader public sector, and employers with 2,500 employees in the private sector.

> *Effective date—Option 2:* Legislation becomes effective two years after its proclamation, irrespective of the number of employees.

> *Disability coverage—Option 3:* Legislation covers persons with physical and developmental disabilities.

Envelope C: Low-Range Package

> *Employer coverage—Option 4:* Legislation covers only public sector employers with 10 or more employees.

> *Effective date—Option 3:* Legislation becomes effective three years after its proclamation, irrespective of the number of employees.

> *Disability coverage—Option 1:* Legislation covers only persons with physical disabilities.

As noted above, Envelope A is the optimal package; it has the strongest impact, a reasonable date for implementation, and broad coverage of persons with all sorts of disabilities. Envelope A is the package most likely to meet the service delivery goal of optimizing services for persons with disabilities. Envelope C is the least likely package to meet the service delivery goal because it is limiting in the scope of employers, persons with disabilities, and the long wait time for the proposed legislation to take effect. Envelope B is somewhere between Envelope A and Envelope C in terms of the extent of the community of persons with disabilities, employers impacted by the proposed public policy, and the timeline in which the policy will take effect. Envelope B will not affect small or medium-sized private or public sector employers; however, it will require employers with more resources to comply. In numerical terms, the majority of employers in the province will not be affected, and this may appease the business sector. Although not all persons with disabilities will be covered under this public policy, the policy will provide services to most of them, and this may appease these communities. Having a lead time of two years will give employers adequate time to prepare and develop the infrastructure and operational systems required to carry out the services. This, too, may appease the employers. For these reasons, Envelope B is likely to be presented as the public policy developer's recommendation.

In the recommendation section of a cabinet submission for this proposed new legislation, a public policy developer may write: It is recommended that Envelope B—employer coverage option 2, effective date option 2, and disability coverage option 3—be adopted by the cabinet. When measuring potential in accordance to the six principles for good public policies, it is clear that each envelope has its own strengths and inherent weaknesses.

TACTICS FOR DEVELOPING POLICY RECOMMENDATIONS

When developing policy recommendations, public policy developers must

- be prepared to follow directions or suggestions from the cabinet and the minister's office;
- take into consideration the concerns of the ministers and deputy ministers when preparing policy recommendations, as they may be conveying the sentiments and comfort level of their constituents;
- exercise due diligence when conducting research related to contentious issues, and always try to find ways to mitigate or alleviate these contentions; and
- be prepared to shuffle and trade off policy options, so that recommendations can be packaged in a way that is more likely to gain support.

SUMMARY

Policy options are different ways to carry out government decisions. To develop policy options, public policy developers must first establish the areas in which cabinet ministers need to make policy-related changes. For each of the major policy areas (or major headings), there are four guidelines for developing policy options: viability, impact, distinctiveness, and balance. With these guidelines in mind, public policy developers prepare policy options. There are several starting points for developing policy options: research findings; input from political parties, think tanks, experts, and community members; instituted policies in other jurisdictions on similar subject matter; best practices from other organizations or jurisdictions; and international standards or recommendations. Policy instruments are presented to cabinet ministers as potential methods for effecting change. Public policy developers may need to distinguish primary (generic) from secondary (specific) policy options. To determine the pros and cons of policy options, several issues are considered, including political factors, stakeholder acceptability, financial costs, organizational constraints, legislative changes, and expected impacts.

After the policy options have been established, public policy developers must put forward their recommendations. As all policy options have strengths and weaknesses, it may be difficult for public policy developers to ascertain the correct course of action. They often use one of the following approaches to identify which policy option to recommend: the policy option with the greatest positive impact; the policy option that aligns best with the six principles of good public policies; the most optimal constellation of policy options; or the most well-balanced envelope of policy options.

QUESTIONS FOR CRITICAL THINKING

1. In addition to the four principles for preparing policy options—viability, impact, distinctiveness, and balance—what other principles could be established?

2. Usually, several policy options are available for each policy issue. How do public policy developers determine which options are put forward for ministers to consider? List these determining factors.

3. Consider the implications of putting forward recommendations based on research findings versus recommendations that the ministers may find politically affirming and organizationally convenient.

DETERMINING PUBLIC POLICIES FOR IMPLEMENTATION

INTRODUCTION

Public policy developers must come up with policy options and recommendations for cabinet ministers to consider; these are usually presented in the form of a cabinet submission. At this point, ministers scrutinize, assess, and discuss the draft public policy; this is followed by a process of intensive, bureaucrat-conducted activities to ensure that government protocol is followed. These activities are pertinent to the cabinet's final decision regarding the fate of a public policy. Some of these activities are formal procedures, but others are informal; these informal procedures take place behind the scenes and are not usually documented. It is often unclear what issues are significant enough to require public policy developers to obtain clearance from the cabinet and what could be dealt with at the ministry level. The entire decision-making process is extremely complicated and fluid, and direction from those involved can change without warning, sometimes on a daily or hourly basis. Even the players involved may change, and decision-making power may be transferred with no advance warning. The twists and turns of the decision-making process cannot be easily represented in a flow chart or diagram. For our purposes, the decision-making process will be illustrated in a simplified and streamlined manner, followed by a discussion of the multiple factors that may impact the decisions of cabinet and parliament members.

DECISION-MAKING PROCESS
Going through Cabinet Committees

After months of meetings, research, and consultations, public policy developers put forward their policy options and recommendations in a cabinet submission presented to the line minister. This does not signal the end of their public policy development work—there may be a series of major and minor revisions that need to be made, additional consultations to be conducted, and more documents to be written and approved before a final decision is reached.

After reviewing various drafts and participating in numerous briefings with the minister, the deputy minister (with the assistance of the minister and his or her political aides) may finalize the cabinet submission. If the draft cabinet submission is acceptable (and by the time the public policy developers have finished all of the successive inputs and revisions, it usually is), the next step is for it to be sent to the relevant cabinet committee members. The draft cabinet submission is then placed on the agenda for a specific cabinet committee meeting.

During the meeting, committee members (ministers from different line departments) discuss the draft cabinet submission. This is not the first time that these committee members are presented with this subject matter, as they are briefed many times during the development process. Very often, the minister introduces the policy topic during the meeting and briefs the rest of the committee members on the various recommendations. If the topic is complex, public policy developers may be asked to supplement the presentation orally or with slides.

Urgency is an important factor in the public policy decision-making process. At any one time, there are usually multiple policy issues competing for cabinet's attention. As the breadth of policy domains in cabinet expands, competition for a spot on the agenda intensifies. The central agencies (such as the planning and priorities board, the management board, and the treasury board) are overloaded with competing policy issues; they can only review those public policy issues that top the political agenda. Policy choices are now more interrelated than in the past, and new policy proposals must compete with existing ones to be justified across policy domains (Chandler and Chandler, 1979, p. 108). This usually results in policy negotiations among ministers, as public policies have political and cost implications that need to be discussed. If there is an urgent need to get the cabinet submission approved, discussions will likely touch on sensitive issues so that a consensus can be reached on the policy recommendations. At this stage, there may be some minor proposed changes to specific recommendations, or there may be none. Any changes will be summarized in the committee meeting minutes.

If the public policy proposed in the draft cabinet submission is not urgent, the members may have to decide whether it should be submitted at a later stage, depending on the agenda of the planning and priorities board and the cabinet. The committee members may put the draft submission on hold until further notice. This scenario rarely happens, because if a policy is not urgent, public policy developers usually receive advance notice that they do not need to complete the draft submission until they receive further instructions from the ministers and the planning and priorities board.

FIGURE 9.1: FROM PUBLIC POLICY DEVELOPERS TO CABINET COMMITTEES

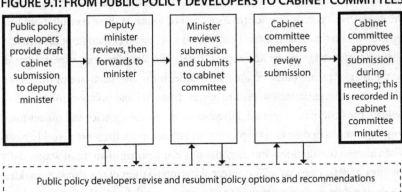

Working with Central Agencies and Line Departments

If the cabinet committee members agree to forward the cabinet submission to the cabinet, the submission follows two common routes, depending on the nature of the policy matter: (1) financial, management, and statutory issues can be resolved and agreed upon by the central agencies—treasury board, management board, statutory committee, and the ministry of finance—before the submission is forwarded to cabinet, or (2) it can be submitted directly to cabinet and it will determine the policy direction prior to any specific discussion of financial, management, and statutory issues.

If financial, management, and statutory issues need to be resolved, there will be a great deal of back and forth between the central agencies and the line department as they consult with each other to negotiate and finalize the financial and management arrangements. Once the financial, management, and statutory issues have been ironed out, the decision-making process usually progresses with minimal complications.

The financial implications of a cabinet submission may be related to the allocation of funds for program implementation—service delivery, information gathering, public education, or transfer payments. Management implications may be related to the allocation of human resources—workforce, operational structure, and communication. The officers of the treasury board secretariat and management board secretariat must scrutinize these implications and pose questions to the line department responsible for the cabinet submission. These conversations and meetings—between officers, public policy developers, and government officials in charge of human resources, financial management, and communication from the line department—will consist of numerous consultations and negotiations to determine the most feasible financial and management arrangements. The department responsible for finance must be aware of these consultations and negotiations on financial matters to maintain a big picture estimate of present and future government revenues and expenditures. The planning and priorities board, the premier or prime minister, and the cabinet must also be aware of these consultations and negotiations to ensure overall financial and policy consistency. To facilitate the flow of information, bureaucrats in central agencies and offices must work together to update and prepare information for briefings on a weekly basis. When these consultations and negotiations are nearing their final stage, daily briefings may be necessary. This internal harmonization of the decision-making process involves many departments and central agencies, at both the political and bureaucratic levels. Depending on the nature of the policy matter, the end of this process is usually signified by a treasury board or management board submission for approval. Once approved, the content of the submission is summarized in minutes along with the draft cabinet submission. Alternatively, the cabinet may choose to determine the financial allocation and send the submission to the treasury board for ratification.

The role of a public policy developer in a line department may be central or marginal, depending on how the ministers and deputy ministers designate tasks. In some ministries, public policy developers work in a team with officials in charge of financial management, human resources, and program and service delivery. In other cases, ministers and deputy ministers determine the type of management arrangement and the amount of funding to be allocated from existing ministry budgets, consulting only with senior government bureaucrats. In this situation, public policy developers must work within the confines of the policy's intents, specifications, and internal allocation of funds.

Some policy matters require a piece of new legislation, a regulation, or an amendment to existing legislation. Legal counsel representing the statutory committee will become involved either prior to or after the approval of the draft cabinet submission, depending on the nature of the policy matter. Public policy developers play an important role in working with legal counsel to ensure that the essence of the draft cabinet submission is maintained and accurate. In some cases, the draft cabinet submission may already include the policy options that legal counsel can use to draft the legislation or regulations; in other cases, legal counsel has to work with public policy developers during the drafting process. The role of the legal counsel is to translate public policies approved by the cabinet into legal language, and to develop a piece of legislation, an amendment, or a regulation. Similar to the consultation and negotiation phase carried out by the treasury board or management board bureaucrats, legal counsel has to work with the legal counsel of other ministries to ensure draft compatibility. The line department, treasury board, management board, cabinet office, planning and priorities board, and premier or Prime Minister's Office all have to be a part of this process to ensure the consistency of policy, legal, finance, and management matters.

FIGURE 9.2: FROM CABINET COMMITTEE TO CABINET

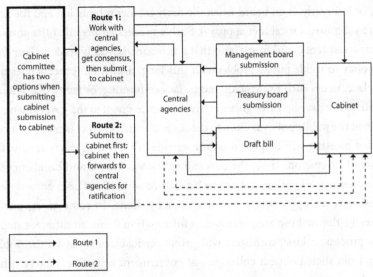

Going through Cabinet

By the time the draft cabinet submission is finally put forward to cabinet for consideration, along with the minutes approved by the treasury or management board, the cabinet members are confident that the financial and management aspects have been agreed upon—at this point, there should not be any other disruptions or disagreement among ministers regarding financial or management matters. The government is now ready to put the policy forward as a piece of legislation or an estimate item to be passed on to members of the legislature or parliament.

Ideally, the draft bill is ready for the cabinet to review and approve at the time of the cabinet submission. However, drafting a bill usually takes a long time, as it requires legal experts' advice, legislative research, and a review by legal counsel of other ministries to ensure legality and compatibility with existing laws. There may be situations in which amendments are needed, especially if the new bill introduces legal inconsistencies or loopholes among existing laws, or exposes grey areas that require further study. Under these circumstances, the new bill, along with the proposed amendments, must be submitted to the cabinet for approval at another meeting. If it is expected that the new bill will be submitted at a later date, the line ministry responsible for the bill must consult with other ministries and central agencies, just as it had previously for the cabinet submission.

This series of extensive consultations and negotiations across ministries and central agencies is extremely complex, labour-intensive, time-consuming, and, at times, dramatic. The objective is to ensure that everyone involved, either directly or indirectly, is on board when the draft cabinet submission and the new bill are submitted for cabinet approval. Such a process ensures that the government is consistent on all fronts, and that it is organizationally ready to launch a new policy to tackle public problems. If this long, drawn-out process does not take place, issues such as inconsistencies, lack of funding, or faulty operational infrastructure can slip through and cause embarrassment to the government.

When the public policy is close to the stage at which cabinet is ready to move ahead, a meeting will be placed on the agenda of the ruling party caucus for an overall discussion. Here, the government's constituents and backbenchers (those members of parliament or the legislature who do not hold government offices) have an opportunity to voice their opinions. In some cases, public policies-in-the-making are presented as information items. At different stages in the process, cabinet ministers will gather feedback or input on the public policy from their political colleagues at government or political party functions. Informal comments constitute a reservoir of ideas to be drawn upon during the review of the draft cabinet submission. Pre-legislative meetings provide opportunities for elected representatives from different political parties and backbenchers to voice their ideas on policy matters—again, ideas and feedback help cabinet ministers shape public policies.

At the cabinet level, many policy proposals cross the desks of ministers. Cabinet ministers must deal with tremendous pressure in terms of time and resources, and have to find ways to address public problems in the most effective and efficient manner (Chandler and Chandler, 1979, p. 121). As a result of the demand on cabinet ministers to make decisions about complex public policy matters under severe time constraints, they increasingly look to the premier, or prime minister, for guidance on whether or not a public policy (as outlined in the draft cabinet submission) is ready for final approval. Cabinet ministers seek cues from their leader about the timing of a public policy, its robustness, and whether it adequately balances priorities. The premier, or prime minister, indicates approval of a public policy, and his or her acquiescence demonstrates that it is ready to be tabled in the legislature or parliament.

When the cabinet minister receives the cabinet submission, the new bill, and the related minutes from the treasury or management board, he or she has an opportunity to discuss these items with the premier, or prime minister. Here, without dwelling too much on the financial and management issues (many of which have been settled by this point), cabinet ministers tend to focus on the political aspects of a proposed public policy.

FIGURE 9.3: FROM CABINET TO LEGISLATURE

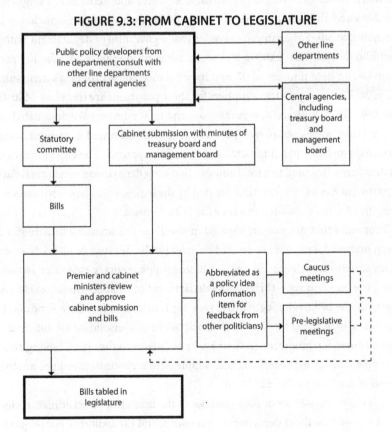

Going through the Legislature

After an extensive internal discussion of the cabinet submission, the cabinet is prepared to table its policy decisions in the legislature or parliament. Despite what many people think, public policies are not usually written as policy statements on a piece of paper. They are manifested in one of two forms: (1) an estimate bill covering the annual operating and capital spending requirements of ministries, including their programs under transfers of payments to external institutions, or (2) legislation.

Estimates

In the estimate bill, each new program in the approved cabinet submission is identified by a vote number and an item code. The vote and item system makes the allocation of funds specific and clear. The vote number denotes the name of the line department. Items, which are the line departments' programs, are listed under each line department. Both votes and items have designated numbers and the amount of funds available for each vote/item is included in the estimate bill. For example, consider that a government department with a portfolio in health has 1400 as its vote number, its long-term care facility program has an item number of 07, and its substance abuse program's item number is 08. The vote and item numbers for these programs are therefore 1400-07 and 1400-08. Additionally, separate vote and item numbers are designated for salaries and wages, employee benefits, transportation and communication, services, supplies and equipment, and transfer payments. The expenditures of all items are calculated to a total amount that each department can access. Each department has its own estimate ratified by the legislature. These estimates are considered main estimates and they are tallied annually.

Programs that are not anticipated at the time the annual estimate bill is being prepared, but that are created to meet public demand or alleviate emergency situations as they arise, are considered supplementary estimates. In these cases, the government—through the department of finance—must revisit and resubmit the bill to the legislature, seeking ratification for more funding. In general, it is in the interest of each department to consolidate all anticipated expenditures for programs in their main estimates, rather than tabling them as supplementary estimates, because supplementary estimates require another round of scrutiny in the legislature.

It is the responsibility of each member of the legislature to scrutinize, review, and ask questions about departments, programs, and expenditures. For programs that have already been approved by the cabinet, the task of the members of the legislature is to ratify the estimates. There may be situations in which sensitive issues are raised in the legislature, but, in general, the passing of an estimate is routine, since most of the items are existing programs. New programs that do not require a new piece of legislation are usually subjected to questioning by the opposition parties. They seldom rise to the level of attracting media attention, unless they introduce controversial issues or unusually high program expenditures.

Legislation

When the cabinet has approved a new program that requires the drafting of a new piece of legislation or amending an existing law, a bill (draft legislation) must be prepared for tabling in the legislature. These two processes—policy and legislative development—are conducted either simultaneously or sequentially. The legal counsel at the statutory committee of cabinet drafts the bill, and by the time of tabling, the bill is ready.

When a new bill is tabled in the legislature, it signifies that the government is planning to take a new policy direction or adopt a new way to resolve a public problem. It should embody the cabinet ministers' consensus. All bills go through three readings in the legislature. During the first reading, the minister responsible introduces the new bill. If the opposition parties raise questions that generate a lot of debate, it may be decided that more time is needed to thoroughly study the new bill. The bill will then be sent to a standing committee made up of elected representatives from all major political parties for review. Most standing committees are responsible for a certain policy domain, though that may encompass more than one department (Kernaghan and Siegel, 1991, p. 389). During the standing committee's study of the bill, the elected representatives may conduct research or seek expert opinions on issues stated within it. The minister responsible for the bill, and its designated experts, may also appear at committee meetings to answer questions from opposition parties. The standing committee members may put forward recommended changes at the end of the review period; these suggestions are considered and decided upon, and the bill is redrafted by the cabinet minister responsible.

When the redrafted bill is tabled again during the second reading, all members of the legislature have an opportunity to review it and ask questions. The minister responsible for the bill has to decide, once again, what changes to accept and how to address contentious issues if there is no consensus in the legislature. After the second reading, some bills that require redrafting go to a legislative committee made up of representatives from all parties, while other bills may go to ad hoc committees, which are usually composed of backbenchers from various political parties. Ad hoc committees are formed to look into specific issues generated by the bill that may require additional research or consultation; this provides backbenchers with an opportunity to offer their opinions. The minister may make alterations to the bill based on questions posed during the second reading, the findings of the ad hoc committee, or the proposed redrafted version of the legislation. Whether or not the bill is revised between the second and third readings depends largely on if cabinet members believe that their party has compromised enough, and if suggested changes from the opposition parties have been incorporated as much as possible. If the minister has the support of the majority of politicians in the legislature, the bill will be passed during the third reading. If a minority government is in power, an astute minister may make some minor changes to appease the other parties to ensure the passing of the bill during the third reading. It is likely that by the time a bill has progressed to the third reading, it will be passed. After the third reading, royal assent by the lieutenant-governor will be sought and the bill will become law.

This process illustrates the power and responsibility of cabinet concerning public policies and the allocation of funds to programs; they are constrained only by the requirement to table these policies and programs in the form of bills for review by the legislature for ratification. Although the legislature does not make public policies, it is still an integral force in the process, especially when the government in power is in a minority position. It acts as "a constraint as well as an impetus for change" (Chandler and Chandler, 1979, pp. 115–121). The legislature calls attention to issues that may not have been addressed by the cabinet, highlighting problems in a democratic system. The lieutenant-governor's role is largely symbolic and does not influence the construction or modification of a public policy.

FIGURE 9.4: FROM TABLING BILLS TO ROYAL ASSENT IN THE LEGISLATURE

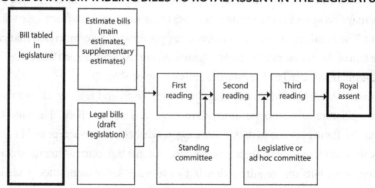

The process of tabling and redrafting a bill is the same for both provincial and federal governments through the third reading; in the federal government, the bill is sent to the Senate after the third reading in Parliament (or the House of Commons). Senate members review and debate the bill in three readings (similar to the process that took place in the House of Commons). After the second reading, the bill is sent to a standing committee for examination. With the committee's report, senators go through the third reading and put the bill, with the appropriate amendments, to a vote. All bills must be agreed upon and passed by both the House of Commons and the Senate before receiving royal assent from the governor general, which is the formal act of approving a bill, and the final step for it to become law.

GOVERNMENT REGULATION, DEREGULATION, AND PRIVATIZATION

Whether or not a politician decides to support a certain public policy depends on the context of the problem in relation to its environment. Not surprisingly, when social context changes, a politician's choice of policy instruments also changes (Hood, 1983, p. 162; Pal, 1992, pp. 166–167). For several decades, neo-liberalism has been gaining momentum in Canada. It emphasizes personal responsibility and the primacy of the market economy. According to this ideology, the market economy (in the absence of government intervention) should be capable of taking care of an individual's livelihood (Barry, 2005, pp. 131–166). However, there is a tendency for the public sector to accumulate high debt and deficit. The need to balance the budget while simultaneously financing programs spurs government to look for alternative sources of financing. The frequency with which neo-liberalism intersects with the government gives the impression that, as government expenses become less sustainable, the private sector may be called upon to provide financial support and play an increasing role in the lives of individuals.

Government regulation and privatization are two major policy instruments that help to produce desired effects on individual behaviour or institutional performance. A growing discourse on whether to regulate, deregulate, or privatize services has been at the forefront of the agenda for decades. If government regulation is favoured, then we must ask how large a role the private sector will be invited to play. Government is constantly trying to find a balance between these policy instruments, which are inherently contradictory. Because privatization alleviates government burden, it may take several forms as a policy instrument. These include establishing public-private partnerships; changing the status of Crown corporations; allowing private ownership of government services; deregulating industries, goods, and services; and diminishing the role of government in funding, education, quality control, and monitoring. Privatization can also manifest itself in indirect ways, such as allowing private donations, fundraising, or outsourcing, and allowing the private sector to assume a larger role in traditionally public domains. In each of these forms, privatization is involved to various degrees. In line with the deregulation process that has taken place in the United Kingdom and the United States, privatization in Canada is reversing the historical trend of government regulation of the environment, housing, heritage, education, training, health, justice, citizenship, and culture (Inwood, 2009; Pal, 1992, pp. 166–167). This is a move towards a free market economy, smaller government, less government intervention, and more personal responsibility.

Depending on the political inclination of the government in power, the process of deregulation proceeds at an uneven pace. During the 1990s, the federal Liberal government observed a tendency to regulate, but in the following decade, the Conservative government came into power, and has attempted some deregulation, or has at least given the appearance that it allows more opportunities for the private sector and individuals to regulate themselves. For example, the federal Conservative government's abolition of the controversial long-gun registry demonstrates its willingness to remove the government's influence from particular issues.

While deregulation as a policy instrument aligns well with neo-liberalism, there is a widespread preference for some degree of government regulation. The water contamination tragedy in Walkerton, Ontario, in May 2000 (described in detail below) illustrates how the deregulation and privatization of quality control of water under the province's Conservative government in the 1990s led to a loss of accountability for essential services. The deregulation was motivated by a drive to reduce the size of the government. The near-collapse of the US financial sector in 2008 is another indication that stronger government regulation and state intervention may be more beneficial for the majority of the population. In this case, the general lack of government regulation of real estate transactions, trading practices, mortgages, and capital holdings of financial institutions made it easy for consumers to take bank loans without a viable repayment capability or adequate capital backing. As a result, financial institutions faced a liquidity crisis, the stock market's value dropped significantly, house foreclosures and evictions rose, and layoffs and unemployment rates multiplied. While the downturn of the US and European economies continued, American and European governments started bailing out banks and strengthened regulations on the financial and housing industries. In this context, many of these countries looked to Canada as a model of strong and effective government regulation of financial institutions.

WATER CONTAMINATION IN WALKERTON, 2000

In 1996, the Government of Ontario permitted the privatization of water testing, and no longer regulated water quality or enforced existing water-testing guidelines. In May 2000, more than 2,300 residents of Walkerton, a town northwest of Guelph, fell sick, and 7 people died as a result of drinking E. coli–contaminated water from the town's supply.

During a public inquiry into the tragedy in 2002, the Walkerton Public Utilities Commission was found to be at fault. The undertrained manager, Stan Koebel, and water foreman, Frank Koebel, of the Public Utilities Commission were found criminally responsible for not adequately testing the water supply. They failed to monitor the chlorine residuals on a daily basis and made false entries in operating records, contrary to the guidelines and directives of the Ministry of the Environment. Both were sentenced in 2004 after they admitted that they falsified reports, and drank while on the job. The tragedy cost somewhere between $64.5 million and $155 million. The recommendations made during the inquiry regarding improving water quality in Ontario have been accepted by subsequent governments, and have also had a positive effect on water-related public policies in other provinces.

Source: O'Connor, 2002.

Although deregulation fits well within an ideology of neo-liberalism, agenda items related to law and order can only be effectively managed through government regulation. A review of the number of bills going through parliament in the provincial and federal governments over the last two decades suggested that deregulation remains a sporadic gesture, and that the overall trend of government regulation remains the norm. Bill C-10 (outlined in detail below) is an example of government's continual interest in using legislation as policy instruments, and a clear effort on behalf of the federal Conservative government to get tough on crime.

BILL C-10: *SAFE STREETS AND COMMUNITIES ACT*

The federal government introduced Bill C-10: *Safe Streets and Communities Act*, also known as the omnibus crime bill, and went through the first reading of the bill in September 2011. The objective of this bill is to institute mandatory minimum prison sentences for drug crimes, harsher penalties for violent crimes and sexual assaults, and the right of victims of terrorism to sue their perpetrators. This bill was part of the Conservative government's anti-crime strategy and was passed quickly. The bill went through the Standing Committee on Justice and Human Rights in November of the same year. The third reading and royal assent were completed in March 2012.

Sources: Government of Canada, 2011; Wikipedia, n.d.

FACTORS THAT INFLUENCE PUBLIC POLICY DECISIONS
Political Ideology
It is common for politicians to make decisions about public policies and assess policy instruments on the basis of their political inclinations. Members of the Conservative Party tend to prefer a small government and free market economy, and to select policy instruments that are less intrusive. Liberal and New Democratic Party members, on the other hand, generally lean toward more government regulation and are prepared to use interventional instruments. Nevertheless, once in power, politicians may deviate from their political ideology to maintain power. These compromises and dilutions of their ideological principles are especially common when in a minority government.

Popularity and Re-electability
Government popularity and re-electability is another factor politicians must consider when they review draft public policies. Because politicians in power often want to be re-elected, they are likely to endorse public policies that enable them to appear favourable to the public. Employing interventionist policy

instruments at the beginning of a term, with the expectation that their negative repercussions will be forgotten by the next election, is a common tactic in
Canadian politics. The Conservative Party in Alberta, led by Premier Ralph
Klein, perfected this model in the 1990s. Since then, other governments seem
to have followed its model of a quick succession of painful changes—layoffs,
budgetary cutbacks, program and service reductions, and the closing of agencies—during the first two years of their mandate, then doling out goodies to
voters—allocating more money to existing programs and services, announc-
ing new government initiatives, and giving out subsidies—during their last
two years.

Stakeholder Interests

One of the key factors to be considered by cabinet ministers when making
public policy decisions is how best to balance stakeholders' competing and
conflicting interests. Because public problems are connected to multiple
stakeholder groups—each of which has its own historical baggage, interests,
likes, and dislikes—public policy developers must balance their demands
and put forward placating bundles of policy options for ministers to consider. Cabinet ministers, due to their political ideologies, may favour one
stakeholder group over another, but they should expect resistance if a public
policy is skewed too much in favour of one group over another. Unless the
government is prepared to battle those groups that are offering resistance to
the policy, cabinet ministers should compromise and attempt to strike a balance among interests. To minimize resistance, the government may remain
firm in its choice of policy instruments as a strategic decision, but prepare to
compromise on tactical issues.

Stakeholder Power

The power of stakeholder groups is another factor that determines policy
options. Some shareholder groups, such as business associations and labour
unions, have strong networks of influence and power and do not hesitate to
make their bottom line known. Some of these groups have their own lobbyists
or public relations specialists who use media and other forms of influence to
get their messages across in an effort to sway the government's position on
policy issues. Under these circumstances, the government must deliberate
before using an interventional policy instrument, which may spur resistance
from these powerful groups. In contrast, stakeholder groups that have smaller

power bases, such as social assistance recipients, may not be able to strike back against coercive measures.

Organizational Readiness

The selection of a particular policy option may also be determined by the degree of organizational readiness to implement that particular policy instrument, also known as "technical efficiency" (Pal, 1992, pp. 163–164). Having an existing infrastructure and technical expertise in implementation reduces preparation time and false starts; it may also save money if the policy instrument requires only a minor extension or addition to the government or the institution that will carry it out. In times of fiscal constraint, any additional allocation of funds for new capital investment and implementation, or revamping the existing infrastructure, diminishes the attractiveness of a policy instrument.

Policy Impact

A policy's impact refers to how effective the policy instrument is at producing results consistent with the policy's goals. If a public policy's anticipated impact is high, then it will likely yield the expected results and heighten the reputation of the government. Pal (1992, p. 164) calls this factor "political efficiency," the importance of which cannot be overemphasized. Some public policies—after taking into account trade-offs among stakeholder groups, financial costs, and public perception—are very moderate in their use of policy instruments and are not expected to be very effective at solving public problems. Some policy instruments are utilized merely to give the impression that the government is doing something to address an identified public problem, but the methods chosen are not expected to have any substantial results. These empty actions are closer to symbolic gestures than substantial policies.

Financial Costs

The public problems that need to be resolved far outweigh the funds available to address them. Consider the broad range of programs and services that the government provides and the seemingly insatiable needs of the public, alongside the general aversion to high taxation. That is why the management board must review, assess, and approve all cost estimates for public policies prior to cabinet making a decision. The combination of an interest in neo-liberalism and a rising debt and deficit has heightened awareness of the financial commitments of our government. Politicians must be able to defend their decisions to implement new public policies and incur their financial costs.

FIGURE 9.5: FACTORS THAT INFLUENCE THE POLICY DECISION-MAKING PROCESS

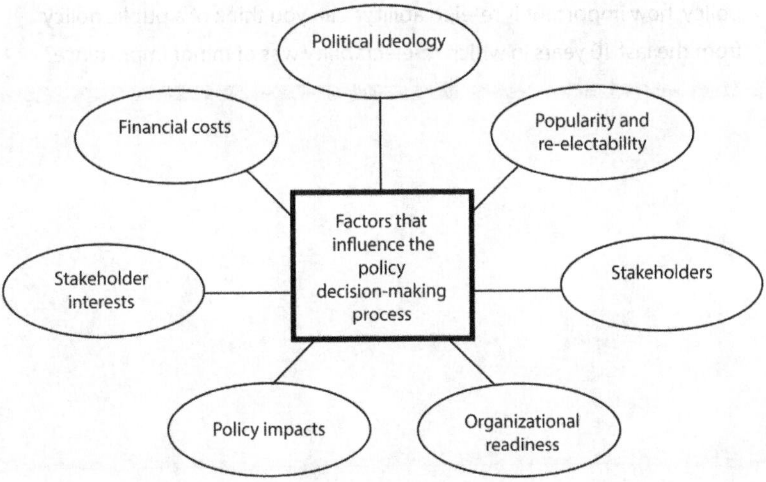

SUMMARY

The decision-making process is long, drawn out, and complicated, taking a public policy from a proposal by line department through the cabinet system to royal assent. Many people are involved in this process. It involves constant consultation and negotiation among central agencies and line departments in a series of collaborative yet competing activities among ministers and bureaucrats. When cabinet approves a public policy, and the bills or estimates have been tabled, the challenges and debates among political parties begin. The policy instruments chosen by ministers tend to be based on a political ideology, popularity, potential re-electability, stakeholder interests and power, organizational readiness, expected policy impact, and financial costs. Though every participant who comes in contact with a developing policy has a specific role and makes a substantial contribution, the cabinet of the ruling party is the most significant advancing agent of a public policy. Understanding the functions, weight, and configurations of all the elements involved helps clarify how public policies are made.

QUESTIONS FOR CRITICAL THINKING

1. Do some research to determine how the public policy decision-making process in the government is different from corporate policy-making in the private or non-profit sector. Why do you think these differences exist?

2. How does the government resolve the competing interests of internal line departments when finalizing a public policy for parliament to ratify?

3. Among all the factors for consideration by politicians in making a public policy, how important is re-electability? Can you think of a public policy from the last 10 years in which re-electability was of minor importance?

CONCLUSION

Public policy is an important way for governments to effect social change. Depending on the nature and comprehensiveness of a policy, it can have a long-lasting impact on people and society. As illustrated throughout this book, public policy developers make an important contribution to this process. Their application of multidisciplinary policy knowledge and skills assists in the proliferation of good and sound policies that positively impact the public. The experience of public policy developers is also invaluable. The skills and knowledge acquired through public policy work—such as familiarity with policy products, the principles of good public policy, awareness of special strategies and tactics used to identify policy issues, research skills, the construction of sensible policy options and recommendations, and cognizance of how the systems work—facilitate the process and ensure that policies are produced that benefit both the public and the government.

As public policy development is a very fluid process that is constantly evolving, an abstract idea has to take a long journey, fraught with twists, turns, and reversals, before it becomes a public policy. Most people have an abstract concept of what constitutes an ideal country or society and what the government can do to get there. Some of these concepts and ideas land on the desks of public policy developers or politicians; from there, they are implemented, shelved, or abandoned. Those that are taken under serious consideration are usually integrated with other ideas, but few make it to the end of the public policy development process.

The success of these ideas depends on the alignment of five factors (known as the *five stars of public policy development*): (a) the social context from which the idea arose; (b) the culture, traditions, values, and beliefs of the society; (c) the stakeholder dynamics; (d) the institutional arrangement; and (e) the decision-making process. If one of these factors does not align well with the others, the policy idea, which may be making its way toward ratification, will fall flat for an indefinite period. These five factors must co-exist for an idea to become a public policy, and the window for them to come into alignment is rather limited. These factors involve many players working under very different circumstances, restrained by numerous conditions (sometimes beyond their control) and representing various interests and power bases. The interplay of these variables makes it difficult to determine whether a policy idea will be ratified by the legislature, receive royal assent, and become a piece of legislation.

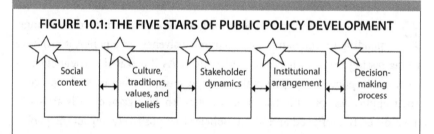

FIGURE 10.1: THE FIVE STARS OF PUBLIC POLICY DEVELOPMENT

Social context: An idea that arises from concrete evidence of a problem has a better chance of being noticed than one that is abstract. This is especially the case when a problem is perceived as growing, persistent, or having a negative effect on the population.

Culture, traditions, values, and beliefs: A potential policy idea must be compatible with a society's dominant culture and traditions, as well as with the prevailing values and beliefs of the time. Without that compatibility, the idea may face strong resistance. Despite this, not all ideas that are compatible or consistent with Canadian culture are bound to become public policies; cultural factors alone are not enough, unless they are reinforced by other institutional and political factors.

Stakeholder dynamics: The relationships among stakeholder groups, the public, and the government are key determinants in whether or not an idea becomes a public policy. To compete with other stakeholder groups for dominance and influence, each stakeholder group must (a) assess its own ideas in relation to those of other groups; (b) determine any benefits to forming alliances; and (c) identify the necessity of undermining other groups' ideas, networks, and power bases.

Institutional arrangement: The federal and provincial governments have different mandates and responsibilities, but their demarcations are often not clear. When an idea is considered for public policy development in relation to a jurisdiction, stakeholder groups must know which level of government has the mandate to deal with the subject matter. Once this is settled, the idea needs to be framed and packaged to fit the institutional arrangement (which includes the roles and responsibilities of specific institutions or departments, organizational directions and priorities, protocols, schedules, and administrative procedures).

Decision-making process: The federal and provincial governments have similar legislatures of elected politicians, cabinets, and central agencies, as well as a parallel structure of bureaucracy that supports the work of elected officials. The decision-making process can be reduced to the resolution of internal stakeholder groups' competing interests. Given the interests of numerous politicians and bureaucrats and the strategies or tactics used to support or undermine ideas, it is never easy to predict the outcome of a decision-making process.

As public policy developers are situated between internal and external stakeholder groups, they must be knowledgeable about institutional arrangements and the decision-making process. While a public policy developer is not in a position to influence the social context or the surrounding culture and value systems, he or she is strategically located in the development process to formulate public policies that balance the interests of various stakeholder groups, and to incorporate the various principles of good public policy. It should be noted that not all five stars will be aligned in the progress of every public policy idea.

The notion that politics and public policy do not mix is a misconception. The perception that public servants are there to serve elected politicians, irrespective of their political stripes, and that they must be apolitical, non-partisan, neutral, objective, or impartial in their policy work is false. A public policy developer must make some political decisions, including which stakeholder organizations to consult, which course of action to take after receiving direction from the minister or the cabinet office, and which policy options and recommendations to put forward. If public policy developers are not politically astute enough to understand the competing interests, rivalries, and power bases of both internal and external stakeholder groups, and to decipher the political implications of various policy ideas, then they may find themselves debilitated. Senior bureaucrats, government officials, and cabinet ministers expect their public policy developers to have some degree of political savvy to navigate the various negotiations that usually take place during the public policy development process, assess the marketability of different policy options and recommendations, and anticipate the implications of information that is communicated to the public.

A good public policy is defined by its achievement of the greatest public good. To achieve this, a policy must balance public interests and an accountability framework; accomplish its impacts as planned, and ensure these impacts are cost-effective and just; and balance short- and long-term considerations. Because there are many individuals and groups with competing interests and agendas involved in the process, the final public policy is destined to contain a mix of these ideas. Compromises are expected. As it is crucial to find agreement on the final version of a public policy, it may come at the cost of diluting one or more of these principles.

Predicting the outcome of a public policy development process is difficult. As outlined above, when the five stars of public policy development—social context; culture, traditions, values, and beliefs; stakeholder dynamics; institutional arrangements; and decision-making process—are aligned, there is an increased chance the specific public policy will come into fruition. However, as noted, there are various factors that may arise and interact with one another to derail the progress of an idea on its way to becoming a public policy. Once the public policy has been ratified, people outside the government—especially external stakeholder groups—are likely to see the product as a diluted version of their expectations that does not properly reflect their interests. However, if compromises had not been made and the principles had not been diluted, there is a good chance that the policy would not have been passed. Public expectation that a government can activate social change is high, as is the expectation that a public policy should be flawless. These expectations are often founded on an inadequate understanding of how government works and how a public policy is developed, which this book seeks to rectify.

There are many windows of opportunity for stakeholders and other interested parties to exert their influence on the development of a public policy. These windows are accessible through politicians and bureaucrats. On the political side, every elected politician can be approached by any member of the public; those in power have greater influence and insider connections. Given the structure of the cabinet system, ministers in cabinet have even more power than elected politicians to affect the development of public policies. Policy directions and decisions can be influenced at the level of politicians, but policy options and recommendations are better influenced at the bureaucrat level. On the bureaucratic side, deputy ministers have the advantage of being situated between the government bureaucrats and the ministers. This may translate into an immense advantage and power to influence, as they have both the trust of the ministers and the institutional memory of the bureaucrats at their disposal. Senior bureaucrats (assistant deputy ministers, executive directors, and senior managers) all wield influence over the public policy development process because they know how line departments work, and how to work with them.

Members of the public and stakeholder groups that are eager to exert their influence on the public policy development process should approach both the political and bureaucratic sides to start marketing their policy ideas. They should do so at the earliest possible stage in the development process, and will need to continue to liaise with both politicians and bureaucrats on a regular basis. It has been observed that knowing when, where, and how to exert influence on the development of public policies is important and has far-reaching implications. However, in spite of what we know of the public policy development process and the factors that influence this process, due to its fluid nature, we cannot confidently predict the outcome of a policy idea until it reaches its final stage, has passed all its readings, and has received royal assent.

POLICY PRODUCT EXERCISES

CORRESPONDENCE
Energy

SCENARIO

Under the *Green Energy Act,* the Government of Ontario has begun to develop renewable energy sources and encourage energy conservation. The government must upgrade old transmission lines and power plants. For a period of 5 years, electricity prices will rise by about 8 percent on an annual basis after which the government projects residential electricity bills will increase by an average of 3.5 percent per year over the next 20 years. This price increase is expected to contribute to infrastructure improvement and renewable energy generation, such as the construction of new hydroelectric projects.

Many homeowners are unenthusiastic about the projected increase in electricity costs, especially those living on a fixed income, and the current 10 percent rebate on electricity costs to homeowners from the government is simply not enough to pacify them.

A retired homeowner recently wrote a letter to the Minister of Energy expressing his concerns over rising monthly electricity bills. You are asked to draft a reply to the letter.

Dear Minister:

I write to express my concerns about rising electricity bills.

My wife and I recently retired and are living in a small town in northern Ontario. Though we try to be as self-sufficient as possible, we do not have much of a pension and depend on the Canadian Pension Plan and Old Age Security.

Rising electricity bills over the last few years have gradually eaten away at our savings and, based on your projection of the continual climb of electricity costs, the next 20 years will likely be worse for us.

Please tell us how we can support ourselves if the amount of electricity bills keeps on increasing. We can only put on so many layers of warm clothing to keep us from shivering in the long winters. We have already minimized our cooking time and insulated our walls and windows.

What are you doing to help people like us survive over the next 20 years?

Sincerely yours,
J. Smith
Timmins, Ontario

REQUIRED FORMAT
Draft a reply in response to the above letter. The Minister of Energy will sign your reply, so it must be professional and respectful. Limit your reply to one page. The letter should include reference to the government's commitment to green energy and the long-term sustainability of the province, as well as to some of the initiatives that the government is planning to roll out to alleviate the hardship that many retired people and low-income earners experience. Information provided in this letter has to be accurate and up-to-date. The tone of the letter should be empathetic and helpful.

BRIEFING NOTE
Employment and Youth

SCENARIO

The federal Minister of Human Resources and Skills Development Canada is attending a meeting with a number of youth organizations this afternoon regarding the dismal state of employment for young people. Although the overall unemployment rate has been decreasing for the last two years, youth employment statistics indicate that prospects remain bleak for those under 25 years old across Canada.

In accordance with the fiscal restraint agenda of the federal government, the minister has decided that over 300 student employment centres across the country will be closed and replaced by online tools, which some student associations have openly criticized as not useful. Given that the average student-loan debt in Canada is almost $27,000, students are concerned about their future job prospects, especially in light of the federal government's recent announcement.

As a policy advisor, you are asked to provide a one-page, single-spaced briefing note to the minister on this matter two hours from now.

REQUIRED FORMAT

Your briefing note should adhere to the following headings and format:

1. *Title:* State the topic of the briefing note in fewer than 10 words. This section is usually written after the briefing note is completed to ensure that the title is a short but accurate description of the document contents.

2. *Issue:* Identify the issue and summarize it in one short sentence in the form of a question. An issue can be framed in a number of different ways; here you must determine whether the issue is the closing of youth employment centres, the high youth unemployment rate, exorbitant student loans, or the future of youth in Canada. You must frame the issue in such a way that the minister can answer the

question based on the evidence and information you provide in the briefing note.

3. *Background:* Provide information by answering the following suggested questions concisely. Answer each question in one sentence.

- What are the current national unemployment rates for adults and youth?
- What is the historical pattern of unemployment rates over the past five years?
- How does the Canadian youth unemployment rate compare with those in other OECD (Organisation for Economic Co-operation and Development) countries?
- What programs has the federal government implemented to help youth gain employment?
- What are the performance records of these programs in alleviating Canada's youth unemployment problems?

4. *Current update:* Provide information in this section by answering the following questions as they relate to the identified issue. Answer each question in one sentence.

- What is the federal government planning to do to strengthen Canada's economy?
- What specific programs or initiatives is the federal government planning to implement in an effort to lower the unemployment rates of both adults and youth in Canada?
- What investment is the federal government planning to make in the future of youth?

5. *Summary:* Summarize the current position of the federal government regarding the employment of Canadians, especially that of young people, in one or two bullet points.

HOUSE BOOK NOTE
Environment

SCENARIO

One of Environment Canada's mandates is the protection of the natural environment. For this reason, environmentalists are likely to target this department when they perceive that the federal government is not doing enough to protect the environment.

Concern has been expressed about the potential environmental harm that could be caused by the transportation of unrefined oil from Alberta through British Columbia to the Pacific Ocean via Enbridge's proposed pipeline. Enbridge's initiative is the result of the postponement of the Keystone XL pipeline, which would have gone through Nebraska, by the Obama government to allow further environmental study. The proposed route from Alberta to the coast of British Columbia covers many acres of land and waterways. Environmentalists claim that an oil spill along this route could be disastrous to the environment. In addition, much of the potentially affected land belongs to Aboriginal groups, many of which are gravely concerned about such a possibility.

Locals and their supporters have launched a campaign condemning this idea and are pressuring the federal government to abandon it. They are organizing a rally in front of Parliament and a demonstration in downtown Ottawa tomorrow at noon.

To prepare the Minister of Environment Canada for this protest and question period in the House of Commons, you are asked to prepare a one-page House book note on this issue.

REQUIRED FORMAT

1. *Issue:* Identify the key issue(s) and pose them in the form of a question (or questions). As each issue will determine the kind of information you have to collect and present to the minister, the framing of the issue is pivotal. Each issue requires a separate House book note, so that the minister is clear on the recommended responses.

2. *Recommended responses:* Prepare the most appropriate response to the identified issue. The recommended responses should be clear, as they may be used for media purposes. These responses should answer the following questions:

- What has the government done to alleviate the concerns of the environmentalists and those living in the areas through which the proposed pipeline would be constructed?
- What plan has the government put in place to tackle their concerns?

3. *Background:* Answer the following questions succinctly. Bullet points (in full sentences) are acceptable.

- What are the recent milestones in the issue of transporting unrefined (bituminous sand) oil in Canada?
- What are the key concerns of environmentalists and Aboriginal communities with regards to this matter?
- What actions have environmentalists and Aboriginal communities taken to make their concerns heard on this matter?
- What are the concerns of other stakeholder groups, including the oil industry?
- What are the key legislative requirements and guidelines related to this issue?
- What has Environment Canada done to address this matter?
- How has the media covered this matter so far?
- What are some popular public opinions on this matter?

DECISION NOTE
Education and Aboriginal Affairs

SCENARIO

Educational matters largely fall under provincial and municipal jurisdiction; however, the federal government plays a significant role in the education of Aboriginal peoples. On paper, the federal government is committed to making sure that Aboriginal children and youth receive the same quality of education as other Canadians.

Some Aboriginal communities that claim their children receive poorer-quality education than non-Aboriginal children are challenging this commitment. Among other serious grievances, some Aboriginal children attend school in portables (regularly criticized for their low-quality construction) that have no running water, libraries, or computers. A perceived asymmetry is the capping of federal education funding to Aboriginal schools at 2 percent since 1996, while the federal funds for provincial education have been increasing by more than 2 percent annually.

Aboriginal youth groups, and organizations that support them, have been requesting the attention of the minister in charge of Aboriginal Affairs and Northern Development Canada (AANDC) in an attempt to set up a meeting. Under the direction of the minister's office, the AANDC's policy division has been instructed to develop some options for consideration for how best to tackle this serious and devastating reality. A decision note is required to facilitate the decision-making process of the minister on the quality of on-reserve federally funded education.

REQUIRED FORMAT

A decision note is usually one single-spaced page, consisting of four major headings. This one-page limit ensures that the note will be concise and specific; it is not uncommon for a document longer than one page to be returned to its submitter for revision.

1. *Issue:* Identify the issue and pose it as a succinct question.

2. *Background:* In bullet points, answer the following questions and add new ones if appropriate and relevant:

- What is the current federal government funding arrangement for Aboriginal education for children and young people on reserves?
- Are there any regional variations in federal government funding?
- What are the current conditions under which these federal funds are provided?
- What is the current operational arrangement of schools on First Nations land?
- What is the current condition of facilities, equipment, curricula, and other quality issues related to education at these schools?
- What programs are currently in place to ensure the quality of on-reserve education?
- What concerns have Aboriginal communities voiced regarding education for children and youth?
- What demands or suggestions have they put forward so far?
- What are the viewpoints of other major stakeholder groups on this issue?

3. *Options:* In this section, three options are usually put forward for consideration. These recommendations should be realistic and resolve some, if not all, of the key concerns of the communities seeking an improvement to on-reserve education. These options must provide a feasible range of solutions to resolve the identified issue. They should be arranged in a gradational manner, for example, from most to least effective. It is critical to avoid advising inaction to the minister.

Following the principles suggested in chapter 5, each one of these options must provide several meaningful pros and cons for the minister to consider. These pros and cons may document the research findings of public policy developers on this matter and reflect their educated judgments on the benefits or risks of the options. Some of the advantages and disadvantages may include information on operational costs, potential results, legislative or program implications, potential reactions from stakeholder groups, political factors, or jurisdictional, federal, and provincial ramifications. Number your options and state each one in a full, but short, sentence. Each option should be followed by a list of pros and cons (commonly one to four); the essence and brevity of each can be best captured as a bullet point.

4. *Recommendation:* The public policy developer should identify one of the options as the most sensible decision the federal government can implement. It is only necessary for the public policy developer to state the recommended option number in this section. He or she may combine two or more options in the recommendation, but may not put forward a recommendation that has not been stated in the decision note. While this section does not require the public policy developer to present his or her rationale for the recommendation, it is important that he or she be able to defend the recommendation in a professional manner when asked.

E X E R C I S E 5

RESEARCH PLAN
Training and Persons with Disabilities

SCENARIO

Each provincial government has a ministry responsible for skill training; its mandate includes strengthening the economy by researching, supporting, and assisting in raising the literacy level of residents. Most research activities are conducted by external centres outside the government, many of which have a special focus.

You are asked to prepare a research plan in collaboration with a university research centre on literacy training for persons with learning disabilities. The university's research findings show a large gap in the knowledge base regarding the literacy training needs for persons with different types of learning disabilities, and the availability of training experts and facilities.

There is ample statistical data on the conditions of unemployment and poverty for people living with a range of different learning disabilities. Because a significant portion of the Canadian population has problems with numeracy, literacy, and computer skills, current training programs are largely customized to able-bodied adults who have not completed the ninth grade. There still remains a gap in data regarding the availability of qualified teachers, effective curricula, generative teaching materials, and facilities that would maximize knowledge acquisition for people with learning disabilities.

REQUIRED FORMAT

There are no length requirements for a research plan; however, in a government environment, the shorter, the better—a two-page plan should be sufficient.

1. *Research topic:* Literacy training for people with learning disabilities is the research topic; however, given the broadness of this subject, it may be beneficial to narrow the scope of the inquiry to something more specific.

2. *Research purposes:* Determine the scope and purpose of the research to ensure that the presentation of it is manageable.

3. *Methodology:* Describe the core research questions and research methods needed to achieve the answers to these questions. List all the major areas that you need information about and the names of organizations or experts you need to contact.

4. *Researchers:* List all researchers involved in this project. As this is a collaborative research project, define the role of each player and the time frame of their involvement. Identify the team's lead researcher.

5. *Timetable:* Determine the number of weeks or months needed to complete the research and write the research report. Prepare a realistic schedule of research activities and, based on the allocated time frame as stipulated by political constraints, determine what can potentially be accomplished.

6. *Budget:* Based on the scope of the research and the human resources required, prepare a research budget.

7. *Sources of funding:* If money is needed for the research, identify the funding sources and whether or not they have been secured.

8. *Deliverables:* Describe what will be provided upon the implementation of this research plan—for example, a report, a verbal briefing, or a collection of resource materials on the subject matter.

RESEARCH PAPER
Tourism

SCENARIO

The provincial ministry responsible for tourism has a priority to conduct research on and ameliorate the relationship between tourism and the economic welfare of an area. You are asked to prepare a research paper on models of growth in tourism by analyzing data that suggests the number of tourists and visitor inquiries in your jurisdiction have been diminishing. A variety of explanations have been put forward, including the currency exchange rate, the lack of marketing both domestically and abroad, and the lack of tourist attractions. The historical reliance on American tourists may also be a factor for consideration.

To strengthen tourism, the ministry has requested that you conduct research on several aspects of the industry, including the projected outlook for tourism over the next five years, as well as cross-jurisdictional models of invigoration, their success and risk factors, and their applicability to the area in which you are working.

REQUIRED FORMAT

There are no length requirements for a research paper—20 to 50 single-spaced pages would be reasonable.

1. *Executive summary:* This section should be written last, as it summarizes the key findings and analysis of the subject matter.

2. *Introduction:* Provide the context for this research project: Why is tourism important to the economy, and why is the government interested in finding out how best to integrate it into the larger economy? You should also describe the core questions, scope, and presentation format in this section.

3. *Research focus:* State the key research questions and outline the research methods that will be used to find the answers to these ques-

tions. Describe the scope of the research by stating the specific areas of research, and the time periods and cities/regions it will cover.

4. *Research findings:*

(a) *Current status of provincial tourism:* Present and analyze data on the major indicators required to answer the core questions. Some cross-jurisdictional comparisons may be helpful, and this may give the minister a better sense of how the performance of your jurisdiction compares to others. You will be expected to explain why the province under examination is not doing well.

(b) *Models of tourism:* Present information on how other jurisdictions in Canada and elsewhere have developed their tourism industries. Report the role of the government in each case and identify best practices.

Transnational models of tourism are not easy to obtain, as there is limited information available on the Internet, and at libraries and embassies. If adequate research funds are available, a fact-finding mission abroad may be a successful way to gather information.

(c) *Applicability:* After collecting relevant information on different models of tourism, you are expected to analyze it and delineate the degree of applicability of one or more of these models. This may require an analysis of the political, economic, social, and organizational prerequisites for each model to ascertain whether or not they exist in your jurisdiction. An analysis of the risk factors embedded in the models and the financial costs for the provincial government should be provided.

5. *Conclusion:* In this section, you are expected to come to a conclusion about the applicability of these models, along with their anticipated success and risk factors.

6. *Appendices:* Attach detailed methodological issues, complex statistical tables, and lists of key resource materials, experts, and organizations consulted.

DISCUSSION PAPER
Health Care

SCENARIO

The federal government has introduced a new federal transfer of payment for health care. Transfers are to be grown at 6 percent per year for five years; after that, increases will be tied to the growth of nominal gross domestic product. Some provinces and territories have accepted this financial arrangement. Your province has not, and the provincial government maintains that such an arrangement will result in funding cuts to health care support and services. Containing the escalation of health care costs is a major concern.

Due to an aging population, the escalating costs of operating health care facilities and providing services, the continued frustration that people feel about health care received, and the perceived ineffectiveness of health care management, you have been asked to prepare a discussion paper on how to reduce the reliance on federally funded care by diverting non–medically essential needs to community care services. The intended audience of this discussion paper is the internal stakeholder groups within the provincial government—health care, community and social services, intergovernmental affairs, and all the central agencies.

In your discussion paper, you are to explore the connection between hospital and community care, specifically how the community (including the family system) can make a contribution to health care services by unloading some of these services from the hospital sector to the community sector. One-quarter of health care resources are employed by the elderly in the last few months or weeks of their lives. It is believed that, given the choice, the vast majority of Canadians would not choose to die in a hospital environment; if we accept this notion, then it may be reasonable to allocate some end-of-life support to community services or family members. This deinstitutionalization would alleviate the financial burden on the federal health care system, as well as improve quality of life for terminal patients. A careful review of literature and an analysis of the current interface between the hospital and community sectors should provide the government with an insight on how to move the health care sector forward.

REQUIRED FORMAT

While there are no strict length or formatting requirements for a discussion paper, 10 to 20 single-spaced pages is acceptable.

1. *Executive summary:* Write this section last, as it should consist of the key elements considered in the discussion paper. It is usually a half to a full page in length.

2. *Introduction:* Provide a description of the nature of this discussion paper. Include background information on the health care system, some key issues of historical importance, and the role of this discussion paper in the overall process of the public policy development.

3. *Historical background:* Here you should include the current federal financial arrangement, the provincial government's financial situation and its allocation of funds to health care, the interests of stakeholder groups, and the social, economic, and cultural contexts of this dilemma.

4. *Current arrangement in the province:* Describe what services the community sector provides, as well as what the local government has done to bridge the gap between federally funded health care and community programs and services. Analyze the strengths and weaknesses of the current system.

5. *Current models in other jurisdictions:* What are other jurisdictions doing to assist in the interaction between hospital and community care sectors? How has their collaboration been implemented? How extensive and successful is the relationship between these two sectors? How successful has their coalescence been? What are the risks involved in bringing the two together? How applicable is the current interaction model to your jurisdiction?

6. *Discussion issues:* Identify and analyze issues related to policy direction, cost, institutional arrangements, and social and cultural readiness, and their implications.

7. *Summary:* Highlight the models discussed and their related issues.

PUBLIC CONSULTATION PLAN
Internet Gaming

SCENARIO

The legalization of provincial lotteries in the 1970s was envisioned as a potential source of revenue, a stimulus to local economies, and a development aid to communities. These remain the primary reasons for the government's involvement in the gaming industry. Gaming has increasingly become an important source of revenue for the government—a method of revenue some segments of the population prefer over increased taxation.

While the social and economic benefits of gaming remain debatable, your provincial government has requested that you determine public receptiveness to gaming and ideas concerning government regulation of Internet gaming through public consultation. A public consultation plan is in order.

REQUIRED FORMAT

There are no length requirements for a public consultation paper; however, 10 to 20 single-spaced pages is reasonable.

1. *Purpose of public consultation:* Clearly describe the purpose of this public consultation, and ensure that all aspects of the public consultation plan are developed in alignment with the purpose(s).

2. *Major topics for consultation:* There are many aspects of online gaming that the government is interested in ascertaining the popular opinion of, including the regulation responsibilities of suppliers and operators; the protection measures available to consumers; the testing standards of equipment; the development of operational standards; and the types and levels of monitoring, assessment, investigation, enforcement, and sanctions. You will need to narrow down the list of these topics for consultation and ensure that the rest of the planning is consistent with the scope of the topics, including the allocation of time and materials.

3. *Major stakeholder groups to be consulted:* Stakeholder groups related to Internet gaming should be consulted; in this section, list the name and contact details of each relevant group. Outreach efforts should be included in the plan.

4. *Consultation methods:* Specify how the public should be consulted. Consider focus groups, town hall meetings, interviews, social media, and other methods.

5. *Geographic locations of consultation:* List the cities, towns, or re-serves where the public consultation sessions will take place. Provide a rationale for your selection.

6. *Schedule of consultation:* Identify the most appropriate time period for the public consultation to take place. Provide a rationale for your selection. It is important to note religious holidays for some stake-holders or groups.

7. *Format of consultation:* Outline the consultation format. What are the agenda items, protocols, and procedures that the facilitator will follow?

8. *Coordination committee:* Recommend and identify the positions of the people who should sit on the coordination committee. Committee members are usually public servants.

9. *Major operational logistics:* Identify all major logistics that are required to make this public consultation a success, including, for example, the size of the venues, seating pattern, electronic devices required, refresh-ments, stenographer, and accommodation measures.

10. *Materials for public distribution:* Describe the types of materials required for public distribution before, during, and/or after the public consultation.

11. *Communication strategy:* Develop a communication strategy that takes into consideration all of the key components of this plan, in-cluding the consultation purposes and schedule.

12. *Expected results and deliverables:* List all expected results of the public consultation, including media coverage, and tangible or intangible deliverables.

13. *Government representatives:* Identify the positions of the government representatives who will be present at the consultation sessions and the roles that they will play.

14. *Budget:* Prepare a realistic budget that covers the operational costs of conducting this public consultation in a manner that is consistent with the scope and complexity outlined in the plan. Identify funding sources and state whether funding has been secured or not.

PUBLIC CONSULTATION PAPER
Immigration

SCENARIO

Canada is a land of immigrants. In the last few decades, immigration has assumed great importance because, among other reasons, much of our economic growth depends on immigrants. However, in spite of an increased target number of immigrants permitted each year and an effort to make finding jobs related to their credentials easier for recent immigrants, there are still some persistent issues that Canada has to wrestle with.

One major issue is the interminable wait time for immigration applications to be processed. The federal government's target range of 240,000 to 265,000 immigrants admitted into Canada per year remained unchanged between 2006 and 2013 (Citizenship and Immigration Canada, 2012). Officials are responsible for matching skilled newcomers with provincial demands to prevent the unemployment of highly educated and professionally trained individuals. Officials must endeavour to create an alignment between the skills and work experiences that the Canadian economy needs and the arrival of immigrants with these skills and experiences.

Due to a lack of alignment between regional demands and placement of skilled immigrant workers to meet those demands, Citizenship and Immigration Canada has requested that you prepare a public consultation paper in the interest of finding new solutions to this problem. The strategy is to have a multi-pronged research approach to diagnose this persistent issue by pooling the observations and experiences of other jurisdictions, experts, stakeholder groups, and the general public.

REQUIRED FORMAT

There are no page requirements for a public consultation paper, but a 10- to 20-page, single-spaced paper is reasonable.

1. *Letter from the minister:* You are asked to draft a one-page letter from the minister responsible for immigration to be placed at the beginning

of this public consultation paper. The letter should provide a brief background of the persistent immigration issues and explain why the federal government has undertaken a public consultation. The letter should also encourage people to participate in the consultation.

2. *Executive summary:* Provide a summary of the immigration issues and the significance of the timing of this public consultation. This section should be written last so that it accurately reflects the contents of the paper.

3. *Background:* Write a summary of Canada's immigration history, its importance to the country's economy and culture, the contributions of immigrants, the current immigration system, and the immigration-related issues that Canada is confronting.

4. *Immigration issues for consultation:* In this section, several immigration issues should be identified for public consultation. For example:

Issue 1: There is a long list of immigration applicants and an abysmally slow processing time.

Issue 2: There are problems related to matching immigrants with provincial needs.

Issue 3: There are limited employment opportunities for highly educated and skilled immigrants.

Issue 4: There is a lack of alignment between the skills needed and the arrival time of immigrants with those skills.

Explain why these issues have been selected for consultation. Each issue should be numbered, and followed by four sections: background (including social context), questions for consultation (the questions the federal government would like answered), things to consider, and possible approaches. The final section will be broken up into subsections that differentiate the various approaches that the federal government is considering.

Example: *Issue 1:* There is a long list of immigration applicants and an abysmally slow processing time.

Background

Questions for consultation

Things to consider
Possible approaches
    Approach A
    Approach B
    Approach C

5. *Conclusion:* Briefly describe what the federal government intends to do with the results of this consultation, and how these results will become an integral part of the development of a public policy on this matter. The conclusion should also include the contact information of the communication coordinator for people who wish to participate in the consultation process.

STAKEHOLDER CONSULTATION PAPER
International Trade

SCENARIO

The Canadian and American economies are closely connected, as 85 to 90 percent of Canada's exports are delivered to the United States. The federal government, beginning with Trudeau's search for the Third Option (trading partners outside of the United States and Europe), has made some effort to minimize Canada's reliance on the American economy, without much success. Driven by the stagnating US economy and the destabilized financial situation of the European Union, the current federal government is looking to broaden its international trading partners by exploring its relationship with India, China, and emerging markets in Eastern Europe and South America.

Strengthening trade relations with countries outside of the United States and Western Europe requires additional considerations. The federal government is interested in the Trans-Pacific Partnership, which includes countries with coasts on the Pacific Ocean. Canada is attempting to ease itself into a trade arena in which there is a lot of competing business from Europe, Japan, and Australia.

To find a new direction in international trade for Canada, the federal government must first deal with some domestic challenges, including the powerful influence of the agricultural sector (which is interested in protecting its traditional base), the relative inexperience of Canadian businesses in trading with Asian countries, and the general lack of an international mindset and cultural etiquette among Canadian businesses, as these may be the factors that slow the expansion of international trade. Agricultural subsidy (for dairy and poultry farmers in Canada) is an issue that some of these countries adamantly oppose. One of the challenges for the federal government is to find a solution for ending agricultural subsidies, or to convince opposing parties of the Trans-Pacific Partnership that agricultural subsidies should not be a determining factor in international trade agreements.

As a public policy developer working for the Department of Foreign Affairs and International Trade, you are asked to prepare a stakeholder consultation paper on the topic of developing international trading relations in Asia. The target groups of the consultation are small, medium, and large Canadian companies. The purpose of the consultation is to identify specific areas in which the federal government can help increase the international marketability of Canadian industry. It is an opportunity for members of the business sector to voice their opinions, participate, and provide suggestions.

REQUIRED FORMAT

There are no length requirements for a stakeholder consultation paper, but 20 to 30 single-spaced pages should suffice. There are a variety of ways to structure a consultation paper, depending on the subject matter. The format outlined below fits the purpose of this particular topic:

1. *Open letter from the minister:* Draft a letter for the minister's signature to be attached as an open introduction to the consultation paper. The contents may include the background of why the federal government is focusing on this issue of international trade now, and what the government has done so far. It should also present the reasons a consultation with stakeholder groups is important. The letter should end by urging stakeholder groups to take this opportunity to participate in the consultation process and provide a point of contact for those who wish to participate.

2. *Executive summary:* Summarize the consultation framework and the important consultation issues. It is best to write this section after the entire consultation paper is completed.

3. *Context of international trade:* Provide a few paragraphs on the changing context of international trade, what other countries are doing, Canadian performance in this area, and the growing importance of international trade.

4. *Why Asian trading now?* Provide, in clear terms, the reasons Canada is now focusing on branching out into growing markets in Asia, in addition to European and American markets. Summarize the benefits and challenges for Canada.

5. *Asian trade issues for consultation:* Put forward three key issues for Canada when trading with Asian countries that the federal government and the business sector must work together to resolve. Briefly provide the context in which the issue arises, an explanation of why Canada has been slow to get involved in trade in Asia, and what the federal government has done so far to augment Canada's role in international trade. Pose one or more questions for the stakeholder groups to think about, and ask them to consider a number of related factors. These factors could be economic, social, technical, cultural, or political. To facilitate the stakeholder groups to provide concrete answers to the consultation questions, you are asked to put forward three approaches for people to think about. These approaches are proposed options from the federal government for stakeholder groups to consider. They are to be written in a specific manner—broad enough to stimulate discussions without giving the impression that the government has already made up its mind. Each issue should be numbered, and followed by four sections: background, questions for consultation, things to consider, and possible approaches. The final section will be broken up into subsections that differentiate the various approaches that the federal government is considering.

Example: *Issue 1*

Background

Questions for consultation

Things to consider

Possible approaches

Approach A

Approach B

Approach C

6. *Conclusion:* Write a few paragraphs describing what the federal government intends to do with the results of consultation, and the general process of developing this subject matter further. Include contact information for people or groups who wish to participate in the consultation process.

CABINET SUBMISSION
Equity and Women

SCENARIO

Establishing equality between men and women has been on the political agenda of the Canadian government for decades. It has led to the implementation of many programs and initiatives to create parity between the life chances of women and men in education, employment, health care, family relations, social participation, and political engagement. Some have been successful, but others have not. The implementation of federal employment equity for the benefit of women has been an ongoing focus for the past three decades; however, none of the provincial governments have a full-blown employment equity program in place. In spite of the apparent failure in Ontario to entrench its social justice effects, there has been some progress in increasing the employment of women in a number of areas (including professional, managerial, and non-traditional technical and trade occupations), accompanied by advances in post-secondary education. This is not enough.

Women are still marginalized among major institutional decision-making circles, namely on boards of directors. A 2012 study released by Catalyst Canada showed that only 14.5 percent of board directors of the 500 largest public sector organizations, Crown corporations, and private companies are women. There has not been much progress in the representation rate for women since 2009. Approximately 40 percent of these boards are still composed entirely of men, with no female participants (Eichler, 2012, p. B17). There are indications that women are making headway into boardrooms, but the rate of progress is glacial (McFarland, 2009, pp. B1, B8; Eichler, 2011, p. B18). At this rate, it has been estimated that it will take 120 years before women reach parity with men on the boards of directors in Canada's 300 largest publicly traded companies (Robertson and McFarland, 2011, pp. B1, B5). The drive to have more women on the boards of directors is the topic of this cabinet submission.

Your provincial government is convinced of the effectiveness of a legislative approach to gender equality, but it is quite cognizant of the lack of public appetite for a quota system in Canada. The failed implementation of a legislative approach to employment equity in Ontario in the 1990s taught politicians that no matter how noble the cause, without proper and adequate investment in public education and stakeholders' buy-in, it is difficult to gain public acceptance.

The proportion of women in Canada's boardrooms is similar to that of European Union member countries (currently 13.7 percent) in which only voluntary measures are in action. Experientially, voluntary measures yield negligible results for gender equality in the boardroom. Consider that after years of urging the private sector to increase the proportion of women on their corporate boards without much success, Norway passed legislation in 2003 to implement a mandated quota system for women on boards of public companies to rectify the situation—it was legislated that 40 percent of the members of each corporate board must be women. By 2009, 40 percent of board members in public limited, state- and municipality-owned, and co-operative companies in Norway were women. This success is based largely on tough government sanctions, the implementation of databases on which women and companies can register, and the launch of training programs. France, Germany, Spain, Iceland, Sweden, the Netherlands, and Australia are reviewing similar policies and some have already committed to these policy changes (Storvik and Teigen, 2010).

As a public policy developer working in the ministry responsible for women's advancement, you are asked to prepare a cabinet submission on legislating organizations in the broader public and private sector, under provincial jurisdiction, to institute a quota system for the number of women on their boards of directors.

REQUIRED FORMAT

A cabinet submission document should be as concise as possible, containing only core information. While there are no length requirements for a cabinet submission, 10 to 20 single-spaced pages is satisfactory.

> 1. *Executive summary:* This section should be written after you have completed the rest of the submission. In a few short sentences, summarize (in 100 words or less) the nature of your policy proposal on gender parity for boards of directors. Include the government's commitment and the policy rationale, as well as the expected impacts, related facts, and costs.

2. *Summary of cabinet decisions:* This section should summarize gender parity as the object of cabinet's approval, and provide its reasons for supporting this movement and the government's commitment to ensuring the success of this endeavour.

3. *Recommendation to cabinet:* Outline background information (such as events, issues, and consultations) that has led to the proposal, the recommendation, and the rationale in support of this decision. Be sure to report major delivery issues, such as delivery agents, timelines, expected outcomes, methods of monitoring, evaluation and communication, and management related to this cabinet submission.

4. *Alternative options:* State all other policy options and their pros and cons. Explain why they are not recommended.

5. *Legislative and regulatory plan:* Some government policies require a new piece of legislation. State the legislative or regulatory plan for gender parity, if it is to be implemented.

6. *Financial analysis:* Provide a cost estimate for the recommended action of instituting gender parity on boards. What are the financial implications for revenue, human resources, and other ministries and governments involved? Describe the impact on the operation of different government services such as labour relations, information technology, and diversity. Furthermore, describe the economic impact of the recommended action on economic growth, stakeholder groups, and regions involved.

7. *Factors for consideration:* Outline the potential risks to the workforce, business, finance, and productivity anticipated in approving the recommended action, and a strategy to address those risks. Include a government strategy to deal with stakeholder groups' reactions to the recommended action. Put forward the consultations undertaken by other ministries and the impacts the recommended actions have had on other ministries. Answer any questions on jurisdictional alignments, such as comparing what other jurisdictions are doing to deal with this problem. Finally, address any legal or constitutional implications related to the implementation of this submission.

8. *Communication:* This section should outline the communication strategy for the approved government actions. This strategy should include how the government should position itself, what media will be used, and what communication messages will be approved.

CABINET PRESENTATION
Telecommunication

SCENARIO

The telecommunication sector has long been protected through government-imposed foreign ownership restrictions. In Canada, several large players dominate this sector, notably Rogers Communications, Telus, and Bell Canada Enterprises; a few small players, such as Mobilicity and Wind Mobile, are also involved. Due to their lack of large capital, among other factors, these small players cannot compete effectively with the large ones.

The federal government is interested in developing a new policy on allowing non-Canadians to invest in the telecommunication sector, including the purchase of smaller domestic wireless companies. At the time of developing this policy, the law limits foreign investment in small telecommunication firms to no more than 46 percent. These small firms have a combined national market share of only 4 percent in the wireless sector.

If the government loosens federal rules on foreign ownership, these small firms may have an influx of international capital, which would allow them to compete more efficaciously with the larger players, but it may also make it difficult for the latter to provide services to a fragmented market or rural areas. These implications are to be considered by public policy developers, as well as issues related to how much foreign capital is allowed to penetrate the telecommunication sector and how much of a company's shares foreign capital can purchase.

As a public policy developer working for Industry Canada, you are asked to prepare a verbal presentation to the cabinet on a proposed new policy for foreign investment in telecommunication companies. This new policy is based on a cabinet submission on the same topic.

REQUIRED FORMAT

The verbal presentation of the cabinet submission may be done in PowerPoint format. This format consists of a deck of slides that contains the key points of the cabinet submission. As cabinet ministers (with the exception of the Minister of Industry Canada) may not have an intimate knowledge of the telecommunication sector, the terminology used in the slides must be simple and colloquial. Ten to twenty slides are usually optimal for this type of presentation. Each slide should contain no more than six lines and the font size should be large. The following is an example of the material addressed in a cabinet presentation:

Slide 1—*Proposal:* In one or two clear, short sentences, state what the ministry is seeking cabinet's approval for.

Slide 2—*Government commitment:* Quote any written government commitment on the subject matter.

Slide 3—*Rationale for government action:* Explain why the government needs to take policy action now on this particular subject, and the implications for the country if the federal government does not act now.

Slides 4–6—*Recommendation:* Outline the policy proposal and give reasons for its necessity.

Slides 7–8—*Delivery:* How will the government deliver the recommended policy? What is the time frame? What are the expected results? How many people will be affected? What will be monitored, measured, and assessed upon implementation?

Slides 9–10—*Assessment and mitigation of risks:* Identify the key risks for the government. What are the impacts of these risks and how are they addressed?

Slide 11—*Additional options:* Outline the alternative options that have been considered. What are their pros and cons? Consider their risks, outcomes, impacts, financial implications, benefits, and anticipated stakeholder group reactions. Explain why these options are not being recommended to the cabinet.

Slides 12–13—*Financial implications:* Note the funding source and the amount (broken down by capital and operational costs) involved in the effectuation of the new policy. Identify the revenue implications, if any. Include a cost-benefit analysis and value-for-money analysis. Identify the impacts on the government's workforce. In presenting these analyses, it is best to arrange them by year.

Slide 14—*Economic implications:* Identify the implications of the recommended actions on the telecommunication sector, the Canadian economy, consumers, corporate competitiveness, and job creation.

Slides 15–16—*Communication:* Describe the communication strategy related to the recommended government actions, including positioning, messaging, expected reactions from stakeholder groups and the public, and implications for other government programs. Identify primary and secondary target groups for communication, and their special communication instruments or media channels.

MANAGEMENT BOARD SUBMISSION
Education and Men

SCENARIO

The post-secondary education sector is undergoing a major demographic shift. In the 1960s and 1970s, students in colleges and universities were disproportionately male. However, in the last few decades the proportion of men and women has been reversed, with an average of three women for every two men among undergraduates. In Canada, gender parity was reached at the undergraduate level in 1987 and at the master's level in 1997. Women now account for 46 percent of PhD candidates (Church, 2009, pp. A1, A5).

Studies have shown that women have higher educational aspirations than men while in high school. This does not necessarily mean that they will pursue post-secondary degrees; nonetheless, this adolescent ambition has some effect on women in Canada. The formative years of high school are crucial for both men and women in setting the stage for their entry to higher education. The government must develop a policy to encourage male students to improve their academic performance and learning experiences, and to continue their education after high school. Otherwise, the trend of skewed post-secondary enrolment for men will continue and may have implications for Canada's labour force, productivity, family relations, and global competitiveness.

Reversing this skewed post-secondary enrolment will require efforts in high schools. These efforts should be built on the following recommendations, included in the Hospital for Sick Children's report *Early School Leavers: Understanding the Lived Reality of Student Disengagement from Secondary School* (2005):

- provide an academic coaching program for those with below-average academic performances
- create an enhanced reading and writing program
- implement a special professional development program for teachers and school counsellors in an effort to address gender-related education issues

- introduce an enhanced career education for students
- develop a special rescue program for disengaged youth and potential school leavers
- encourage and facilitate a joint orientation program between high schools and colleges or universities
- encourage and facilitate a joint mentoring program between high schools and colleges or universities

This package of programs has to be budgeted and documented in the form of a management board submission. As a public policy developer in the ministry responsible for education, you are asked to prepare a management board submission on this new program package to be implemented in schools to encourage male students to stay in school and improve their academic performances.

REQUIRED FORMAT

The management board has a special format that must be adhered to. Please include the following headings:

1. Nature of the request

   Purpose of the request: Explain the purpose of this funding request in one concise sentence.

   Issue(s): Identify the core issues first and address the following questions: How will the proposed funding affect stakeholder groups and other interested jurisdictional parties? What are the social and economic factors to consider?

2. Description of the request

   Program description: Briefly describe the purpose, operation, target groups, and expected impacts of the entire package of programs. How is this program package related to the ministry's overall strategy?

   Policy support: State the cabinet committee's policy approval for the program, and the date this occurred.

   Background of request: Briefly outline the social changes that have occurred and prompted the new package of programs, as well as previous relevant management board minutes and past funding changes.

   Substantiation for the request: Briefly provide evidence and data that can explain the request and trend analysis.

3. Analysis of the program

Business case for the request: Consider financial options and their cost-benefit analyses in this section.

Impact on fiscal plan: Briefly describe the impact of the request on approved ministry expenditure over a period of years.

Options considered and proposed action: Describe various options that have been considered and cost-estimated. What results are to be expected? Project their multi-year financial implications. Describe the expected achievement of the proposed action.

Performance measurement: Provide measurement indicators and units of analysis for the performance of the proposed package of programs. How is the anticipated funding invested in the achievement of program objectives to be expressed? Identify the standard used for measurement and the target of short- and long-term accomplishments.

Assessment of risks: Identify all major potential risk factors (demographic, economic, and technological) and develop realistic assumptions and plans.

Implications: Identify and analyze the implications of the proposed package of programs for existing programs, stakeholder groups, ministries, and jurisdictions. Describe consultations with the above and their reactions and resolutions.

Impacts: Determine the time frame for the management board to evaluate the program results to ensure that they are consistent with the approved plan. This includes legislation, workforce, labour relations, information technology, customer service, privacy, facilities, regions, and other factors as the government sees fit.

Time frame: Outline the schedule for the implementation of the programs from start to maturity.

Approval sought: State the exact wording of the approval sought.

Communication plan: Describe the communication plan for the proposed programs.

ROLE-PLAYING THE DECISION-MAKING PROCESS
Public Housing

SCENARIO

Public housing has not been a priority policy item for the Canadian government in many years. The issue of housing has largely been an individual responsibility. Though there are temporary housing solutions available for people in need, they are almost always in short supply.

In light of growing income inequality among Canadians, this lack of access to affordable housing, combined with growing homelessness statistics and a rising unemployment rate, has increased the need for provincial governments to be involved in the production and maintenance of public housing. To this end, public policy developers in Ontario's Ministry of Municipal Affairs and Housing have been instructed by the minister to prepare a cabinet submission on a new public housing policy. The draft public policy envisions the rendering of funds for additional public housing projects for low-income individuals and families. Consider this initiative part of a larger anti-poverty policy that the provincial government adopted a year ago.

The draft policy will earmark $200 million each year for the next five years to invest in building public housing stocks. This is proposed in partnership with municipal governments and the private sector to build and operate new public housing projects targeting specifically, but not exclusively, the homeless, persons with disabilities, and single-parent families. The exact type of housing, numbers of dwelling units, funding and operational arrangements, and other issues have yet to be developed.

This exercise is intended to enable students to cultivate an understanding of how a draft public policy moves through the decision-making process in the government. By enacting this simplified version of a discussion among different internal stakeholders within government, participants may take on the role of internal and external groups that either plead a case or assess a policy recommendation.

REQUIRED FORMAT

This exercise requires at least two hours. Students should be divided into the following groups:

- Group 1: The minister and the public policy developers in the Ministry of Municipal Affairs and Housing, tasked with preparing the cabinet submission
- Group 2: Members of the treasury board and management board of cabinet, who will provide input on money and management issues
- Group 3: Cabinet members, who will review and approve the final version of the cabinet submission
- Group 4: Opposition party members, who must raise questions and debate the policy position of the government as it is presented

Stages of Role Play

Stage 1: Time allocated for this component is 30 minutes.

Stage 1A: The session starts off with the Ministry of Municipal Affairs and Housing's public policy developers (Group 1) discussing among themselves the public housing policy. Discussion topics include policy goals, housing types, funding arrangements with municipalities and the private sector, funding conditions and amount of funding, target residents and the potential number of residents benefitting, and other factors. During this discussion, the public policy developers will identify potential questions from other stakeholder groups within the government regarding public housing. One member from Group 1, identified as the spokesperson, will act as the Minister of Housing and will present the cabinet's policy position later in the legislature.

Stage 1B: While the public policy developers of the Ministry of Municipal Affairs and Housing (Group 1) are working on the ministry's policy position, each of the other groups (Groups 2, 3, and 4) will discuss internally the most feasible public policy options for the province and assess each potential policy's pros and cons.

- Group 2, the treasury board and management board of cabinet, will focus on the financial and management aspects of public housing.
- Group 3, the cabinet, will focus on the overall government position after assessing public housing from various perspectives, including

the economy, the business environment, and the issue of poverty, as they relate to housing, sources of funding, benefits and risks for the government and the provincial residents, etc.

- Group 4, opposition parties, will focus on assessing the value of public housing funding from the perspectives of their constituents in light of the current socio-economic situation.

Stage 2: Time allocated for this stage is 15 minutes.
After the internal group discussion, the Minister of Housing (from Group 1) will present the Ministry of Municipal Affairs and Housing's policy position on public housing.

Stage 3: Time allocated for this stage is 15 minutes.
The treasury board and the management board of cabinet (Group 2) work with the Ministry of Municipal Affairs and Housing and come to an agreement regarding management issues and the allocation of resources based on the policy position on public housing. While the Ministry of Municipal Affairs and Housing (Group 1) and the treasury board and management board of cabinet (Group 2) are discussing the management and resource issues, the cabinet (Group 3) and the opposition parties (Group 4) will assess the Ministry of Municipal Affairs and Housing's presentation internally to determine whether or not they support it.

Stage 4: Time allocated for this stage is 20 minutes.
After the Ministry of Municipal Affairs and Housing (Group 1) and the treasury board and management board of cabinet (Group 2) come to an agreement on the policy position and the funding and management issues, they then jointly present to the cabinet (Group 3). The cabinet (Group 3) will have to decide on the final public housing policy. The cabinet must also identify potential questions from the opposition parties (Group 4) and prepare answers accordingly.

Stage 5: Time allocated for this stage is 10 minutes.
The Minister of Housing then presents the ministry's position in the legislature. All groups will listen to the presentation.

Stage 6: Time allocated for this stage is 15 minutes.
After the ministry's presentation, the opposition parties (Group 4) will debate the cabinet (Group 3) on its public housing position. Opposition parties may

ask questions and challenge the cabinet's position. The Minister of Housing (Group 1) will answer these questions. Opposition parties may request that the government (the cabinet, in this case) revise its policy position.

Stage 7: Time allocated for this stage is 15 to 30 minutes.

After the above role play, a debriefing session should be held regarding the entire decision-making process within the provincial public management framework.

GLOSSARY

Accountability: Accountability in the public sector usually refers to a highly valued criterion of measuring the extent to which politicians and public servants are answerable to taxpayers in terms of allocation and usage of funds, program performance, work productivity, and quality of service delivery. (See also *auditor general.*)

Ad hoc committees: Ad hoc committees are work arrangements consisting of politicians and backbenchers who review specific issues or bills in the legislature. The duration of such a work arrangement depends largely on the nature of issues or bills and dissolves upon the completion of the work.

Advocacy: Advocacy is the act of promoting and advancing a cause or viewpoint. It is carried out by a group of people or an organization with the objective of influencing the public and the government to adopt its perspective.

Amendment: Amendment is the act of making a revision to a piece of legislation or regulation following parliamentary or constitutional procedures.

Auditor general: Canada's auditor general reports to Parliament, and not to the government. The auditor general is responsible for independently reviewing the activities of the federal government, paying special attention to the cost-effectiveness and operational efficiency of government administration and programs. The auditor general's key objective is to hold the government accountable.

Backbenchers: Backbenchers are members of parliament who do not hold government offices. They have not been selected by the prime minister to be responsible for special portfolios, usually for one of the following reasons: they are new and perceived to be inexperienced, they have been demoted from the government, or there are simply not enough portfolios for distribution (especially when the government is in the majority). They do not have much power to influence public policies or government administration. Occasionally, they are nominated to sit on parliamentary committees, where they may exercise influence over legislative matters.

Bill: A bill is a piece of draft legislation introduced by the party in power in the legislature with the objective of having it ratified by the members of parliament. In provincial government, a bill has to go through three readings in the legislature before receiving royal assent and becoming a piece of law. In the federal government, a bill usually goes through three readings in the legislature before being forwarded to the Senate for approval. Only after Senate approval and royal assent is a bill enacted into law. At that stage, it becomes a statute or an act.

Briefing notes: Briefing notes are short documents written for the purpose of informing ministers about issues of significance to the government. It is common for briefing notes on policy matters to be circulated on a daily basis. They are often written by public policy developers.

British North America Acts: The *British North America Acts* are a series of acts enacted by the Parliament of the United Kingdom and the Parliament of Canada between 1867 and 1975. They were later renamed the *Constitution Act of 1982*, after several acts were amended and others were repealed. The first act was established in 1867 to create the self-governing Dominion of Canada. Other acts deal with representation in Parliament or the Senate of Canada, the addition of provinces, boundaries of the country, transfer payments, power sharing between provincial and federal governments, power over changes to the Constitution, and other issues.

Bureaucrats: Bureaucrats are people working in an organization with a hierarchy of people with different roles governed by written administrative rules and defined lines of authority. In the public sector, they are public servants, government employees paid to provide services to elected politicians. They are non-partisan and serve whichever party is in power. (See also *public servants*.)

Cabinet: In Canadian government, a cabinet is a formal committee made up of ministers chosen by the prime minister, in the federal government, or the premier, in provincial government. Each of these ministers is responsible for a particular domain (e.g., foreign affairs, industry, or human resources); the cabinet comes together to make decisions about everything within their mandate of government, including public policies.

Cabinet minutes: Cabinet minutes are brief documents that record the decisions made by cabinet ministers during cabinet meetings.

Cabinet presentation slides: Cabinet presentation refers to the verbal summarization of public issues by public servants. Visual slides, usually in PowerPoint, are used to make these presentations. They provide the necessary information for cabinet ministers to make policy decisions.

Cabinet submissions: Cabinet submissions are documents written by public policy developers to provide information about public policy issues to cabinet ministers. These submissions include research findings, analyses, policy options, and recommendations. Based on this information, cabinet ministers make decisions about proposed public policies. These submissions are the backbone of public policies.

Canada Act 1982: The Canadian federal government requested that the Parliament of the United Kingdom pass this act. It is the act that ended Canada's dependency on the British Parliament to amend parts of the Constitution of Canada. With this act, Canada became a sovereign country.

Canada Pension Plan (CPP): The Canada Pension Plan is one of two public retirement income systems. It is based on the contributions of employers and employees. The other system is Old Age Security (OAS). CPP is administered by the federal government on behalf of employees in Canada, with the exception of Quebec.

Capitalism: Capitalism is an economic system based on private property, accumulation of profit, and the competitive market economy. Western capitalism was developed out of the decline of feudalism. There are various forms of capitalism, including laissez-faire and welfare capitalisms. The changing nature of contemporary socialism with an increasing tone of capitalism further complicates its definition. Currently, common usage of the term focuses on the primacy of market competition over state intervention and the supremacy of private property over state ownership of means of production. Capitalism has been viewed as the source of inequality of wealth and power among social classes.

Caucus: A caucus is a group of elected politicians, ministers, and backbenchers from the same political party that meets regularly to discuss matters related to politics, public policies, or administration. These meetings are usually a sounding board for new or emerging political issues during which backbenchers have the opportunity to voice issues that matter most to their constituents. Here, cabinet ministers have the opportunity to get an overview of the issues facing different communities and stakeholder groups in their jurisdiction.

Central agencies: Central agencies are government bodies that review and approve public policies, legal issues, management, and funding issues. As they usually have a macroscopic view of the functioning of the entire government, they are also in a better position to find balanced solutions to the multiple demands of various government departments.

Charter of Rights and Freedoms: The Charter of Rights and Freedoms is a bill of rights entrenched in the Constitution of Canada. The Charter guarantees political rights to Canadian citizens and civil rights to everyone in Canada. Fundamental freedoms identified in the Charter include freedom of conscience, religion, thought, belief, expression, the press, peaceful assembly and association, mobility rights, equality rights, and minority-language education rights. The Charter applies to government laws and the actions of the federal, provincial, territorial, and municipal governments, as well as public school boards. Since the Charter was signed into law on

April 17, 1982, it has generated many judicial reviews. The Charter is explicit on the guarantee of rights, the right to exclude evidence in trials (if it is in conflict with the Charter), and the role of judges to enforce them. The courts have struck down unconstitutional federal and provincial statutes and regulations that are in violation of the Charter.

Collaboration: Collaboration is the process of two or more persons or parties working together. Its objective is to find alternatives to an existing situation that are acceptable to all of the people or parties involved. Collaboration is one method the government uses to find solutions that balance the interests of various stakeholder groups.

Committees: Committees are work arrangements, made up of a limited number of people, with specific mandates, membership, roles, responsibilities, decision-making mechanisms, and meeting schedules. Unlike task forces, committees are not limited to a single task or specific time period. They have multiple tasks and are generally formed for a longer duration, often evolving as a permanent structure of an organization.

Common Sense Revolution: The Common Sense Revolution was a political platform introduced by Mike Harris' Progressive Conservative Party, which was in power in Ontario from 1995 to 2002. The platform focused on reducing the role of the provincial government, broadening the role of the private sector in activities that were traditionally government regulated, reducing taxes and the size of the government's complement, balancing the budget, and increasing individual responsibility.

Conservative Party: The federal Conservative Party was formed as an amalgamation of two former parties, the Progressive Conservative Party and the Canadian Alliance Party, in 2003. This merge was a pragmatic way to end the division of the political right and gain enough electoral votes to attain power. Its central values are smaller government, freer market economy, and more individual responsibility.

Constellated recommendation: A constellated recommendation is a policy proposal strategy presented to ministers as a package of several policy options that are deemed worthy of acceptance and approval by the ministers. These recommended policy options are packaged in such a way that when taken together, they are in the best interest of the public and the government. When the policy options in the package are taken apart and considered separately, they may not be the best options in their own right.

Consultation: Consultation is the process of having a conversation between two or more persons or parties with the objective of exchanging ideas and, sometimes, finding solutions to a problem. In the area of public policy development, government increasingly uses this process to determine public needs and wants, as well as to explore their ideas for social change.

Consultation highlights: Consultation highlights are the major findings of a consultation session or a series of consultations with the public or various stakeholder groups. These major findings reflect the themes, competing or conflicting viewpoints, and suggestions expressed by members of the public or stakeholder groups. Public policy developers often use these highlights to guide their development of policy options.

Co-operative Commonwealth Federation (CCF): The Co-operative Commonwealth Federation was founded in 1932 in Alberta and became the first social-democratic government in North America. It was rebranded as the New Democratic Party in 1961. Its objective was to carry out economic reform to alleviate the suffering of people during the Depression era. Its political platform was to establish a socialized planning economy to replace capitalism. Tommy Douglas was CCF's first provincial premier in Saskatchewan. In 1944, he introduced a universal health care system in Saskatchewan, and this system was replicated by other provinces, as well as the federal government under Lester Pearson.

Correspondence: Correspondence is a communication tool using various written formats, including social media, texting, email, and blogs.

Decision notes: Decision notes are similar to briefing notes. They provide pertinent information on specific policy issues. Decision notes provide options for ministers to weigh and decide on to resolve issues, whereas briefing notes merely present information.

Deinstitutionalization: Deinstitutionalization is an ideology that encourages the reduction of personal dependency on institutions. One example of deinstitutionalization is the process of moving patients from hospital care to community or family care, thus shifting the burden of responsibility from government services to individual responsibility. The idea began in the 1960s, gained momentum in the 1970s, and continues to be popular among more conservative politicians.

Demarcation: Demarcation is the line of separation between two or more objectives, issues, values, or activities. It sets them apart so that people are aware of their differences or uniqueness.

Demographic data: Demographic data is statistical information on human population that focuses on fertility, mortality, and migration, as well as the distribution patterns and trends of various segments of the population, including gender, ethnicity, and age. This data is of great value to government activities, especially for planning and priorities, revenue and expenditure, policies and programs, services and delivery mechanisms, industrial growth, and economic development.

Department of finance: The department of finance is one of the many departments in a government. As a line department, its main activities are to collect and analyze financial data and to forecast and plan for the government and its jurisdiction. Although it is a line department, it is also a central agency (due to its strategic oversight of the economy and finance). As a central agency, it reviews, evaluates, and endorses financial proposals and estimates from other line departments. It works closely with other central agencies (such as the planning and priorities board, treasury board, and management board) to determine how much money should be generated as government revenue and how much should be spent on programs and services.

Deputy minister: A deputy minister is the operational head of a line department or a central agency in the government. With a mandate to manage a government organization, a deputy minister is the person between the government bureaucracy, where public servants work, and the political office, where politicians and political aides work. His or her role is to provide support to the minister.

Difference principle: The difference principle is one of John Rawls' three principles of social justice. The principle maintains that social inequality is permissible only when unequal situations work to the advantage of those who are the most disadvantaged and marginalized. This implies the acceptance of inequalities in a society, as long as such inequalities benefit the poor. (See also *fair opportunity principle* and *liberty principle*.)

Disability allowances: Disability allowances are a form of income support for persons with disabilities. At the federal level, the Canada Pension Plan (CPP) Disability Benefits provide a monthly benefit to people who have made contributions to CPP and cannot work because of their life-threatening or lasting disabilities. There are also weekly disability allowances, which are additional social welfare benefits or supplementary welfare payments for persons 16 years or older with disabilities.

Discussion papers: Discussion papers are documents written for the purpose of stimulating discussion on specific public policies. They usually include a review of the literature pertinent to the subject matter and raise core questions for further discussion, with the objective of formulating new policies.

Draft legislations and regulations: Draft legislations and regulations are documents written by legal counsel in the government. Legislations are always in draft form prior to their introduction by cabinet ministers in the legislature. Regulations are done internally with the approval of the cabinet. Each piece of legislation or regulation usually goes through many drafts, as many individuals within the government are involved in the review process and contribute their viewpoints on how best to perfect legislations and regulations.

Drug subsidies: All provinces have some form of drug subsidies for residents aged 65 and over. All have some degree of co-payments or deductibles that have to be paid to senior citizens. In Alberta, for example, senior citizens have to pay 30 percent of the cost up to a maximum of $25 for each prescribed drug. These subsidies help individuals manage the costs of their prescription drugs.

Employment equity: Employment equity is a concept of addressing systemic unfairness in employment for different segments of the population that have been discriminated against. The federal government created the *Employment Equity Act* in 1986, and employment equity programs are established in federally regulated organizations and organizations with federal contracts to make the workplace more equitable for Aboriginal peoples, persons with disabilities, visible minorities, and women.

Employment Insurance (EI): Employment Insurance provides temporary financial assistance to the unemployed who have lost their jobs through no fault of their own while they are looking for work. In addition, employment insurance is available to people who are pregnant, sick, looking after a newborn or adopted child, and those caring for a family member who is very sick or has a life-threatening disease.

Enveloped recommendation: Public policy developers sometimes package their policy options into different recommendation envelopes, developed for ministers. An enveloped recommendation is a recommendation package with several policy options selected for their potential impact, cost-effectiveness, balance of stakeholder interests, balance of short- and long-term considerations, justice, and accountability. Enveloped recommendations consist of a mix of these principles or different gradations of adherence to these principles. While a constellated recommendation is based on selecting the best mix of policy options, an enveloped recommendation is based on selecting one of the recommendation envelopes with different gradations of scope and effectiveness.

Equality: When used in a legal sense, *equality* implies the same treatment of people before the law or the same entitlement for all without discrimination. When used in a sociological sense, this term covers two types of equality: equality of opportunity and equality of condition. Equality of opportunity denotes fair competition for everyone without limiting the chances of individuals to access to the competition for housing, services, and employment. Equality of condition means the same or similar social conditions and material wealth. Without equality in condition for people, equality of opportunity may be meaningless.

Equity: Equity is a concept that centres on the notion of fairness. Unlike the concept of equality, it does not equate fairness with sameness in treatment. According to the objective of equity, people must be treated differently based on their inherent or acquired differences. Equity is viewed as a means to attain equality.

Estimates: Estimates, in the context of the public sector, are requests for approval from line departments to the cabinet regarding financial allocations to their capital and operational, program, and service expenses. There are two types of estimates. Main estimates are presented once a year as an estimate bill to the legislature for ratification. Supplementary estimates are presented to the legislature throughout the year if and when line departments need additional funds. Once the main or supplementary estimates have been ratified, they become the budgets for the line departments. (See also *main estimates* and *supplementary estimates*.)

External stakeholders: Stakeholders are groups of people or organizations that have a vested interest in specific issues, domains, or territories. External stakeholders (e.g., business organizations, labour unions, citizen groups, and service agencies) are groups that are not part of the political or bureaucratic side of the government; the term *external* implies that they are outside of government.

Facilitation: Facilitation is a process through which an environment is created with the help of a group leader so that people can contribute their ideas with ease and without being intimidated or ridiculed. The leader, called a facilitator, encourages people to voice their concerns, preferences, demands, and suggestions in relation to issues. Facilitation by a third party, who remains neutral and objective, is especially important when the discussion topics are contentious or emotion-laden.

Fair opportunity principle: The fair opportunity principle is one of John Rawls' three principles of social justice. It maintains that positions of public responsibility or private advantage should be open to all on the basis of fair equality of opportunity. (See also *difference principle* and *liberty principle*).

First reading: The first reading is the first of three occasions during which a bill is presented in the provincial or federal legislature. The minister responsible for the subject matter of the bill usually introduces the bill in the legislature and, depending on the bill, some debate may occur. The bill is then sent to a standing committee made up of elected members of all political parties for more detailed review. After that, the bill, with some amendments, will be brought to the second reading in the legislature. The amount of time between the first and second readings varies. In federal government, the Senate also has a three-reading system. First reading refers to the first time a bill is read in the Senate. (See also *second reading* and *third reading*.)

Flexible formats: Flexible formats for policy products means that there are no rigid requirements regarding the headings, font size, spacing, margins, and number of pages used for documents written by public policy developers.

Foreign affairs: Foreign affairs refers to international relations. The federal government of Canada has the Department of Foreign Affairs and International Trade, which has a mandate to manage Canada's diplomatic and consular relations and to encourage international trade.

Funnel of causality model: The funnel of causality model views the development of public policies as the result of various contributing factors at work, starting with the macroscopic (e.g., political, cultural, economic, and social frameworks). When policy issues are in alignment with these frameworks, they are then filtered through intermediate factors, such as the organizational and decision-making mechanisms in the government. When these policy issues are aligned with intermediate factors, they are filtered through the agenda-setting process of the government and considered by cabinet ministers. This funnelling process includes a filtering process that narrows the range of public policies in cabinet discussion.

Globalization: Globalization is a process through which ideas, goods, and services are transmitted quickly among markets and countries, with political, social, and economic ramifications, increasing the interdependence of many nations. This process is usually associated with the disappearance of paid work, wage constraints, polarization of wealth, growing impoverishment, global inequality, privatization of former state institutions, and escalation of militarization, criminalization or imprisonment, and international intervention in local politics. These phenomena are usually viewed as capitalism going through a stage of mass expansion.

Global justice: Global justice is both a concept and a social movement. As a concept, it embraces each individual's impartiality to produce good for everyone without preference to one individual or population segment over another. Such impartiality transcends institutional and territorial lines and extends globally. The idea of benefitting everyone raises the issues of its scope, wealth distribution, and the institution responsible for justice across the globe. Social movements for global justice encompass humanitarian assistance, anti-cultural colonialism, anti-dictatorial regimes, transfers of wealth from the rich to the poor, and the building of international governing bodies to monitor and enforce international laws on global justice.

Government intervention: Government intervention refers to action taken by the government to alter the courses of action taken by individuals, groups, or organizations. The nature of these government actions depends on the policy instruments used by the government, which can range from moderate symbolic or educational tools (e.g., advertising and public awareness campaigns), to financial means (e.g., taxation and subsidies), to strong coercive means (e.g., police and military activities). (See also *interventionist*.)

House book notes: House book notes are a collection of short briefing notes on topics of interest to ministers. These notes are usually placed in a binder so that ministers can access them during question period in the legislature to refresh their memories on these topics. These topics may vary from contentious issues, to public policy issues, to existing program or service specifics.

House of Commons: The House of Commons is the lower house of Parliament, in which members of Parliament (elected politicians) congregate. It is here that these members review and debate government bills. It is also known as the legislature.

Human resources: Human resources are the individuals who work for an organization. These individuals constitute the internal workforce of the organization. While the business sector tends to view human beings as assets to organizations, some people object to the use of the term *human resources,* as they believe that human beings should not be treated as resources, assets, or commodities. Human resources are highly connected to demographic changes and diversity, labour migration, occupational structure, and the transferability of knowledge and skills.

Ideology: An ideology is a system of abstract ideas that constitute the worldviews and social values of individuals. In political science, an ideology can be interpreted as a set of ideas and visions that those in power use to socialize people for the purpose of justifying the status quo.

Image: In the context of public policy, image refers to the public perception of policy ideas. The government attempts to create this image as it frames its position.

Impact model: An impact model shows a public problem at one point in time and the removal of the problem at another point in time. A change in the nature or magnitude of the public problem may be the result of the implementation of a public policy, or another intervening variable, between these two points in time.

Income support: Income support is an additional financial provision for people whose incomes are below the low-income cut-off (LICO) point, generally known as the poverty line. *Income support* is a generic term that covers a variety of financial support systems (e.g., Old Age Security) provided by the federal or provincial governments.

Institutional memory: Institutional memory is a recollection of observations of things that happened in an organization in the past. This may include how things were done, how the organization was structured, where information has been stored, who has moved from one position to another, and what ideas or projects have succeeded or failed. These observations are usually retained by people who have been in the organization for a reasonable period of time.

Interest group: An interest group is broadly defined as an advocacy group that seeks to promote and create advantages for its cause. Although interest groups are primarily concerned with influencing government decisions, they often quarrel among themselves in an effort to protect their competing or conflicting interests.

International Monetary Fund (IMF): The International Monetary Fund is an international organization that promotes economic co-operation and trade among nations, employment, economic growth, financial stability, and the reduction of poverty.

Countries contribute money to the IMF, which makes financial resources available to its members. There are 188 countries in its membership.

Interventionist: An interventionist approach is an approach taken by the government that interferes with the actions of individuals, groups, or organizations. (See also *government intervention*.)

Invisible hand: Adam Smith coined the phrase *invisible hand* to describe the self-regulating function of the market economy. He believed that, in a free marketplace, without the intervention of the government, the marketplace channels the (profit-driven) self-interest of individuals as buyers and sellers to a socially desired goal of higher productivity and lower costs, minimizing the need for government intervention in the marketplace.

Issue-attention cycle: The issue-attention cycle is the period of time in which specific issues become the focus of public attention. This cycle is usually short in duration, unless it is tied to regular government events that catch media attention.

Jurisdiction: Jurisdiction denotes the authority of a sovereign power over a broad range of people and institutions. It usually has a geographic boundary, and a legal framework that spells out its mandates and obligations.

Keynesian economy theory: Keynesian economic theory is heavily tied to public policy, as it stresses the important role of the government in smoothing out the ups and downs of capitalist business cycles. It calls for government intervention in unemployment and investment during recessionary periods. As a public policy, it paves the way for an active and larger government with emphasis on more state ownership and regulations.

Legislation: Legislation is a piece of law enacted by a legislature. It is one of the three major functions of government. The other two functions are judicial and executive. Legislation is usually introduced as a bill by a member of the legislature, and is debated among all members or reviewed by committees prior to being passed. Legislation has the power to authorize, declare, sanction, regulate, and allocate funds.

Legislative committee: A legislative committee is a committee of legislators with experience and expertise in the requisite field assembled for the purpose of examining a government bill. The work of a legislative committee begins after the second reading of the bill.

Legislature: Legislature is a body of elected members who have the authority to make, amend, and repeal laws. It also has the authority to determine levels of taxation and budgetary allocation. Internationally, the term *legislature* can refer to parliament, congress, or national assembly. In the federal system in Canada, the legislature is known as Parliament, in which there are two houses: the House of Commons and the Senate.

Liberal Party: The Liberal Party of Canada was formed in the 1870s. Its gain in political power was based on its success in holding onto the middle ground between conservative and social democratic forces. Its central beliefs are free choice, individual rights and equality, democracy, and private property. Its emphasis on government intervention and a free market system has varied throughout history.

Liberty principle: The liberty principle is one of John Rawls' three principles of social justice. It maintains that each person is entitled to the most extensive set of basic liberties compatible with the same liberty for all. (See also *fair opportunity principle* and *difference principle*.)

Line department: A line department is a bureaucratic unit under the leadership of a minister. Each line department has its own mandate and responsibilities. On the bureaucratic side of the government, there are public servants working in the line department headed by a deputy minister, who works for the minister. On the political side, there are ministers and political aides. A line department is also known as a line ministry. The two terms are often used interchangeably; however, in common usage, people tend to use the term *department* only for an office in the federal government, while *ministry* is used to refer to offices in a provincial government.

Line ministers: Line ministers are elected members of the legislature who have been appointed by the provincial premier (or the prime minister in the federal government) to be in charge of a portfolio (e.g., natural resources or agriculture). Line ministers have a bureaucracy of public servants who provide services to support them and carry out the responsibilities of the ministries or departments.

Lobby groups: Lobby groups are groups of people with the same or similar perspectives on politics, economics, morality, or religion. These groups may be private companies, trade councils, medical associations, industrial associations, advocacy groups, or religious groups. Their key role is to inform, influence, and promote changes in government policies that favour their positions or causes. Lobby groups usually know how the government system works and are knowledgeable and skilful at building networks within the government and utilizing opportunities to meet and communicate with politicians and public servants.

Lobbying: Lobbying is the attempt to influence decision-makers in government. Decision-makers include ministers, opposition politicians, and members of regulatory agencies. Lobbying can represent the interests of a minority group or wealthy and powerful groups that are attempting to gain an advantage in the law. Governments usually establish rules and regulations to contain lobbying activities.

Long-gun registry: The long-gun registry was a program introduced by the Liberal government under Prime Minister Jean Chrétien in 1993. From 1995 to 2012, all firearms in Canada were required to be registered. As of April 6, 2012—with the enactment of Bill C-19, *An Act to Amend the Criminal Code and the Firearms Act*, by the Conservative Party of Canada—non-restricted firearms no longer required registration and all records of non-restricted firearms on the registry were to be destroyed, with the exception of those in Quebec, pending litigation. One downfall of the registry was its costs. It was originally estimated that the cost for the registry was around $2 million, but it was reported to be $66.4 million for the fiscal year of 2010–2011. The sources of the high cost of administration may be related to administrative inefficiency and information technology. The impact of the discontinuation of the registry on public safety remains a contentious issue.

Macroscopic: The term *macroscopic* implies a big-picture approach to viewing a phenomenon, object, or issue. This broad perspective usually focuses on historical and structural factors and excludes the specifics of the subject matter.

Main estimates: Main estimates are the annually proposed budgets of government departments and central agencies introduced in the legislature for review and ratification by legislators. They contain the breakdown of capital and operational costs, as well as program costs, for each department. (See also *estimates* and *supplementary estimates*.)

Management board submissions: Management board submissions are documents requesting funds for program operation from line departments. They document the purposes of the funding request, program description, business case for the program, performance measurement, risk assessment, time frame, communication plan, and any other pertinent information on which the management board's decision may be based.

Methodology: In the context of research, methodology is an integral part of a scientific inquiry. Methodology includes indicators of evidence to be identified, research methods, measurement instruments, collection of information and data, verification, tabulation and analysis of information and data, sequences of research tasks, and quality-control processes.

Negotiation: Negotiation is the act of discussing with the objective of arriving at a settlement or compromise on issues. The idea of give and take is inherent in the process, though there is a tendency for each party to seek an advantage for themselves in this process. Negotiation can be carried out formally or informally, and each party involved in the negotiation process develops its own strategy. Unlike mediation and arbitration, negotiation does not involve a third party in the process.

Neo-liberalism: Neo-liberalism is a school of thought that emphasizes the importance of a free market economy and minimal government intervention. According to neo-liberalism, a welfare state is detrimental to people and society, and deregulation will make the society better. It values individualism and personal responsibility. Neo-liberalism is seen by some as a right-wing ideology that should therefore be called neo-conservatism.

New Democratic Party (NDP): The New Democratic Party was established in 1961 as a replacement for the former Co-operative Commonwealth Federation (CCF). It has been strongly associated with the trade union movement and social democrats. Historically, the party has been more successful in gaining political power at the provincial level than at the federal level, although this changed when the NDP became the official opposition in the House of Commons in 2011. Its central values are social democracy, freedom and equality, and a stronger government role.

New public management: New public management is a model of operation for government that became fashionable in the 1990s. Philosophically, it emphasizes that the core business of the government is to provide direction (i.e., steer) and not to administer programs or services (i.e., row). Its focus is on making individuals take responsibility for and regulate themselves, as opposed to requiring government interference. It strives for a limited government, especially in terms of roles, responsibilities, and employees. Its operational model is based on increasing the role of the private sector to maintain government cost-effectiveness and cost-efficiency and promotes outsourcing government programs and services, as well as establishing public-private partnerships. New public management is closely aligned with neo-liberalism.

Non-profit alliances: Non-profit alliances are a form of coalition among non-profit organizations to fight for a common or similar cause, or to demand special concessions from the government. They may involve labour unions, interest groups, community organizations, and political organizations. These alliances are usually short-lived, as they are often dissolved upon winning concessions from the government, gaining recognition of a cause (or causes), or because of internal conflicts.

Non-starter: A non-starter is an idea, proposal, candidate, or action that is not expected to be acceptable or successful and is destined to fail, at least in theory.

***Official Languages Act,* 1969:** The *Official Languages Act of Canada* was enacted in September 1969. It declared English and French as the two official languages of Canada, with equal status in the federal government. Under this act, federal government departments and Crown corporations must provide services in both English and French; federal courts must provide services in the language chosen by Canadians; Parliament has to publish regulations in both languages; and the government is obligated to hire civil servants who are bilingual or provide current civil servants with the opportunity to learn the other official language.

Omnibus bill: An omnibus bill is a draft legislation that covers a broad range of unrelated policy matters that the government deems suitable to be tabled for ratification in the legislature as a package.

Outsource: Outsourcing refers to the act of contracting a process or a task to an external organization. In some cases, outsourcing involves the transfer of employees or assets to the separate organization.

Partisan: Partisan is a political term that describes a commitment to a political ideology or a political party. Its current connotation is often connected to individuals who are militant proponents of something despite evidence that it is not factual.

Polarization: Polarization is a state of opposing opinions or conditions (for example, in attitude, or wealth distribution). Economic polarization can be summed up by the adage, "the rich get richer, and the poor get poorer." Social polarization implies that people are divided into two conflicting groups, each of which believes that the other is wrong in thought or action. In situations of this nature, people have a tendency to espouse a selective perception in which objective facts are interpreted in a way that benefits their cause, while opposing groups select interpretations that justify their positions, thus further polarizing the situation.

Policy idea: A policy idea is a vague concept of how a certain aspect of society or human behaviour can be changed. A policy idea has not yet been articulated to the extent that it is convincing or suitable for a government to work on, but represents an early stage of public policy development.

Policy instrument: A policy instrument is a form or method of government intervention used to translate a policy idea into a concrete action. This action may effect change in society or human behaviour. Some policy instruments are moderate or symbolic in nature (e.g., public education), and are usually slow to get results. In contrast, some are intrusive and coercive (e.g., law enforcement and punishment), and tend to see results more quickly.

Policy issue: A policy issue is the delineation of a policy idea on a particular subject for the purpose of further articulation, research, and analysis. A policy idea may contain several policy issues, which are more specific and have implications for the government. These policy issues are specific enough for research purposes, and they are often translated into policy questions to be answered.

Policy products: Policy products are written documents or the verbal presentation of material related to public policy ideas or issues. In the public sector, some of these documents are for internal use and some for external use. Each of these documents is constructed for a particular purpose—briefing, discussing, consulting, responding to requests, educating, or making decisions.

Policy question: A policy question is a policy issue phrased in question format so that it can be answered in specific detail. Without a policy question, there will be no specific answer to a policy issue.

Policy research: Policy research covers a broad range of research activities that are similar to those used in academic research. Policy research follows similar research processes, methodologies, research instruments, and analytical tools; however, unlike academic research, it is pragmatic, simplified, and is often not modelled on any theoretical school. Due to the fact that policy research is often done in a limited time frame with minimal resources, the process is often truncated and the evidence it presents is often grounded in secondary or proxy data and information. Primary research is done only when resources are available, and it often takes the form of a commission or task force.

Policy statement: A policy statement is a document that summarizes the government's policy position on a particular subject. There are variations in the way policy statements are written, but they usually include the nature of the policy matter, the principles upon which the policy was formulated, the policy scope, the stakeholder groups involved, and time frame of effectiveness.

Policy windows: Policy windows are opportunities for people or groups inside or outside the government to influence the direction or outcomes of the public policy development process. Some of these policy windows are regular features of the government (e.g., throne speeches) and some are unexpected and unpredictable (e.g., natural disasters).

Poverty line: The poverty line is a threshold demarcated to distinguish people who have only the minimum level of income assumed to be adequate for living in a certain jurisdiction or geographic area. This level is usually determined by reviewing the cost of essential goods and services that an average adult person uses in one year, the most expensive of which is rent, which varies according to the location of residence. Demographic factors, such as marital status and age, are also taken into consideration. Canada does not have an official poverty line. The poverty threshold used in Canada is Statistics Canada's low-income cut-off (LICO) point, although Statistics Canada has never endorsed the LICO as the official poverty line for Canada. In 2012, 9.4 percent of the Canadian population was living below that line.

Pragmatism: Pragmatism is a philosophical school of thought that argues that the practical consequences of something are the criteria of the knowledge, meaning, and value of it. For this reason, the common use of the term focuses on practical effects. Pragmatism, in public administration, denotes a focus on the results of government programs and services. Critics of pragmatism maintain that the results that government focuses on are in its own interest only, rather than the interests of citizens, and that too much focus on getting results often leads to ignoring the process itself.

Premier: The term *premier* is applied to the head of a province in Canada. The premier is the first minister of the Crown for a province, and he or she is the head of the provincial cabinet.

Press releases: Press releases are written documents, usually a page or two in length, that communicate newsworthy items to the mass media. Governments use press releases to inform media and the public about their new public policies and programs, legislative changes, organizational changes, and new cabinet members. They are transmitted to sources, journalists, or editors by email or facsimile. Commercial press release distribution services make these communications widely available on the Internet.

Primary research: Primary research is the collection and analysis of first-hand (or raw) information and data by researchers. Researchers typically review secondary research, including publications or unpublished reports written by other people, prior to conducting their own research. Primary research methods include survey questionnaires, face-to-face or phone interviews, social media dialogues, and participatory observations. Primary research projects are customized for specific issues or topics, and are usually expensive and time-consuming. (See also *secondary research*.)

Prime minister: The prime minister is the top minister of the federal government in Canada, appointed by the governor general on behalf of the Queen. The Canadian monarch, represented by the governor general, is the head of state; the prime minister is the head of the government, the cabinet, and the Canadian Forces. The prime minister has increasingly assumed more authority by performing duties traditionally assigned to the governor general, and has the power to appoint the governor general, senators, cabinet members, justices of the Supreme Court, heads of Crown corporations, provincial lieutenant-governors, ambassadors, and many other government-related positions.

Privatization: Privatization is the transfer of ownership from the government to the private sector, or the act of outsourcing government services to private companies.

Privy Council: The Privy Council is made up of current and former cabinet ministers. The chief justices of Canada, former chief justices, former speakers of the House of Commons, former speakers of the Senate, former governors general, distinguished individuals, and heads of opposition parties are appointed to the Privy Council. On occasion, provincial premiers are appointed. All members are appointed by the governor general, as advised by the sitting prime minister. Membership on the Privy Council is for life, unless the governor general withdraws the appointment. Privy Council members advise the Queen on issues related to state and constitutional affairs.

Program designs: Program designs are administrative frameworks for long-term initiatives and projects or services provided by the government. When public policies are approved at the cabinet level, some of these policies are manifested in the form of programs that benefit or affect the public or various stakeholder groups. Program development involves a budgetary process, as well as a statement of program objectives, the mapping of the structural arrangement and process of program implementation, target groups and their eligibility, operational details and tools, accountability, and program evaluation mechanisms. Each of these elements is part of the program design. They are best established jointly by public policy developers and front-line program workers, so that the public policies are concretized and the administrative aspects of the programs are effective and user-friendly.

Progress: Progress is often associated with the improvement and betterment of human life. It often acts as a belief that propels people to sustain their faith in the future. There is a lack of consensus on how to measure progress.

Protest: A protest is an expression of disagreement with an idea, a policy, a decision, an event, a proclamation, or an action. It can be expressed in writing, verbally, or through action. It can take many forms, such as individual hunger strikes, demonstrations, rallies, petitions, boycotts, or organized mass movements that involve thousands of people.

Proxy: A proxy is a placeholder or substitution, due to a lack of availability of the exact object or concept. In research, a proxy indicator for measurement approximates the exact, but unavailable, indicator to the closest extent possible. A proxy measurement unit may enable the determination of the degree or extent of a phenomenon or movement in the absence of an exact measurement unit. In policy research, secondary data is often used as proxy data; this commonly occurs because the exact data that public policy developers are seeking is not available and time or resources will not permit the policy developers to conduct the primary research necessary to obtain it.

Public consultation papers: Public consultation papers are documents written by public policy developers with the objective of stimulating public discussion of policy ideas or issues. These papers usually outline the parameters of consultation topics and seek opinions or suggestions from the public on these topics. They are usually written in an easy-to-read format and are distributed to the public prior to consultation sessions.

Public consultation plan: A public consultation plan is a document that outlines the purposes, methods, topics, schedule, communication, responsibility centres, and evaluation criteria of a public consultation. It is an internal document circulated to select people within the government with the objective of ensuring that the public consultation is in sync with government priorities, agendas, and time frames.

Public interest: Public interest implies the well-being of the public; however, there is no consensus of what constitutes public well-being, as different segments of the population have different interests and visions. In terms of developing public policies, public well-being is often projected by the government before policies are implemented. Everyone in society will not necessarily agree with this prejudgment; therefore, the term *public interest* remains vague and largely undefined.

Public policy: A public policy is the embodiment of both formal and informal actions (or inactions) carried out by the government in relation to specific issues that have a significant social, economic, political, or environmental impact on particular population groups or the public at large. Public policies are usually implemented in the name of the public good or public interest. These actions represent the government's position. Over time, these positions are often, but not necessarily, supported by human and financial resources, organizational structures and processes, ideological justifications, or legal, financial, military, or other government-sanctioned endeavours.

Public-private partnership: A public-private partnership is a special collaboration between the public sector (government) and the private sector (business) on specific projects or programs. The division of roles and responsibilities is agreed upon prior to the signing of a contract to officially establish the relationship. The nature of the contractual relationship varies based on the involved parties.

Public problem: Issues of concern to some segments of the population are considered to be public problems when there is a critical mass of people seeking government intervention. Issues of concern that are limited to some people and are not able to command the attention of the government to take action may not be viewed as public problems.

Public servants: Public servants are salaried employees of the federal, provincial, territorial, and municipal governments. They are sometimes called civil servants. They are hired to serve the public by providing services to elected politicians. Regardless of the political party in power, to ensure smooth functioning of the government, public servants are expected to be non-partisan, objective, neutral, and able to serve politicians of all political stripes.

Question period: Question period is the time in the legislature during which elected members of all parties participate in a debate. Members of the opposition parties may ask questions, and the political party in power must answer them in a highly procedural process with specified protocols. Question period occurs during almost every session while the legislature is in process. It is an opportunity for the political party in power to clarify its positions on issues raised by the opposition, and is often broadcast to the Canadian public.

Ratification: Ratification is the act of legally binding a piece of legislation by members of the legislature. While the cabinet of the government can only approve public policies, programs, and budgets, it must introduce them as bills for ratification by all members of the legislature before they can become law.

Regulations: Regulations are parts of a piece of legislation in which certain legal issues (usually concepts, procedures, and processes) are spelled out more specifically. Unlike legislation, which must be passed through the legislature, regulations can easily be changed by ministers without formal legislative debates. While legislation provides the framework of a public policy, regulations spell out its necessary details.

Royal assent: Royal assent is the formal act of approving a bill and making it a law, with the signature of the governor general. This signing is largely symbolic in nature in Canada.

Royal commissions: Royal commissions are a form of public inquiry into a major issue of concern to the public. Commissions are created and issues of public concern are researched and analyzed by the governor general at the advice of and adhering to the terms prepared by the government. Due to the magnitude of work, royal commissions usually last for years and their findings are documented in publications. Royal commissions have ample avenues and resources to gather information and defeat many protective mechanisms used by politicians or government bureaucrats. Commissioners are usually retired judges and they have immense investigative power to summon witnesses under oath, seize documents, offer indemnities, and hold hearings. Overall, the value of royal commissions varies—the government adopts some commission recommendations, while ignoring others.

Second reading: When the government introduces a bill for debate in the legislature, the bill goes through three readings. During the second reading, the bill is debated. The magnitude and intensity of the debate depends largely on how controversial the bill is and the extent to which the amendments made following the first reading meet the expectations of all political parties. Between the second and third readings, a legislative committee may more closely examine the bill. (See also *first reading* and *third reading*.)

Secondary research: Secondary research is a review of existing literature on specific topics; it does not include any fieldwork, experiments, interviews, surveys, focus groups, or participatory observations. Secondary research is usually done prior to any primary research; it is a useful way to determine what research has been done on a specific subject before, in an effort to ascertain what to do next. (See also *primary research*.)

Senate: The Senate is the upper house of Parliament, and has 105 appointed members. It was created in 1867, under the *Constitution Act,* to counterbalance representation by population in the House of Commons. It was intended to provide Parliament with a second perspective when considering bills before they are passed. The Senate may propose amendments to a bill if it breaches the constitutional rights, consists of technical errors, or is simply a bad policy. The Senate Chamber, where senators debate legislation or other government issues, is often called the Red Chamber.

Seniority rights: Seniority rights refer to the priority status, based on the length of time in continuous employment, held sacred by labour unions. Many collective agreements have this right enshrined for the protection of union members, affecting promotions, job transfers, and terminations.

Silo effect: The silo effect is the outcome of working in isolation without awareness of others' research or work. In an organization, the term applies to the compartmentalization of activities to the extent that employees in one branch of an organization do not know what the other branch is doing. Consequently, there is minimal coordination of organizational activities, which may lead to duplication of efforts or counterproductive activity.

Social democrat: A social democrat is a person who believes that democracy should extend beyond political democracy, and should include the right of co-determination in the workplace, universal child care, free education, free health care, and accessible public services.

Stakeholder consultation papers: Stakeholder consultation papers are documents written with the objective of stimulating discussion between the government and stakeholder groups centring on specific topics. The papers are usually written by public policy developers and distributed to stakeholder groups prior to a consultation session. (See also *stakeholder group.*)

Stakeholder group: A stakeholder group is a group of people with specific claims on specific issues. These groups can be unorganized, or belong to formal organizations or institutions. They have a vested interest in protecting, maintaining, promoting, and advocating on their own behalf to further their cause.

Standardized formats: Standardized formats are prescribed methods of presenting and arranging information in documents prepared by public policy developers for government line departments or central agencies.

Standing committee: A standing committee is established by the standing orders of the legislature. A standing committee will review or study public policy issues, administrative issues, and budgetary estimates of departments and agencies within its field. There are also standing committees that examine issues of national or provincial importance.

Statutory committee: A statutory committee is established by the Rules of the Senate or the Standing Orders of the House of Commons to study public policies with statutory implications or to examine regulations and statutory instruments.

Supplementary estimates: Supplementary estimates are additional budgets proposed by government departments. These proposed costs go beyond what has been approved and ratified in the annual main estimates. Supplementary estimates are introduced in the legislature for ratification. (See also *estimates* and *main estimates*.)

Think tanks: Think tanks are policy research and advocacy institutes that are usually non-profit in status. Their interests cover a broad range of areas, including policies, economic strategies, politics, trade, business, defence, social development, international relations, and culture. These think tanks often use their research findings as a platform for advocacy. Some think tanks in Canada are quite influential, as governments utilize their research findings to develop public policies.

Third reading: The third reading is the final reading session for a bill in the legislature. After this reading, the bill goes to the lieutenant-governor of the province for royal assent, and the bill becomes law. In the federal government, the term *third reading* also refers to the last of the three reading sessions of the Senate. After the third reading of the Senate (if the Senate has amended the bill), the bill goes back to Parliament for final agreement between the House of Commons and the Senate, then to the governor general for royal assent. After royal assent is given, the bill becomes law. (See also *first reading* and *second reading*.)

Throne speech: A throne speech is also known as a speech from the throne. It is a verbal presentation prepared by the ministers of the Crown in cabinet, but it is read by the lieutenant-governor in the provincial government or the governor general as the head of the state in the federal government. The speech is addressed to the members of parliament and highlights the national condition, legislative agenda, and national priorities for the coming parliamentary session. This is a formal event and is conducted annually.

Treasury board: The treasury board is a central agency in both the federal and provincial governments. Its focus is on the workforce of the government, accountability, and financial and administrative management. In the federal government, the Treasury Board is a committee of the Privy Council. In provincial governments, it is part of the provincial cabinet. The functions of the treasury board are sometimes merged with those of the management board; when that happens, the central agency is sometimes called either the management board or treasury board.

Typology: A typology is a classification scheme based on subject matter.

Vote and item numbers: Vote and item numbers are associated with the name of a line department and the programs it administers. The vote number denotes the name of the line department, and its programs (listed beneath it) are identified as items. Each vote and item has a designated number and corresponding funds, as identified in the estimate bill.

Welfare state: A welfare state is a form of government in which the social and economic welfare of citizens is actively protected by the government. It works on the premise that there are situations in which certain segments of the population cannot support themselves, and therefore need the assistance of the public sector. To this end, funds from the government are transferred to public services for the provision of child care, elderly care, health care, and education, as well as direct income supports for those who are eligible. In this sense, a welfare state redistributes wealth among its citizens to ensure the greater public good.

World Health Organization (WHO): The World Health Organization is an organization within the United Nations with a mandate to lead global health issues, develop health research agendas, establish health norms and standards, formulate policy options, provide technical support, and assess international health trends.

BIBLIOGRAPHY

Bardach, Eugene. (2009). *A Practical Guide for Policy Analysis: The Eightfold Path to More Effective Problem Solving.* Washington, DC: CQ Press.

Barry, Brian. (2005). *Why Social Justice Matters.* Cambridge, UK: Polity Press.

Bergerson, Peter J. (1991). *Teaching Public Policy: Theory, Research, and Practice.* New York: Greenwood Press.

Bernier, Luc, Keith Brownsey, and Michael Howlett, eds. (2005). *Executive Styles in Canada: Cabinet Structures and Leadership Practices in Canadian Government.* Toronto: University of Toronto Press.

Boase, Joan Price. (1996). "Trends in Social Policy: Towards the Millennium." In *Provinces: Canadian Provincial Politics,* edited by Christopher Dunn, 449–477. Peterborough, ON: Broadview Press.

Boswell, Peter G. (1996). "Provincial-Municipal Relations." In *Provinces: Canadian Provincial Politics,* edited by Christopher Dunn, 253–274. Peterborough, ON: Broadview Press.

Campbell, Robert M., Leslie A. Pal, and Michael Howlett. (2004). *The Real Worlds of Canadian Politics.* Peterborough, ON: Broadview Press.

Capeheart, Loretta, and Dragan Milovanovic. (2007). *Social Justice: Theories, Issues and Movements.* New Brunswick, NJ: Rutgers University Press.

Chandler, Marsha A., and William M. Chandler. (1979). *Public Policy and Provincial Politics.* Toronto: McGraw-Hill Ryerson Ltd.

Chase, Steven, and Tavia Grant. (2013). "Experts Debate How Much These Statistics Count," *Globe and Mail,* May 7: A10–A11.

Church, Elizabeth. (2009). "Who's in the Know: Women Surge, Men Sink in Education's Gender Gap," *Globe and Mail,* December 7: A1, A5.

Citizenship and Immigration Canada (CIC). (2012). "Backgrounder—2013 Immigration Levels Planning: Public and Stakeholder Consultation," July 7. Retrieved from www.cic.gc.ca/english/department/media/backgrounders/2012/2012-07-31.asp#app-b

Cobb, Roger W., J. K. Ross, and M. H. Ross. (1976). "Agenda Building as Comparative Political Process," *American Political Science Review,* 70(1): 126–138.

Craig, Gary, Tania Burchardt, and David Gordon, eds. (2008). *Social Justice and Public Policy*. Bristol, UK: The Policy Press.

Cramme, Olaf, and Patrick Diamond. (2009). "Rethinking Social Justice in the Global Age." In *Social Justice in the Global Age*, edited by Olaf Cramme and Patrick Diamond, 3–22. Malden, MA: Polity Press.

Cross, William. (2007). "Policy Study and Development in Canada's Political Parties." In *Policy Analysis in Canada: The State of the Art*, edited by Laurent Dobuzinskis, Michael Howlett, and David Laycock, 425–442. Toronto: University of Toronto Press.

Ditchburn, Jennifer. (2013). "Survey: Will Experts Revel in the Details?" *Globe and Mail*, May 6: A4.

Dobuzinskis, Laurent, Michael Howlett, and David Laycock, eds. (2007). *Policy Analysis in Canada: The State of the Art*. Toronto: University of Toronto Press.

Doern, G. Bruce, and Richard W. Phidd. (1983). *Canadian Public Policy: Ideas, Structure, Process*. Toronto: Methuen Publications.

Dunn, Christopher. (1995). *The Institutionalized Cabinet: Governing the Western Provinces*. Montreal: McGill-Queen's University Press.

Dunn, Christopher. (1996a). "Premiers and Cabinets." In *Provinces: Canadian Provincial Politics*, edited by Christopher Dunn, 165–204. Peterborough, ON: Broadview Press.

Dunn, Christopher, ed. (1996b). *Provinces: Canadian Provincial Politics*. Peterborough, ON: Broadview Press.

Dunn, Christopher. (2002). "The Central Executive in Canadian Government: Searching for the Holy Grail." In *The Handbook of Canadian Public Administration*, edited by Christopher Dunn, 305–340. Don Mills, ON: Oxford University Press.

Dyck, Rand. (1996). *Provincial Politics in Canada: Towards the Turn of the Century*. Scarborough, ON: Prentice Hall Canada.

Dye, Thomas. (1978). *Understanding Public Policy*. Englewood Cliffs, NJ: Prentice Hall.

Eichler, Leah. (2011). "Quotas Would Get More Women into the Board Room." *Globe and Mail*, October 22: B18.

Eichler, Leah. (2012). "Breaking the Boardroom Gender Barrier," *Globe and Mail*, March 10: B17.

Eienberg, Avigail I. (1996). "Justice and Human Rights in the Provinces." In *Provinces: Canadian Provincial Politics*, edited by Christopher Dunn, 478–502. Peterborough, ON: Broadview Press.

Fyfe, Toby, and Paul Crookall. (2010). *Social Media and Public Sector Policy Dilemmas*. Toronto: Institute of Public Administration of Canada.

Geva-May, Iris, and Allan M. Maslove. (2007). "In Between Trends: Developments of Public Policy Analysis and Policy Analysis Instruction in Canada, the United States, and the European Union." In *Policy Analysis in Canada: The State of the Art*, edited by Laurent Dobuzinskis, Michael Howlett, and David Laycock, 186–215. Toronto: University of Toronto Press.

Government of Canada. (2011). "Government of Canada Introduces the *Safe Streets and Communities Act*." Retrieved from www.justice.gc.ca/eng/news-nouv/nr-cp/2011/doc_32631.html

Hood, Christopher C. (1983). *The Tools of Government*. London, UK: Macmillan.

Hospital for Sick Children. (2005). *Early School Leavers: Understanding the Lived Reality of Student Disengagement from Secondary School*. Toronto: Ontario Ministry of Education and Training.

Howlett, Michael, and Evert Lindquist. (2007). "Beyond Formal Policy Analysis: Government Context, Analytical Styles, and the Policy Analysis Movement in Canada." In *Policy Analysis in Canada: The State of the Art*, edited by Laurent Dobuzinskis, Michael Howlett, and David Laycock, 86–115. Toronto: University of Toronto Press.

Howlett, Michael, M. Ramesh, and Anthony Perl. (2009). *Studying Public Policy: Policy Cycles and Policy Subsystems*. Don Mills, ON: Oxford University Press.

Hurd, Larry D. (1981). "Drafting Legislation." In *Provincial Policy-Making: Comparative Essays*, edited by Donald Mowat, 166–182. Ottawa: Department of Political Science, Carleton University.

Imbeau, Louis M., and Guy Lachapelle. (1996). "Comparative Provincial Public Policy in Canada." In *Provinces: Canadian Provincial Politics*, edited by Christopher Dunn, 401–422. Peterborough, ON: Broadview Press.

Inwood, Gregory J. (2009). *Understanding Canadian Public Administration: An Introduction to Theory and Practice*. Toronto: Pearson Education Canada.

Jackson, Robert J., and Doreen Jackson. (2001). *Politics in Canada: Culture, Institutions, Behaviour and Public Policy*. Toronto: Prentice Hall.

Johnson, A. W. (2004). *Dream No Little Dreams: A Biography of the Douglas Government in Saskatchewan, 1944–61*. Toronto: University of Toronto Press.

Johnson, David. (2006). *Thinking Government: Public Sector Management in Canada*. 2nd ed. Peterborough, ON: Broadview Press.

Kernaghan, Kenneth, and David Siegel. (1991). *Public Administration in Canada: A Text*. 2nd ed. Scarborough, ON: Nelson Canada.

Kingdom, John W. (1995). *Agenda, Alternatives and Public Policies*. Boston: Harper Collins.

LaPlante, Josephine M. (1991). "Research Use in Policy and Decision Settings: Closing the Gap." In *Teaching Public Policy*, edited by Peter J. Bergerson, 57–65. New York: Greenwood Press.

Linder, Stephen H., and B. Guy Peters. (1989). "Instruments of Government: Perceptions and Contexts," *Journal of Public Policy*, 9: 35–58.

Lipset, S. M. (1959). *Agrarian Socialism: The Co-operative Commonwealth Federation in Saskatchewan—A Study in Political Sociology*. Berkeley, CA: University of California Press.

Lister, Ruth (2008). "Recognition and Voice: The Challenge for Social Justice." In *Social Justice and Public Policy*, edited by Gary Craig, Tania Burchardt, and David Gordon, 105–122. Bristol, UK: The Policy Press.

Margai, Florence. (2010). *Environmental Health Hazards and Social Justice: Geographical Perspectives on Race and Class Disparities*. Washington, DC: Earthscan Ltd.

McArthur, Doug. (2007). "Policy Analysis in Provincial Governments in Canada: From PPBS to Network Management." In *Policy Analysis in Canada: The State of the Art*, edited by Laurent Dobuzinskis, Michael Howlett, and David Laycock, 238–264. Toronto: University of Toronto Press.

McFarland, Janet. (2009). "Women on Board," *Globe and Mail*, November 25: B1, B8.

Miljin, Lydia. (2008). *Public Policy in Canada: An Introduction*. Don Mills, ON: Oxford University Press.

Mintrom, Michael. (2007). "The Policy Analysis Movement." In *Policy Analysis in Canada: The State of the Art*, edited by Laurent Dobuzinskis, Michael Howlett, and David Laycock, 145–162. Toronto: University of Toronto Press.

O'Connor, Dennis. (2002). *Report of the Walkerton Inquiry: The Events of May 2000 and Related Issues. Part I: A Summary*. Toronto: Ontario Ministry of the Attorney General.

Pal, Leslie A. (1992). *Public Policy Analysis: An Introduction*. Scarborough, ON: Nelson Canada.

Pal, Leslie A. (2010). *Beyond Policy Analysis: Public Issue Management in Turbulent Times*. Scarborough, ON: Nelson Education.

Palmer, Randall, and Louise Egan. (2011). "Chrétien Says Austerity Measures Work," *Globe and Mail*, November 22: B8.

Phidd, Richard W. (2001). *Public Sector Management in Canada: Development, Change and Adaptation*. Toronto: Captus Press.

Prince, Michael J. (2007). "Soft Craft, Hard Choices, Altered Context: Reflections on Twenty-Five Years of Policy Advice in Canada." In *Policy Analysis in Canada: The State of the Art*, edited by Laurent Dobuzinskis, Michael Howlett, and David Laycock, 163–185. Toronto: University of Toronto Press.

Robertson, Grant, and Janet McFarland. (2011). "Big Bank Shareholders Vote No to Board Quota for Women," *Globe and Mail*, April 6: B1, B5.

Rowat, Donald C., ed. (1981). *Provincial Policy-Making: Comparative Essays*. Ottawa: Department of Political Science, Carleton University.

Speers, Kimberly. (2007). "The Invisible Private Service: Consultants and Public Policy in Canada." In *Policy Analysis in Canada: The State of the Art*, edited by Laurent Dobuzinskis, Michael Howlett, and David Laycock, 399–421. Toronto: University of Toronto Press.

Statistics Canada. (2011). "Aboriginal Peoples in Canada: First Nations People, Métis, and Inuit." Retrieved from http://www12.statcan.gc.ca/nhs-enm/2011/as-sa/99-011-x/99-011-x2011001-eng.pdf

Statistics Canada. (2012). "National Household Survey: Data Quality." Retrieved from www.statcan.gc.ca/survey-enquete/household-menages/nhs-enm-eng.htm

Storvik, Aagoth, and Mari Teigen. (2010). *Women on Board: The Norwegian Experience*. Berlin: Friedrich-Ebert-Stiftung.

Toner, Glen, Leslie A. Pal, and Michael J. Prince. (2010). *Policy: From Ideas to Implementation*. Montreal: McGill-Queen's University Press.

Voyer, Jean-Pierre. (2007). "Policy Analysis in the Federal Government: Building the Forward-Looking Policy Research Capacity." In *Policy Analysis in Canada: The State of the Art*, edited by Laurent Dobuzinskis, Michael Howlett, and David Laycock, 219–237. Toronto: University of Toronto Press.

Waugh, William L. Jr., Ronald John Hy, and Jeffrey L. Brudney. (1991). "An Assessment of Research Skill-Building in MPA Curricula." In *Teaching Public Policy*, edited by Peter J. Bergerson, 49–56. New York: Greenwood Press.

Waugh, William L. Jr., and Edith Kelly Manns. (1991). "Communication Skills and Outcome Assessment in Public Administration Education." In *Teaching Public Policy*, edited by Peter J. Bergerson, 133–143. New York: Greenwood Press.

Wikipedia. (n.d.). "Safe Streets and Communities Act." Accessed June 6, 2013. Retrieved from http://en.wikipedia.org/wiki/Safe_Streets_and_Communities_Act

Wolff, Jonathan. (2008). "Social Justice and Public Policy: A View from Political Philosophy." In *Social Justice and Public Policy*, edited by Gary Craig, Tania Burchardt, and David Gordon, 17–31. Bristol, UK: The Policy Press.

Woodside, K. (1985). "Policy Instruments and the Study of Public Policy." In *Public Policy and Administrative Studies, Volume 2*, edited by O. P. Dwivedi and R. Brian Woodrow, 42–57. Guelph, ON: Department of Political Studies, University of Guelph.

Wu, Xun, M. Ramesh, Michael Howlett, and Scott A. Fritzen. (2010). *The Public Policy Primer: Managing the Policy Process*. New York: Routledge.

INDEX

decision-making, 31, 32, 41, 98
　circles, 225
　mechanisms, 244, 249
　power, 171
　process, 25, 30, 67, 114, 123, 171, 172, 173,
　　174, 187, 188, 191, 192, 203, 237, 240
　See also cabinets; legislature;
　　parliament; senate
decision notes, 49, 50, 51, 55, 245
　See also policy products
deinstitutionalization, 211, 245
demarcation, 100, 157, 191, 245
demographic data, 139, 141, 245
　See also data; databases; evidence
demonstrations, 115, 201, 258
departments, xiv, 13, 35
　budget and, 11, 44
　decision-making process and, 174, 179
　estimates and, 253, 254, 261, 262, 263
　external stakeholder groups and, 132
　federal, 37
　government, xiv, 6, 9, 10, 11–12, 22, 25,
　　27, 36, 39, 45, 46, 68, 133, 160, 178,
　　201, 243, 247, 253, 261
　internal stakeholder groups and, 128
　needs, 18
　policy development and, xiv, 22, 82,
　　133, 172, 174, 184
　policy products and, 54, 123
　See also line departments; line
　　ministries; ministries
department of finance, xiv, 245
　federal government, 37, 39
　provincial government, 178
deputy ministers, 246
　cabinet committees and, 43
　cabinet minutes and, 71
　cabinet submissions and, 66, 172
　communication materials and, 61
　concerns of, 169
　direction of, 27, 174
　external stakeholder groups, 114
　influencing, 193
　as an internal stakeholder, 47
　management arrangement, 174, 252
　office, 64, 71
　policy issues and, 46, 52, 94, 95, 99
　policy options and, 151
　replacing, 44

reporting relations, 10
　See also assistant deputy ministers;
　　bureaucrats; civil servants; public
　　servants
deputy minister's office, 64, 71
deregulation, 181–183, 254
determining public policies for
　implementation, xiii, 30, 171–188
difference principle, 82, 246, 248, 252
　See also Rawls, John
diversity, 66, 113, 227, 250
disability allowances, 8, 246
　See also persons with disabilities
disability services, 164–169
　See also persons with disabilities
discussion papers, 17, 50, 51, 58, 211–212, 246
　See also policy products
documentary reviews, 56, 129–130, 139, 144
　See also research methods
draft legislations and regulations, 51, 71, 246
　See also legislation; legislature; policy
　　products
drug subsidies, 8, 246–247

economy, 110, 133, 134, 217, 239, 246
　American, 221
　forecasting, 14
　immigrants and, 218
　implications for, 39, 68, 209, 231
　market, 40, 181, 182, 184, 243, 244,
　　251, 253
　risk assessment of, 70
　socialized planning, 245
　stabilizing, 7
　strengthening, 200, 207
education
　Aboriginal affairs and, 203–205
　access to, 83, 160
　departmental mandate, 10
　early childhood, 95
　funding for, 263
　government roles and responsibilities
　　in, 100, 182
　life chances of women and men in, 225
　men and, 233–235
　ministry of, 27
　physical, 161
　post-secondary, xi, 14, 18
　prejudice in, 112, 113